D1474037

Developmental
MANAGEMENT

EXECUTIVE LEADERSHIP

Developmental Management

General Editor: Ronnie Lessem

Charting the Corporate Mind
*Charles Hampden-Turner**

Managing in the Information Society
Yoneji Masuda

Developmental Management
Ronnie Lessem

Foundations of Business
Ivan Alexander

Greening Business
John Davis

Ford on Management
*Henry Ford**

Managing Your Self
Jagdish Parikh

Managing the Developing Organization
Bernard Lievegoed

Conceptual Toolmaking
Jerry Rhodes

Integrative Management
Pauline Graham

Executive Leadership
Elliott Jaques and Stephen D. Clement

Transcultural Management
Albert Koopman

The Great European Illusion
Alain Minc

* *For copyright reasons this edition is not available in the USA*

Requisite Organization Library

A collection of the printed works of Elliott Jaques, and writings, audio tapes, videos, software packages, and training materials developed by others using the principles of Stratified Systems Theory.

Book Titles:

Requisite Organization

Time-Span Handbook

Progression Handbook

Measurement of Responsibility

Levels of Abstraction in Logic and
   Human Action (*with R. O. Gibson and
   D. J. Isaac*)

Free Enterprise, Fair Employment

The Form of Time

The Changing Culture of a Factory

Health Services

Glacier Project Papers *(with W. Brown)*

Project Analysis Pricing *(with W. Brown)*

Executive Leadership *(with S. Clement)*

Also available by Elliott Jaques:

Creativity and Work (*International
Universities Press*)

A General Theory of Bureaucracy
(*Heinemann*)

Video Presentations:

Requisite Organization

Executive Leadership

Software:

Stratified Systems Theory Tool Kit (SSTK)©:
   SSTK/TPD-   Talent Pool Development
   SSTK/OAA-   Organization Analysis and Alignment

Progression Data Charts©:

Roll-up wall chart, $4' \times 5'$ with static cling symbols
Metal boards, $11'' \times 14''$ with magnetic symbols

Executive BriefCase Tool Kits©:

Metal Progression Data Charts© and blank metal boards, $11'' \times 14''$ in black briefcase, for talent pool development and organization work, with magnetic and static cling symbols.

Executive/Conference Room Wall Units:

Cabinet style presentation systems with three metal panels, three $4' \times 4'$ rollup Progression Data Charts©, for organization and talent pool development planning, with magnetic and static cling symbols. Cabinet exteriors available in a variety of woods.

Requisite Organization Library©
Cason Hall & Co., Publishers
P.O. Box 2346
Arlington, Virginia 22202
1–800–448–7357

To
Danielle
and
to
Kathryn

Executive Leadership

A PRACTICAL GUIDE TO MANAGING COMPLEXITY

ELLIOTT JAQUES
AND
STEPHEN D. CLEMENT

WITH A FOREWORD BY
RONNIE LESSEM

Cason Hall & Co. Publishers

Copyright © Elliott Jaques and Stephen D. Clement 1991
Foreword © Ronnie Lessem 1991
Potential Progress Data Sheet and Time Horizon Chart © Elliott Jaques, 1963, 1990
All other illustrations © Elliott Jaques and Stephen D. Clement 1991
"How to win the battle and live" *Army Magazine* 1988, p. 28, reprinted with permission

First published 1991

Basil Blackwell, Inc.
3 Cambridge Center
Cambridge, Massachusetts 02142, USA

Basil Blackwell Ltd
108 Cowley Road, Oxford, OX4 1JF, UK

Cason Hall & Co. Publishers Ltd
1101 S. Arlington Ridge Road
Arlington, VA 22202
Editorial Offices: 703-920-4050

Library of Congress Cataloging in Publication Data
Jaques, Elliott.
Executive leadership / by Elliott Jaques and Stephen D. Clement.
p. cm. – (Developmental management)
Includes bibliographical references and index.
ISBN 0–9621070–1–8
ISBN 1–55786–2575
1. Leadership. 2. Executive ability. I. Clement, Stephen D., 1943–
II. Title. III. Series.
HD57.7.J36 1991 658.4'092–dc20 90–49138 CIP

British Library Cataloguing in Publication Data
A CIP catalogue record for this book is available
from the British Library.

Illustrations by Rebecca Cason-Oates, R CO Design/USA

Typeset in 11 on 13 point Ehrhardt
by Hope Services (Abingdon) Ltd
Printed in Great Britain by
T.J. Press Ltd., Padstow, Cornwall

Contents

Foreword: Requisite Leadership – Managing Complexity   xiii
by Ronnie Lessem

Preface   xxiii

Special Acknowledgment   xxviii

Acknowledgments   xxix

PART I CONCEPTS AND PRINCIPLES

1 The Demystification of Leadership   3
The Process of Leadership in Role   6
Leadership Accountability and Authority   7
Authority Vested and Authority Earned   10
"Leaders" and "Followers" Together   11
The Great Leadership Shortfall   14
Must a Good Manager Necessarily be a Good Leader?   17
Management without Leadership Accountability is Lifeless   19
The Debasement of the Role of Manager   19
What is a Manager?   21
Minimum Managerial Authority   23
Conditions of Leadership: Psychological Conditions   25
Conditions of Leadership: Organizational Conditions   28
Unto the Breach   30
General Leadership Responsibility   32

2 Human Nature at Work   35
Leadership and Competence   35
Who are the Great "Leaders"?   37
The Nature of Work and Tasks   39
The Importance of having a "Big Enough" Manager   42
Leadership Competence is a Function of Role Competence   44
Cognitive Processes and Cognitive Power (CP)   48
The Four Cognitive Processes   51
The Worlds People Live in: Orders of Information Complexity   53
The Categories of Potential Capability (Quintaves)   57
Hollow Language and Ideas   65
Values and "Motivation," or Why People do Things   69
The Importance of Values   72
Knowledge and Skills   74
Wisdom   76
T and Minus T (-T): "Personality, Temperament, and Style"   79
Self-control and Requisite Behavior   82
Maturation of Potential Capability   83
Individual Development   88

3 Role Complexity and Task Complexity   91
The Four Types of Task Complexity   91
Second Order Categories of Task Complexity   93
Third Order Categories of Complexity: Corporate   95
     Strategic Levels
Time-span and the Measured Level of Work in a Role   97
Time-span and the Boundaries between Categories of   100
     Task Complexity

4 Basic Concepts of Organizational Structure   102
What is Organizational Structure?   104
Why Structure Comes First: Who "Leads" Whom?   106
The Heart of Organizational Structure for Managerial   109
     Leadership
Hierarchical Layering and the "Real Boss"   111
The Big Finding about Hierarchy   113
Span of Control and Leadership   116
Complexity and Organizational Magnitude   118
Maximum Unit Sizes for Effective Managerial Leadership   120
Leadership in the Immediate Mutual Knowledge Unit   123
     (MKU)

Supervisory Leadership Roles: First Line Managerial Units 126
Leadership in the Mutual Recognition Unit (MRU) 128
Organizational Structure and Organizational Leadership 131
Specialist Roles without Leadership Accountability 134
Interaction of Level of Capability and Level of Work: 137
  Case Studies
Deploying Managerial Leadership to Win 145

PART II REQUISITE PRACTICES

Introduction 151

5 **Task-Assigning Role Relationships (TARRs)** 154
Working Expectations in TARRs 156
Individual Contributors as Managers 158
Communication 161
Immediate Subordinate Teambuilding 163
Team Business Meetings 167
Team-Working Mode 168
Some Key Principles 170

6 **Managerial Leadership** 173
The Planning Function 175
Task Formulation and Assignment 178
Context Setting 184
Performance Accounting and Feedback 188
Personal Effectiveness Appraisal 191
Coaching 195
Training 198
Recognition of Personal Effectiveness 200
Penalties and Dismissal 202
Remuneration 204
Annual Review of Personal Effectiveness 207
Selection 210
Induction 212
Deselection 215
Retrenchment and Downsizing 218

7 Supervisory Leadership   221
Supervisory Task Formulation and Assignment   223
Personal Effectiveness Appraisal by Supervisors   225
Training   226
Continuous Improvement Project Teams   227
Recognition and Merit Award   228
Use of Penalties   228
Selection   230
Induction   230

8 Project Teams and Expert Leadership   233
Requisite and Anti-requisite Project Teams   234
The Project Team Chief   234
Specialist Expert   237
A Note on "Matrix Organization"   238

9 Manager-Once-Removed (MoR) Leadership Accountability   240
Overseeing the Quality of Managerial Leadership   244
Assessing SoR Potential   247
Gearing the MoR's Judgments of Current and Future Potential Capability of SoRs   250
Mentoring   253
Equilibration   256
Handling Tough Situations and Hearing Appeals   258
Three-Stratum Teamworking   260

10 Organizational Leadership   264
Corporate Culture   267
Corporate Values   270
Corporate Vision   274
The Gearing Function at Stratum–VI   277
Stratum–V Business Unit Leadership   279
Stratum–IV Site Leadership   283
Organizational Communication   285

11 **Managerial Leadership Development Program**   287
   Mapping the Corporate Talent Pool   290
   The Corporate Talent Pool   293
   CEO Succession and Other Mappings   295
   Stratum–V BU Talent Pools and Graduate Interns   298
   Development of Individual Talent: Coaching and Mentoring 300
   Managerial Leadership Teaching and Practice   301

   Outline and Summary   305

   Bibliography   312

   Index   313

Foreword: Requisite Leadership – Managing Complexity

by Ronnie Lessem

The Third European Force

Elliott Jaques, like other authors in this developmental series such as the American Henry Ford,[1] the Englishman Charles Hampden-Turner,[2] and the Japanese Yoneji Masuda,[3] is a wholly original management thinker. He is also strongly influenced by his continental European heritage. A Canadian by birth, Jaques has brought his impeccable logic to bear upon the problem of organizing for complexity over the course of some forty years. In that time he has been a psychotherapist, a management consultant, a prolific author, and a professor on both sides of the Atlantic, making both America and Britain his adopted homes.

For Jaques and his co-author Clement, tackling the problem of how to manage large-scale enterprise has not led them away from organizational hierarchy but has led them instead towards making such hierarchies responsive to human and social needs. It is in fact these responsive hierarchies that have formed the organizational basis for the German economic miracle. Moreover, Jaques and Clement are at pains to point out, again and again, that charismatic leadership is not the key to business success. (Whoever has heard of the chief executive of Bayer, Daimler Benz or Siemens?)

Jaques has therefore been providing the underpinning over the last thirty years for what might today be termed a continental or central European approach to management. This can be clearly differentiated from the Anglo-American approach,[4] on the one hand, and the art of Japanese management,[5] on the other. Whereas the action-centred Anglo-American way is behaviorally lodged in the tradition of the great leader, with a succession of charismatic attributes to boot, the feeling-centered Japanese approach bypasses the individual entirely as the formative unit of account, focusing instead on the affective group. Jaques, as a third, thought-centered European force, concentrates on the individual-in-role, in the process of maturation, via his or her potentially unfolding grasp of cognitive complexity.

In introducing Elliott Jaques's work, I shall thus be providing a backdrop to the increasingly evident superiority in recent economic performance of the German, Swedish, and Swiss over the American, Dutch, and British. It would seem as if, in the industrialized nations, the effective counterpart to the group-oriented Japanese is not the individual "enterprise culture," so feverishly espoused in the 1980s by Ronald Reagan and Margaret Thatcher, but rather the development of requisite managerial leadership, whereby managerial cognitive complexity evolves to match ever-growing task complexity.

Requisite Leadership

Requisite leadership, Jaques and Clement maintain, is particular to role and circumstance. For example, Churchill was a great wartime leader, but was ineffective in peacetime. Bob Geldof was able to lead a major relief effort, but not to sustain it over the long haul. Generalized leadership attributes, such as courage and persistence, are meaningless as far as Jaques is concerned.

The qualities that do make for good managerial leadership, Jaques and Clement argue, are precisely those that bring about effective managerial work. Their argument therefore cuts completely across the contemporary popular grain, whereby overall management and leadership traits are compared and contrasted. What Jaques and Clement have done is to buck the trend "back to leadership basics." Instead they have effectively moved in the opposite direction, towards leadership that is requisite for a particular time and place, both individual and circumstantial. The qualities that managerial leaders are required to have, they say, are:

- The necessary level of cognitive complexity to carry the level of task complexity of the specific managerial role.
- A strong sense of value for the particular managerial work, and for the leadership of others.
- The appropriate knowledge, and skills, plus experienced practice in both.

- The necessary wisdom about people and things.
- The absence of abnormal temperamental or emotional characteristics that disrupt the ability to work with others.

The particular pattern of qualities that constitutes a manager's emotional make-up thus has little effect upon his or her in-role leadership work, unless the qualities are at abnormal extremes.

Requisite Organization

In fact the authors, ever distrustful of the vagaries of personal and primal charisma, have picked up from where Max Weber left off, attempting to evolve bureaucracy into "requisite organization"[6] rather than to get rid of it altogether. While they are concerned, on the one hand, with maximizing the effectiveness of organizations, they are preoccupied, on the other, with giving everyone who works in them creative fulfillment as well as economic security through their work.

A "requisite" organization starts with its mission, from which flows its values and culture. Every institution, the authors maintain, must embrace a number of core values which are fundamental to developing effective working relationships within it. As a minimum, they suggest, the organizational philosophy needs to place strong value on:

- Mutual trust, confidence, and reliability, embodied in what Jaques terms "mutual recognition units".
- Fairness and justice, whereby recognition is related to personal effectiveness. A sound company philosophy with respect to recognition starts from an employment contract which assumes energetic and effective collaboration.
- Recognition of the value of the individual. Everyone is entitled to be treated with dignity and respect as a valued employee of the institution. Management recognizes that people want the opportunity to use their fullest capability in their work, so that recognition by pay increases needs to be linked to taking on increasing levels of work.
- Openness, with freedom from fear and from central decree. Everyone must feel free to express their true opinions within working relationships; opportunities for participation in context setting and policy making should be freely available.

The corporate organizational structure, systems, principles, and policies must thereafter be consistent with these organizational values. Moreover, a "requisite organization" should expect particular kinds of behavior from its employees, involving, in the authors' opinion, five attributes. These are: (1) integrity: to behave honestly; (2) commitment: to express one's full potential capability and energy at work; (3) reliability: to be counted on consistently to do what is expected or required; (4) initiative: to originate new ideas or methods without being asked; (5) co-operativeness: to work together with others towards a common purpose.

From these underlying values and the overarching corporate mission, business functions arise, and these need to be appropriately aligned. Thereafter, a requisite organizational structure must be established. There is, Jaques argues, an optimum pattern of organizational layering. In other words, there is one organizational layer for each quantum step in cognitive and task complexity. Within that layer, in each case, information, planning, and control sub-systems bring the structure to life.

Organizational Strata

Layering makes it possible to have an organizational structure in which each stratum contains roles within the same category of task complexity. The highest level of task complexity in each role will therefore need to be within reach of the cognitive capacity of the individual who is given the work.

The level of work within each role can be measured, according to Jaques, by its so-called time-span of discretion. The longer the time-span of a role, therefore, the greater is its felt level, scope or responsibility. Any and every task has a target completion time, that is, the maximum time that the individual has been allocated in which to complete it. The time-span of the role defines the degree of its complexity.

Forty years of continuous research has led Jaques and his colleagues to conclude that firm boundaries of real managerial layers exist at time-spans of 3 months, 1 year, 2 years, 5 years, 10 years, 20 years, and 50 years. These seven time-spans correspond with the desired number of organizational layers in a large-scale organization.

Organizational leadership accountabilities vary by strata, each stratum being in a nested relationship with all lower strata. In particular, stratum-VII leadership is concerned with setting and sustaining an effective corporate vision and culture. Likewise stratum-VI is concerned with aligning corporate culture and vision, while stratum-V business unit heads and stratum-IV general managers need to develop and maintain appropriate strategies and cultures at their respective levels. The output of effective organizational leadership is the establishment of a valued and valuable corporate context within which people can work together, effectively and creatively, towards achieving the overall direction set.

Orders of Complexity

Complexity is a function of the number of variables operating in a situation, the ambiguity of these variables, the rate at which they are changing, and the extent to which they are interwoven so that they have to be unraveled in order to be seen. The real point about scale of organization has therefore to do with requisite capacity to handle complexity. If one increases the number of subordinates of a manager, one inevitably increases the complexity of the manager's role. But if one goes on increasing the numbers, there comes a point where any further increase not only raises the level of diversity but also raises the managerial role by one whole category of task complexity. In other words, there are certain boundaries in numbers of subordinates beyond which one cannot go without shifting upwards the stratum of the role itself.

For every upwards shift in the stratum of task complexity, an upward shift in cognitive complexity is required of the requisite managerial leader. Jaques cites four orders of complexity that, by and large, correspond with the four domains of primal, rational, developmental, and metaphysical management that Lessem has established.[7] The first order world is the world of childhood and adolescence. The second verbal and numerical order is the everyday world of business discourse through which we discuss our work, issue instructions, maintain information systems, and organize the flow of work. These variables can all be broken down into a myriad of concrete first order things and actions, all of which are put together into useful second order categories so that we are able to see the wood and not be lost in the trees.

The third order of complexity takes us into the conceptual world of senior management. The factors at work in corporate problems are vast in number, very ambiguous, continually changing, and inextricably tangled together. They need to be gathered together into all-embracing concepts, such as group balance sheets, Europe 1992, global ecosystems, and third world development. In fact we cannot readily go directly from such higher order concepts to concrete things. For example, within the third world are countries at varying stages of development, each of which will have its particular foreign exchange problems and its stable or unstable political regime. Finally, the fourth universal order transcends the corporate world, though it inevitably impinges upon it. This is the world that is inhabited by true universal ideas and the language required for handling the problems of whole societies, social movements, ideologies, and philosophies. It is a world entered into only by "the greats," such as – in the business world – Henry Ford in America, and more recently perhaps by Agha Hasan Abedi in Pakistan. It may be apparent that universal ideas encompass a large number of concepts, each of which in turn can be referred to a large number of things.

Maturation of Potential Capability

Managerial leadership thus increases in scope with the maturation of cognitive capacity, knowledge-in-application, value integrity, balance of temperament and overall wisdom. However, according to Jaques, it is potential as reflected in cognitive complexity which holds the key to managerial capability at a given time. Such cognitive complexity, moreover, grows by true maturation, developing in a regular and predictable manner through youth, adulthood, midlife and maturity, as Bernard Lievegoed[8] and Lessem[9] have already indicated. It is this maturation process that makes it possible to evaluate a person's potential.

By contrast, Jaques argues, none of the other components of capability develops by predictable maturation. The development of knowledge and skills depends on experience and education. Values change, or otherwise, depending similarly both on experience and on managerial scope and influence. Wisdom may or may not be enhanced over time. Personality characteristics tend to endure unless modified by intense worldly experiences or by psychotherapy.

The art of facilitating individual development, therefore, involves taking note of the rate of growth of a particular person's potential, and providing work opportunities consistent with that growth. Such opportunities should also provide scope for the progressive integration of values, for the cumulative acquisition of knowledge and skills, for steady accumulation of wisdom in dealing with people, and for the elimination of the expression of damaging quirks of personality into personally and socially enhancing characteristics.

Such overall managerial development will necessarily involve an appropriate combination of teaching and training, counseling, coaching and mentoring. Teaching, for Jaques and Clement, entails the imparting of knowledge to individuals, and is unspecific to any managerial role. Through training, by contrast, managers are helped to develop their skill in the use of knowledge in practice; such training is specific to a particular role. Counseling involves advice on a personal problem, either internal to the individual manager or as a result of external circumstances. Coaching is the process whereby a manager helps his or her subordinate to understand the full range of his/her role, including his/her strengths and weaknesses in relation to it. Such coaching has a particularly important influence on values and wisdom, and on knowledge. The balancing act involved is, on the one hand, to release the subordinate's full capacities and energy by providing him or her with sufficient opportunities for creativity and innovation in achieving continuous improvement, while, on the other hand, guiding him or her in such a way as to avoid wasting resources or undue energy. Finally, mentoring is a process in which a manager-once-removed helps a subordinate-once-removed to understand his or her potential, and how that potential might be developed, career wise, to the full.

Communication Strata

Jaques's and Clement's view, finally, is that conventional incentives, bonuses, and other "pigeon-theory conditioning approaches" should be disbanded. Instead, requisite conditions should be established for managerial leaders to recognize good work, to encourage it, to pay fairly for it, and to provide opportunities for everyone to get on with work that befits their potential. The solution, they say, is arranging the organization structures and orchestrating communication processes through which managerial practices conform, simultaneously, to the properties of hierarchical organizations and of human nature.

If a manager communicates in too complex a manner with a subordinate, that person may not be able to take in the message. For example, a stratum-IV general manager may provide a stratum-III functional manager with control data, in terms of variances, which by their very nature have multi-functional implications. It does no good for the functional manager to be told by the general manager that he or she is within a number of such interrelated variance norms. Managers build trust by setting limits at levels consistent with their subordinate's cognitive complexity.

Communication is enhanced, moreover, by what Jaques terms solid, as opposed to hollow, language and ideas. When solid language is being used, a person will uniformly not only describe more general ideas by reference to specific illustrations but also relate general ideas to one another via these personally owned concrete examples.

Requisite Leadership and the Developmental Manager

At the heart of Jaques's developmental perspective is the layering of orders of complexity that he perceives within the individual, cognitively, and within the organization, hierarchically. Transcending the limits of primal leadership traits and rationally based management principles, Jaques unravels the processes involved in the cognitive maturation of individuals, from concrete childhood to levels of abstraction in adulthood. Similarly, he documents the progressive unfolding of an organization through prospectively seven strata, from shop floor to chief executive officer.

Jaques, with his European heritage, always maintains a strongly cognitive orientation. Whereas, for example, Jaques's European and Austrian compatriot, Rudolf Steiner, shares this pre-emphasis on the cognitive, he pays relatively more attention to the affective and behavioral aspects of our human and organizational being.[10] Similarly the great British and European management thinker, Reg Revans, is both preoccupied with action (cognitive) and with reflection (behavioral), as his concept of "action learning" indicates.[11]

In the final analysis it would seem that original European management thinkers place particular emphasis on cognitive processes in management. However, the degree of emphasis varies, at least partly because of their cultural heritage within Europe. To the extent that they link this orientation to the maturation of the individual or to the evolution of the organization, both of which Jaques has done, they turn towards the developmental realm.

Not surprisingly, over the past forty years, Jaques has pursued a dual career as management consultant and psychotherapist, thus keeping in close touch with processes of individual and organizational individuation. His books on "Requisite Organization"[12] and now with Clement on "Requisite Leadership" serve as landmarks in managerial thought. Through them, together with the work of Steiner and Lievegoed, we also gain real insight into the central European approach to management and organization. I have a sneaking suspicion that, over the course of the next decade, this art of European management may assume seminal influence around the globe, in the same way as the arts of American and Japanese management were respectively so formative in the 1970s and 1980s.

Ronnie Lessem
London, 1990

Notes

1 Henry Ford, *Ford on Management*, Blackwell, Oxford, 1990.
2 Charles Hampden-Turner, *Charting the Corporate Mind*, Blackwell, Oxford, 1990.
3 Yoneji Masuda, *Managing in the Information Society*, Blackwell, Oxford, 1990.
4 T. Peters and, R. Waterman, *In Search of Excellence*, Harper and Row, New York, 1982.
5 R. Pascale and A. Athos, *The Art of Japanese Management*, Penguin, Harmondsworth, 1982.
6 Elliott Jaques, *Requisite Organization: The CEO's Guide to Creative Structure and Leadership*, Cason Hall, Arlington, VA and Gower, Aldershot, Hants, 1989.
7 Ronnie Lessem, *Global Management Principles*, Prentice Hall, Englewood Cliffs, NJ, 1989.
8 Bernard Lievegoed, *Managing the Developing Organization*, Blackwell, Oxford, 1990.
9 Ronnie Lessem, *Total Quality Learning*, Blackwell, Oxford, 1991.
10 Rudolf Steiner, *Towards Social Renewal*, Rudolf Steiner Press, London, 1977.
11 Reg Revans, *Action Learning*, Blond Briggs, London, 1980.
12 Elliott Jaques, *Requisite Organization: The CEO's Guide to Creative Structure and Leadership*, Cason Hall, Arlington, VA & Gower, Aldershot, Hants, 1989.

How to win the battle and live

Military commanders are aware of the seminal importance of operational command (managerial) work underlying effective leadership.

Command and control means many things to different people. To some, it evokes the image of a communication network; to others, the qualities of leadership. Increasingly, it has been described as an information exchange system. An officer who aspires to successful command must understand that behind these ingredients is a process designed to concentrate the immense combat power of an AirLand Battle force against the enemy in order to win engagements, battles, campaigns and wars. It is a process that unifies the efforts of thousands of men performing a bewildering array of battlefield functions, each one of which is utterly essential to success. This process produces unity of effort from a diversity of means.

Yes, it will use modern communications and even computers, and it will require leadership of the highest order; but at the heart of the process lies the mind of the commander. From the mind of that single person, a dominating concept of operation must emerge. That concept must be appropriate to the mission of the command and to all the circumstances that are unique to that time and that place, and that mental construct must be propagated through the minds of the whole hierarchy of subordinate leaders to animate the entire command and to concentrate its actions before the opposing commander can place a counter concept in operation.

Concepts are cannibalistic. The better concept, based on the most recent realities, will devour the older, opposing concept based on information that has been overtaken by events. His concept of operation is the supreme contribution of the commander to his command and to success. The absence of a powerful and dominating concept concedes the initiative to his opponent; and his other qualities of leadership, however many he may possess, and however admirable they may be, will be simply irrelevant and ineffectual. This article focuses directly on that central, seminal creative act – the starting point and cohesive theme of every successful operation.

Gen. William E. DePuy
U.S. Army retired

Quoted from ARMY
August 1988, p. 28
(reprinted with permission)

Preface

The aim of this book is to provide a foundation for decisive, value-adding managerial leadership. In order to do so, we propose to bring the subject of leadership down to earth into practical everyday usable form. We shall thus limit ourselves to managerial leadership. There are many different roles – political, religious, and others – in which leadership accountability is to be found, and in each of which the nature of the leadership work is very different. By thus limiting ourselves to managerial work we hope to provide a sharp focus that will be of genuine help to business organizations and to managers at all levels.

Decisive value-adding managerial leadership is the true key to competitive effectiveness in business. It is what gives the drive, the imaginativeness, the zest, the personal satisfaction, the good working relationships; above all, it gives the productive working effectiveness at all levels from top to bottom of the managerial organization that produces a continuously successful business, thrusting into the future, and makes working a pleasure.

But everyone is familiar with the fact that we have become hamstrung by excessively bureaucratic organizational structures and practices that stymie decisiveness and make it very difficult for managers to add value to the work of their subordinates. The difficulty is that most of the organizational and human resourcing procedures that we use, and the so-called managerial and leadership training that is provided, are seriously counter-productive. They serve to undermine and destroy managerial leadership, leaving our businesses to do the best they can in spite of the contribution of the leadership field rather than with its help.

Democratic Values in the Workplace

In addressing the subject of managerial leadership, therefore, one of our prime values is that of business effectiveness and profitability through time. But whereas this business value is an essential element in free enterprise democracy, there are certain other basic ethical values that must be assumed, values that exist in their own right and that have an overriding priority in their own right. These basic ethical values lie at the very core of free enterprise democracy, and are further discussed in Chapter 10. They include such primary values as the dignity and integrity of the individual, the establishment of mutual trust and confidence, fairness and justice, openness, and absence of fear and autocratic decree. The acceptance of these values is taken for granted as the basic philosophy essential for sound managerial leadership.

These values are not, however, merely taken for granted and left at that. We believe that the requisite managerial leadership practices that we shall describe in Part II express the essence of democratic values applied to the managerial hierarchy. Thus our approach contrasts sharply with the approach that is, unfortunately, prevalent today; namely, that the managerial hierarchy is not only outdated, outmoded and limping along on its last legs, but that it needs to be dead and buried and replaced by some kind of non-hierarchical organization.

This "non-hierarchical" organization is variously described in terms of self-management teams, network organization, continuous improvement councils, quality circles, cluster organization, matrix frames of mind, adhocracy, information-generated project teams, and semi-autonomous work groups. Underlying these proposals are good democratic-value intentions. It is too bad that they have to be linked to a "down with hierarchy" slogan, presumably because all authority is seen as inevitably evil, and managerial hierarchy and managerial roles are thus seen as coercively autocratic and democratically beyond the pale.

The fact is, however, that none of these schemes ever gets rid of hierarchy. That they are thought to do so is mere wishful fantasy. Nor, as we shall argue, is the managerial hierarchy likely to disappear in the foreseeable future. It is an essential form of organization for effective and efficient democratic free-enterprise societies.

What needs to be done is to recognize that all authority is far from necessarily evil and that managerial leadership, to be effective, must be authoritative and not autocratic. We shall show that our requisite managerial leadership practices accomplish just such an outcome. They accomplish all that democracy-wishers could possibly seek – and more – in the way of valuing of individual dignity and participation. And they do so in such a way as to strengthen the constructive use of the managerial hierarchy. That is what we mean by requisite. This view is easily tested by examining whether or not our requisite practices really do provide for full-scale participation and team-working. We think they do, fulsomely so, and for the right reasons economically, socially and psychologically.

The False Concern with "Personality"

The book may seem strange to those who take it for granted that leadership derives from certain key personality characteristics that are said to be possessed by good leaders. We believe that effective managerial leadership is connected not with personality make-up but with managerial competence based upon cognitive capability, values and knowledge and wisdom (so long as there are no seriously deleterious personality characteristics), which are all used in a requisite organization with requisite procedures.

Our view is that far too much emphasis is being placed upon personality make-up these days, and that far too many of the problems of management and of managerial leadership are being seen in terms of interpersonal relationships and interpersonal conflict. It is impossible to tell how much an apparent interpersonal conflict is the result of a clash of personality or of inadequate managerial organization. In the vast majority of cases it is the latter. A good rule of thumb to use is that, until and unless a requisite organization has been established, it is fair to assume that interpersonal stresses and strains and inadequate managerial leadership are the products of poor organization rather than of personality problems. "Cherchez l'organisation" every time.

Thus, for example, if managerial roles are too tightly stacked on top of each other, conflict will arise. The managers will feel insecure in dealing with subordinates who are too close to them in capability, and the subordinates will feel frustrated and irritated at having a manager who "breathes down our necks." And managerial decisiveness and value-adding will not exactly be flowing freely around the place.

This problem of the excessive preoccupation nowadays with personality issues, and of the handling of managerial problems in terms of interpersonal conflict, also highlights the importance of our confining our attention to only one topic, that of managerial leadership. There are indeed circumstances that might well call for dealing with interpersonal conflicts. Thus, for example, the above observations do not apply to family businesses; that is to say, businesses in which members of a family or of interrelated families are appointed to positions because they are family. In such cases, the family members may not always be appropriate to the roles they occupy. It may be necessary to try to work out all kinds of interpersonal problems between the relatives. But that problem arises because family members of a company cannot be placed in true managerial, hierarchical relations with each other, since they are not true employees: they have to put up with one another's shortcomings. Experience in working out interpersonal conflicts between related family members must not be applied to the true managerial hierarchy, and vice versa.

Thus, we shall confine our attention to the functioning of the managerial hierarchy, and to managerial leadership within the managerial hierarchy, and not to political parties, church hierarchies, partnerships, families, universities, or any other type of social institution. To confine our task leaves us with a worthy endeavor. Despite the currently popular but utterly unrealistic view that hierarchy is doomed, the managerial hierarchy will become the dominant type of social organization as the world of the twenty-first century becomes completely industrialized and the employment society comes to full fruition.

We shall show that a no-nonsense approach is required for effective managerial leadership. This no-nonsense approach says that companies must establish a managerial organization structure that makes it possible to deploy competent managerial leaders into realistic roles. And it says that every managerial role must, as an absolute requirement, be filled by a person with the necessary competence to carry the accountabilities in the role, including the leadership accountability. Failure to carry out this requirement without equivocation, in every single case from CEO to shop and office floor, must become recognized as being so seriously disruptive that it will never knowingly be tolerated. Every single instance that is allowed to continue shrieks its message that the company is not serious about sustaining decisive value-adding managerial leadership. Success in carrying out this requirement will produce the decisive value-adding managerial leadership that will bring prosperity to the company and contribute to the social well-being of the nation.

Special Acknowledgment

Kathryn Cason has made a special and particular contribution to this book. It is as a result of her collaboration with Elliott Jaques over two years (while this book was being written), on a research project in which they were engaged, that the present formulations about the nature of mental processes in work and about individual potential capability were made. This work will be published by them shortly.

In addition to this contribution, she carried out a final editing of the text which has improved it substantially in form and content; a job that could have been done only by someone with a comprehensive and thorough understanding of the material. We have indeed been fortunate in our publisher and editor.

Acknowledgments

Readers of Elliott Jaques's book, *Requisite Organization*, will know of the debt of the authors to CRA, the Australian mining corporation. It was in the course of collaboration over numerous years in organizational development work and preparation of materials for managerial leadership training with members of that company that we were able to fashion many of the ideas we have presented. We have worked intensively with Jack Brady, the company's Human Resources director, and the two members of his staff who are accountable for the leadership training development, John Fairfield and John Tynan. All of this work was done with the strong support of John Ralph, the company's CEO, and against the background of development work initiated by the previous CEO, Sir Roderick Carnegie.

It will also be clear to those familiar with leadership development work in the US Army that our work has been influenced by our experience with Army training: Stephen Clement over many years of active duty and Elliott Jaques as a research consultant. We have both worked closely with Dr T. Owen Jacobs, of the US Army Research Institute for Behavioral and Social Science, one of the Army's professional experts in the leadership field. In addition, valued support has come over the years from Gen. Maxwell Thurman, from Col. (ret.) Neale Cosbie, Col. (ret.) Harry Buckley, and Col. (ret.) Mike Malone, and from working colleagues in the Human Resources Development (HRD) Division in the Office of the Deputy Chief of Staff Personnel.

Dr Harry Levinson and Dr Charles Redding have been rich sources of ideas and stimulation.

The illustrations were designed and created by Rebecca Cason-Oates of R CO Design, continuing the fine work she did in preparing the drawings for *Requisite Organization*.

Nancy Lee, of Info-Ed Inc., has ably assisted with the final editing of the text. Leslie Dougherty and Rhoda Fowler were responsible for preparing the text for publication.

PART I

Concepts and Principles

I

The Demystification of Leadership

Good leadership is one of the most valued of all human activities. To be known as a good leader is a great accolade – as true for a youngster at school as it is for the great political, or corporate, or military leaders. It signifies the talent to bring people together, to get them to work effectively together to meet a common goal, to co-operate with each other, to rely upon each other, to trust each other. It evokes the warm and gratifying prospect of being part of a successful team, or organization, or nation, of being a winner in association with other winners. And everyone loves to be a winner.

But good leadership is also seen as one of the most mysterious of human activities. This view is wrapped up in the notion of charisma (or its close relative, style), that divinely bestowed magnetism and talent with which some special people have been graced and which enables them – almost magically it would seem – to win the staunch devotion of others and to get them to work together. This most common view is a discouraging one, because it fixes on the notion that if you are born with only a limited amount of God-given leadership personality then you must rest content with giving only a limited amount of leadership in your lifetime. Such a view is, however, not only discouraging but also, we would argue, simply incorrect.

In order to show why this personality-cum-charismatic view of leadership might be misleading, and to bring leadership down to earth for the ordinary and straightforward activity it can be (see figure 1.1), two crucial points must be established. We should like to clear them away before going any further. We believe that the whole field of leadership is in stalemate because of the failure to recognize these two principle concepts.

The first point is that the concept of leadership is rarely defined

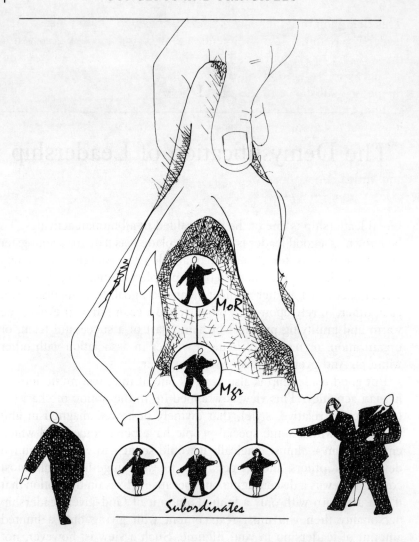

Figure 1.1 The demystification of managerial leadership

with any precision. We shall define it as follows, and will use the term consistently in this way and only in this way:

Leadership is that process in which one person sets the purpose or direction for one or more other persons, and gets them to move along together with him or her and with each other in that direction with competence and full commitment.

This definition of leadership as a process is intended to express what leadership is about. It is not intended to describe how one goes about the process of achieving it, or the mental characteristics and organizational conditions necessary for doing so. These issues are the theme and substance of this book.

The second point is that leadership is not a free-standing activity: it is one function, among many, that occurs in some but not all roles.

Let us examine this second point. It stems from the self-evident and fundamental point that all relationships between people take place within established role relationships. These role relationships set the basic ground rules – the mutual accountability and authority – that let us know where we stand with each other.

Role relationships are established for social purposes. Examples are parent–child, manager–subordinate, teacher–pupil, doctor–patient, priest–parishioner. But, puzzling as it may seem, and however much it may run counter to the way most of us think, there is no such thing as a detached, free-standing leader–follower role relationship. There can be no purpose in setting up a leadership role *per se*: lead who, where, why? Get everybody going in what direction? For what purpose?

There are many roles that carry leadership accountability as part of their functions. Managers, commanders, parents, teachers all do so. John Watson of IBM was a great manager, Churchill was a great wartime prime minister, Alexander the Great and Napoleon were great commanders; as part of their work they effectively carried out their leadership duties. But none of them had an abstract leadership role *per se*, however much it might feel like that.

This last feeling, indeed, is very interesting to consider. It would seem that when we have someone in a role with leadership accountability and when that person is extraordinarily competent in that role, two things happen. First, people are happy to follow along together with such a person. Second, from the feeling that they want to do so arises another feeling; namely that the person is endowed with certain great personal leadership qualities. It is an almost mystical feeling, of everyone's being at one with everyone else. In other words, under circumstances where we have a person exercising great competence in a role with leadership accountability, the effect is to bind people together; the binding together touches the deep recesses of our values for social cohesion, and we are suffused by warm feelings that we tend to associate, incorrectly, with personal qualities in our leaders rather than with effective competence.

The Process of Leadership in Role

In short, then, our theme is that leadership takes place not in a vacuum but in relationships between people. Similarly, relationships between people take place not in a vacuum but always within some kind of role relationship; that is to say, within a social structure.

But, as we have suggested, there can be no such thing as a "leadership" role, no such thing as a leader–follower role relationship. By the same token, there is no such thing as a leader *per se*, and so we shall not use the term "leader" on its own in this book but will use "managerial leader" or "political leader" as appropriate.

We have found that the notion of "a leader" or "the leader" simply gets in the way. It brings about, for example, those fruitless discussions about whether a manager is really a leader, or about whether an Army Division Commander, or a Brigade Commander, or an Army Commander, should be a commander or a leader. That is to say, once we separate a role called leader from that of manager or commander, we simply land ourselves plumb into the middle of a false dichotomy, and there's no way out.

The point we are making can be illustrated by asking whether Winston Churchill was a great "leader." Did he not have great charisma? Was he not a great speaker and communicator? Did he not have a great leadership presence and personality? The answer must be that it seemed so during World War II. But not before the war, or after it. Does that mean that he somehow grew a new personality for the war, and then lost it again? That hardly seems possible. What happened was that he got into a role during the war, in which he was able to use his capabilities to the full and to function with extraordinary competence and effectiveness. A better statement, therefore, would be that Churchill was a hugely effective wartime commander–prime minister, but was not effective as a peacetime prime minister. The roles were very different.

Churchill was at home as a wartime commander–prime minister and as part of that role was not only able to set a clear direction for Britain but was also successful in getting the British people to move willingly and enthusiastically in that direction. He exercised effective leadership in his prime ministerial role and was a great communicator.

After the war, however, Churchill was lost as a peacetime prime minister. He was unable to set a clear direction for Britain, and was unsuccessful in getting the British people to follow along together with him. He was unable to carry effectively the role of peacetime prime minister; he was unable to exercise effective leadership. Did Churchill thus undergo a great personality change? Absolutely not; what we see is the same person with great competence to cope with one role but not with another.

It is therefore no use asking whether a person is a great "leader." The real question should be whether a person is a great manager, or a great commander, or a great political representative, or a great wartime president, or a great peacetime prime minister, or is great in any other role that carries leadership accountability.

Does this example thus lead us to a so-called situational theory of leadership, the notion that people's ability to "lead" will depend upon the surrounding circumstances? Not quite. The proposition we shall pursue is that everyone is capable of exercising effective leadership in roles that carry leadership accountability, so long as they value the role and are competent to carry the basic requirements of that role, and so long as that role is properly structured and the organization has properly instituted practices.

Leadership Accountability and Authority

We have stressed the point that there can be no such thing as a specific and exclusive leadership role, for someone to be "the leader." Slack usage of the term creates trouble and confusion the moment we consider the question of the kinds of ability needed to exercise leadership: the prime ability is that required for carrying the total work of the particular type of role and role relationships within which the leadership accountability happens to be embedded. The significance of this fact will become apparent when we consider the conditions for effective leadership in different types of role. In order to do so, we must be clear about the nature of roles and role relationships.

The roles we occupy set the framework within which we conduct ourselves in relation to one another. They tell us what we are entitled to expect of one another as we work together, play together, live together. Those limits are set primarily by the accountabilities and the authorities that attach to the role.

"Accountabilities" are those aspects of a role that dictate the things that the occupant is required to do by virtue of the role. Success in carrying out the tasks for which one is accountable will ordinarily lead to positive recognition from the person or persons who have established (sanctioned) the role. Failure to carry out those tasks will lead to some kind of negative recognition.

"Authorities" are those aspects of a role that enable the person in the role to act legitimately in order to carry out the accountabilities with which he or she has been charged. In order to discharge accountability, a person in a role must have appropriate authority; that is to say, authority with respect to the use of materials or financial resources or with respect to other people making it reasonably possible to do what needs to be done. It is the authority with respect to other people that we shall focus upon in this book.

Take, for example, Robert who is a 45-year old man: he is the father of three children, a boy aged 15, a girl aged 12, and a boy aged 9; he works as a manager of a research department employing 32 people; and he is the elected president of his neighborhood association. He is accountable for exercising leadership in connection with each of these roles.

As father, he must endeavor along with his wife to ensure that the children follow along with them in the directions set by their values and that they willingly and enthusiastically adopt those values.

As manager, he is accountable for setting direction for his subordinates, and gaining their full collaboration in achieving the goals he sets for the department.

As elected representative, he is accountable for articulating the direction desired by the majority of the neighborhood association, and for using his best endeavors to get members to move in harmony with each other in that direction.

The strongest leadership accountability ought to rest in his parental role, where his parental authority extends for many years, very powerfully at the beginning but gradually weakening in the children's adolescence.

The next strongest lies in his managerial role, where his managerial authority (elaborated later) ought to enable him to ensure among other things that he has no immediate subordinates whom he judges to be really incapable of doing the work he needs to get done.

Figure 1.2   The process of leadership in role

The weakest leadership responsibility lies in his elected representative role, since his authority with respect to the association members is limited to the authority to help them to articulate the direction they desire and to attempt to persuade them to support the program of the association committee.

It may be noted, therefore, that leadership accountability and authority may vary considerably depending upon each role we occupy (see figure 1.2). If we are to understand leadership, we must understand the role in which the leadership accountability appears. A major point, however, is that the authority vested in a role is never sufficient to make it possible to gain the fullest co-operation from those to be influenced.

Parents must earn the love and respect of their children; managers must earn the trust and respect of their subordinates; and elected representatives must earn the confidence of their constituents. Without this personally earned component of authority that engenders trust and respect, leadership effectiveness will fall flat; it will not be a total loss, but will not be exciting either. We should like, therefore, to consider in more detail the possible significance of this distinction between the authority we pick up by virtue of the role we occupy, and the authority that each one of us must win personally by what we do in the role.

Authority Vested and Authority Earned

Because we are dealing with leadership, we shall of course focus upon authority with respect to other people with whom we are connected by virtue of a role relationship. This focus upon authority with respect to other people can be better appreciated if we compare it with authority with respect to material and financial resources. The role we occupy is vested with the necessary authority. We pick up that authority by virtue of our being in the role. We use the authority as we require, and that is that. We do not need to earn the trust or the respect of the material or of the financial resources.

In the case of authority with respect to other people, however, the matter is totally different. We must be vested with certain necessary authority to get the work done. It is this role-vested authority that enables us to require others to do things at our bidding; for example, to listen to us, or to take note of what we say, or even to follow orders or instructions that we might issue.

Role-vested authority by itself, properly used, should be enough to produce a minimal satisfactory result, by means of subordinates doing what they are role-bound to do. What it cannot do is to release the full and enthusiastic co-operation of others. In order to achieve full, enthusiastic, willing collaboration between role-related people, we have substantially to supplement our authority by winning the full personal support of those people; by gaining, in other words, what we shall term personally earned authority.

Thus it is that, in roles that carry accountability and authority with respect to other people, the response we get from those people comes in two parts: first, from the authority vested in the role itself, and second, from their willing and enthusiastic commitment of full capability, which is personally earned by the person in the role.

It should be self-evident that personally earned authority is a crucial issue for anyone in a role with leadership accountability.

Personally earned authority is needed if people are to go along with us, using their full competence in a really willing and enthusiastic way; it carries the difference between a just-good-enough result and an outstanding or even scintillating one. Roles with leadership account-ability are not special in this respect. It is an important feature of all interaction between human beings that we affect one another, partly by whatever vested authority we pick up in the role that we occupy in the interaction and partly by whatever personally earned authority we can muster (see figure 1.3).

Personally earned authority in established roles with leadership accountability needs to be built up over time and accumulated in our social bank account for use in crises, as, for example, by managers when circumstances get tough, or by commanders in combat.

We shall devote much attention to how to amass a solid bank balance in this regard. But it might be useful to summarize at this point the approach we shall use with respect to achieving personally earned authority in managerial leadership roles. First, we should ensure that we are in a requisite organizational situation which is one full organizational stratum and one full category of cognitive capability above our subordinates (we shall elaborate these points in Chapters 2 and 3). Second, we must be operationally competent in that role so that our subordinates can have confidence in us. Third, we must discharge with consistency the requisite managerial practices that we shall describe later. Fourth, we all should be encouraged to express our own natural personality and to be our own natural selves, while at the same time being required to exercise sufficient self control so as not to behave in ways likely to be disruptive of working relationships.

"Leaders" and "Followers" Together

There is a point in our definition of leadership that we should like to emphasize. It is important to an understanding of leadership. It is a point that all people with leadership accountability must have deeply ingrained in the way they see others towards whom they carry leadership accountability.

The point to be stressed is that the true meaning of leadership should arouse a strong and indelible mental image of people moving along together in synchrony, and not one behind the other.

Leadership is not like a game of "follow the leader" in which the leader does things that the followers must emulate, nor like a mother goose followed by her goslings strung out in a straight line behind her, nor like a "Follow me, men!" heroic in which the leader is out in front getting killed.

It is interesting that leading and following have only recently come to take on this meaning of the "leader" in front and the "followers"

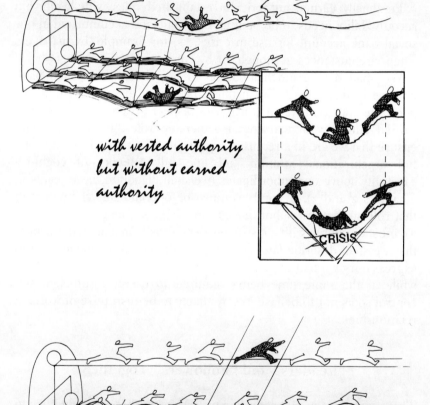

with vested authority
but without earned
authority

CRISIS

with vested and
earned authority

CRISIS

Figure 1.3 Authority vested and authority earned

trailing along behind. Such a meaning is a decided handicap for anyone in the managerial leadership hot seat. Managers need their people to be up with them, and with one another, all going in the same direction, working together when necessary, in pursuit of the common goal that has been set (see figure 1.4). Each person should be free and able to use his or her own initiative within his or her manager's framework. The managers too are then free to get on with what they have to do, safe in the knowledge that, unless they hear otherwise, all is going well and that things will come together as they want them to. Managers need to have the togetherness concept fixed firmly in their minds if they are to be effective in communicating that feeling and outlook to everyone else.

Figure 1.4 "Leaders" and "followers" together

Leading and following are both from old Anglo-Saxon terms that have the sense of going along together. "To lead" comes from *läden*, which means to go or to travel together. "To follow" comes from *ful-gangen*, which means to go together in a crowd or to go as a full company. As we hope to demonstrate convincingly, it is exactly this perspective that defines what a managerial leader really has to do if he or she wants to get the very best out of subordinates. In short, leading and following are about going along together. How that going along together is best arranged is a theme we shall take up in the sections on task assignment in Chapter 6.

The Great Leadership Shortfall

Leadership has to do with certain types of role relationship in which people work together in order to get things done. Under optimum conditions they will share in the desire and the aspirations to achieve common goals which are related to their roles. At the very least, the conditions ought to provide for their moving along together, willingly and enthusiastically. That is what the discharge of leadership accountability is all about.

But everyone is all too familiar with the fact that many situations provide far from optimum conditions for encouraging, or even allowing, people to work together co-operatively, sensibly, enjoyably. One of the most significant of such situations is the managerial hierarchy. This type of hierarchy, in which generally poor circumstances are to be found, has been the form of organization of the military for over 3,000 years, dating back to Chinese and Assyrian history. It has since become the most common type of social institution in our industrially developed nations during the second half of the twentieth century.

For reasons that we propose to go into as we progress through the book, the managerial hierarchy has become noteworthy for its deleterious impact upon human creativity, innovativeness, cohesion, pulling together, satisfaction and morale. This negative circumstance holds widely for all managerial organizations whether in industry, commercial and other services, civil and public service, or in education, health and social services. It holds also for military organizations in peacetime, and may even hold true in combat if the values of a nation are not clearly and unequivocally driving the effort.

In the same vein, the exercise of leadership in our managerial hierarchies has not been outstanding for its brilliance. It is sometimes excellent, but more commonly it ranges from passable to abysmal. The cost is greatly reduced organizational effectiveness and human morale, and wasted effort. There has even been a widely echoed cry to get rid of hierarchy altogether and to substitute some vague and ill-defined alternatives that might somehow work better and make people happier.

Apart from this unrealistic cry for some new kind of organization for the twenty-first century, most of the descriptions of leadership have focused on superiority or shortcomings in personal qualities in people and their behavior. Thus, much has been written about surveys that describe what executives do who are said to be good at leadership, or about the lives of well-known individuals who had reputations as "good leaders," as though somehow emulating such people can help.

This widespread fixation upon the lives and practices of great leaders, and teaching about them, as a way of improving leadership "skills," is incorrectly posited on the notion that effective leadership calls for certain specialized personality characteristics and personal qualities and certain specific skills (see figure 1.5).

We shall argue that this individualistic psychological approach is barking up the wrong tree. It has led to the widespread use of spurious leadership training by means of a bastardized mass psychotherapy administered to all managers. It has wasted great effort and yielded little fruit up till now, and is unlikely to do any better in the future. People are by and large no better or worse, no more or less smart, no more or less responsible, than they used to be, or than they are likely to be in the future. What has occurred, however, is that our structuring of our managerial hierarchies and our procedures for assigning accountability and managing them, have lacked sound guiding principles and will continue to suffer from chronic under-effectiveness unless something radical is done about the problem.

We shall present our own radical approach to removing the difficulties, in terms of two major sets of proposals. First we shall consider the almost universally held and damaging misconceptions about the nature of human nature – and of leadership – that lead to convoluted and impaired organization processes, and we will offer a decidedly different set of conceptions to replace them. Second, we shall present a system of organizational structures, accountabilities and practices that, if followed, will make it possible for ordinary people to exercise effective leadership when held accountable for doing so, and for equally ordinary people to enjoy working together

Figure 1.5   The great leadership shortfall

THE DEMYSTIFICATION OF LEADERSHIP 17

and to do so willingly and enthusiastically while behaving as their own natural selves.

Must a Good Manager Necessarily be a Good Leader?

The fact that there are no free-standing leadership roles, or leader–follower role relationships, points to what leadership is really about. We have argued that it is a particular aspect of accountability in some but not all roles, namely, the accountability for getting others to move in the same direction. Here are some roles that do carry leadership accountability: managers towards subordinates; elected politicians towards constituents; parents towards children; teachers towards pupils. And here are some that do not: friend to friend; opposing tennis players; salesperson to customer; spouse to spouse.

The answer, therefore, to the question of whether a manager should also be a leader is that managers carry leadership accountability by the nature of their roles (see figure 1.6). But be absolutely clear: the role is that of manager and the role relationship is manager–subordinate. Part of the work of the role is the exercise of leadership, but it is not a "leadership role" any more than it would be called a telephoning role because telephoning is also a part of the work required.

Here is our simple and down-to-earth formulation. The particular leadership accountability we are talking about (please see our definition on p. 4) is that which occurs in institutions in which work is being done in a hierarchy of roles, with people (managers) at given levels being held accountable for the work of others at subordinate levels. We call these systems managerial hierarchies, and will elaborate their most important characteristics in Chapter 4.

There are other types of system (e.g political, families) that also have roles that carry leadership accountability. But our point is that the essence of managerial hierarchies lies in managerial roles, and that those roles carry leadership accountability as one of a wide range of duties.

From the point of view of this formulation there is no conflict between management and leadership. All managers carry leadership accountability. There is no such thing as an effective manager who is not able to discharge the leadership accountability in the role effectively. Good managership includes good leadership as an

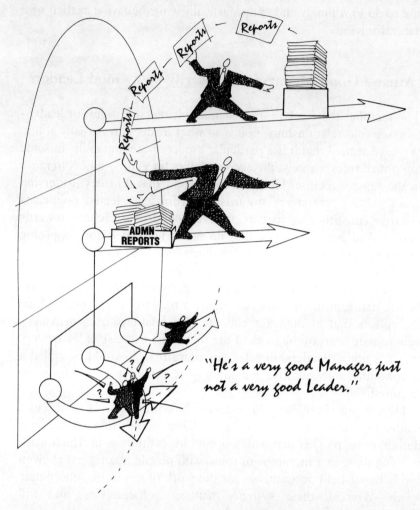

Figure 1.6 Must a good manager necessarily be a good leader?

integral part of its functions, without which managership *per se* cannot exist.

In short, we start the discussion with managerial roles. Planning, communicating, setting operational targets, resourcing, follow-up and control, appraising effectiveness, coaching, merit recognition, selection and induction, are everyday parts of ordinary managerial work. And so also is it an everyday part of the successful discharging of the managerial task to get the willing and enthusiastic collaboration of subordinates in this work. We would suggest that a useful slogan for every managerial organization would be "Each and every manager must exercise decisive value-adding leadership."

Management without Leadership Accountability is Lifeless

Despite the self-evident fact that leadership accountability should automatically be an ordinary part of any managerial role, the past 20 years have seen a continual plague of books, articles and memoranda on the theme of whether a manager is also a leader or should be a leader or whether we need leaders rather than managers or whether we need leaders who are also able to manage and to administer.

The common notion is that it is somehow possible to be a good manager without necessarily being a good leader; or to be a good leader in a managerial hierarchy without being a good manager. This almost universal separating of leadership and management (and administration) is a sign of the powerful confusion and vagueness that exist about the meaning both of leadership and of managing.

The basis of this confusion between management and leadership is that leadership is endowed with virtue, strength and creativity whereas management (and administration) are seen as concerned with the mundane, dull and tedious everyday routines of work. Therefore, from this point of view, someone who is a good manager (administrator) might be a good unimaginative bureaucrat but is unlikely to be able to engage others to scale the heights. Whereas someone who is a good leader will enjoy building excitement in others but will be unlikely to have much taste for the drab routines that are supposed to comprise managing.

Once this unfortunate separation is made between management and leadership, the problem then is to try to put them back together again. And that proves inevitably to be an impossible task. Our advice is not to make this unrealistic and incorrect separation in the first place (see figure 1.7).

The Debasement of the Role of Manager

This separation of "manager" from "leader" has reinforced the modern-day tendency to debase the idea of the managerial role. A

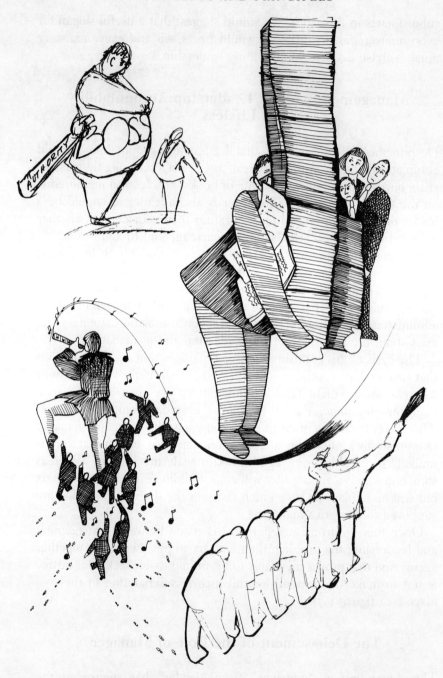

Figure 1.7   Management without leadership accountability is lifeless

manager is seen as "boss"; a boss is seen as someone who has hierarchical authority; and hierarchical authority has had a bad name for a long time as autocratic and coercive domination of others. A leader, however, is not seen as a boss but as someone who gets things done exclusively by a "good personality" without exercising any "nasty," one-way downwards, oppressive authority.

But it is simply not true that "hierarchical authority" and "manager" must mean oppressive relationships. Just because many managers tend, in the absence of effective organization, to behave in this way and to be bureaucratic, mechanistic and coercive, does not mean that the managerial hierarchy must inevitably be like that. Nor does it mean that there is any gain to be had by swinging to the equally unrealistic pole of denying the overwhelming value of the constructive use of authority. We shall show that the effective exercise of authority, which must exist in any role in which leadership accountability may appear, is an absolutely essential element in the effective discharge of that accountability.

More specifically, with respect to this book, we shall establish the proper meaning of managerial roles and manager–subordinate role relationships, replete with managerial accountability including leadership accountability, and the equivalent managerial authority to go with it (see figure 1.8). And we shall use the term "authority" in its correct sense of being authoritative in requiring others to do things, rather than in the all too commonly distorted and debased sense of its being authoritarian or autocratic.

By doing so, we hope to show that managership and leadership are not different, but rather that it is unacceptable for managers to ignore their leadership accountabilities, and that managers who do so must be made to move over and make room for those who want to exercise leadership accountability and can.

What is a Manager?

We have described leadership as a particular kind of accountability that appears in some but not in all kinds of roles, and that has to do with direction setting for others, and getting them all willingly and effectively working and moving together in the same direction. But we are confining our attention to leadership accountability only in

Figure 1.8 Shifting the aim of managerial leadership

managerial roles. It would be useful at this stage, therefore, to define precisely and unequivocally what we mean by a managerial role.

A manager is someone in a role (a managerial role) that carries the following three critical accountabilities:

- For the outputs of others (subordinates).
- For maintaining a team of subordinates who are capable of producing the outputs required.
- For the leadership of subordinates so that they collaborate competently and with full commitment with the manager and with each other in pursuing the goals set.

These accountabilities need to be made explicit, and every manager at every level needs to be taught clearly and unequivocally that he or she is accountable for these critical functions. Our experience has consistently been that effective managerial leadership is not possible unless every manager is aware of and carries out these explicit duties. It is also the bounden duty of the manager of every manager to oversee the work of those managerial subordinates, and to appraise their personal effectiveness in discharging their managerial accountabilities as we have defined them.

Managerial leadership is thus not just a nice thing to have if the managers in an organization happen to be "natural-born leaders with the right personalities." It lies at the heart of the ability of an organization to muster every ounce of creative human energy from its people, and to get that energy driving in the right direction. All managers need to know that they will actually be judged in terms of their discharge of leadership accountability, and that ineffective leadership is unacceptable: that is what accountability is about.

Minimum Managerial Authority

By the same token, we propose to take seriously the notion that a person cannot discharge accountability unless he or she has the concomitant authority. That is an ancient principle but one that is insufficiently enforced in management. There are in fact four basic minimum authorities that are essential if managers are to be held accountable for managerial leadership. Failure to teach and implement these authorities, indeed failure even to articulate them in the first place, is the Achilles' heel of managerial leadership development.

The overriding authority that managers must have is to be able to have a team of subordinates who are at least not unacceptable. That is to say, managers cannot expect to have nothing but subordinates who are "just right" for the work to be done; that is expecting too much. But they can expect not to have subordinates who simply cannot do

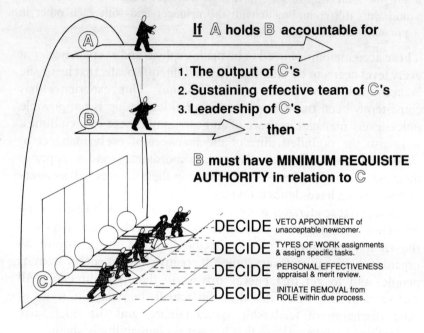

"Accountability for..."
"Authority in relation to..."

If Ⓐ holds Ⓑ accountable for

1. **The output of Ⓒ's**
2. **Sustaining effective team of Ⓒ's**
3. **Leadership of Ⓒ's**
   ----- **then** -----

Ⓑ **must have MINIMUM REQUISITE AUTHORITY in relation to** Ⓒ

DECIDE VETO APPOINTMENT of unacceptable newcomer.

DECIDE TYPES OF WORK assignments & assign specific tasks.

DECIDE PERSONAL EFFECTIVENESS appraisal & merit review.

DECIDE INITIATE REMOVAL from ROLE within due process.

Figure 1.9   What is a manager?

the work for which the manager is being held accountable. Managers therefore require at the absolute minimum the following four authorities:

Veto on appointment   While not having absolutely free rein in making a new appointment, the manager must be able to reject any candidate whom he or she judges not to be capable of doing the work required.

Decide task assignment   The manager, and not his or her manager or anyone else, must decide what types of work their subordinates are given to do.

Decide personal effectiveness appraisal and merit awards   The operative word here is "decide" (as against recommending to a higher manager or to a committee for them to decide) but the manager must maintain regular appraisal and coaching as part of the price of having the authority to make these decisions.

Decide to initiate removal from role   If, after fair warning and coaching, a manager has decided that a subordinate can really no longer do the work required to be done, then that manager must be able to determine that that subordinate will no longer work for him or her. But it should be noted that the manager does not need the authority to fire anyone, in the sense of dismissing him or her, from the organization (other than for gross misdemeanors), since the subordinate might be competent to work in some other area of the company.

An effective managerial leader will learn to exercise these authorities properly in discharging his or her accountabilities (see figure 1.9). It is extraordinarily frustrating for someone to be put in a position of managerial accountability without these authorities. It is soul-destroying for a manager to have unacceptable subordinates foisted upon him or her, and certainly inconsistent with the demands of managerial leadership.

Conditions of Leadership: Psychological Conditions

The argument we are pursuing is that the ability to exercise leadership is not some great "charismystery" but is, rather, an ordinary quality to be found in Everyman and Everywoman so long as the essential conditions exist. These conditions may be summarized under the psychological qualities that must be possessed by the people involved and the social conditions within which the leadership situation occurs.

We have described why there are no specific leadership roles but only leadership accountability as part of the accountability in some specific roles. The formulation becomes of first importance when we consider the psychological conditions necessary for the exercise of leadership accountability.

The major psychological condition in managerial leadership is the individual's personal capability to exercise the functions and duties of the managerial role. One cannot exercise managerial leadership, for example, or combat command leadership, or political leadership, unless one has the necessary capability to carry out the managerial work, or command work, or political representative work, required in the role, at a level of complexity or capacity that matches the level of work in the role.

If we cannot discharge all the functions of our role we do not stand the ghost of a chance of exercising leadership in relation to others, since there is no way in which those others will have confidence in us.

For a manager to rely solely upon charisma or other aspects of social personality or charm or artificial style, without the basic capabilities required in the managerial role, is an utterly counter-productive manipulation. People will follow a charismatic manager for the wrong reasons and moreover will follow along behind, rather than with him or her, because the manager cannot give them the framework of understanding that is needed for effective leadership of the going-along-together kind. Charisma is a quality relevant only to cult leadership.

The other psychological condition in managerial leadership is the ability to gain personally earned trust and respect from others. We shall show that to gain this trust and respect is mainly a matter of sensible and consistent application of requisite practices which we shall describe and which need to be specified by the organization. In addition, one needs personally to value the work in the role, including the leadership work and its necessary valuing of others and their work.

We propose to show that, given these values and abilities, anyone who is not functionally disabled by inhibitions or other disturbances that might impair work and working relationships will be capable of gaining the personally earned authority from others that is the goal of leadership accountability.

Some people will be marginally better and some marginally poorer at gaining the confidence of others, depending upon the strength of their values and of their wisdom in dealing with others. But we are all engaged day in and day out in gaining people's confidence, and fortunately there are no great skills that have to be learned. The most important thing is to be able to carry out the level of work complexity in the role rather than to apply some special personality qualities or style (see figure 1.10).

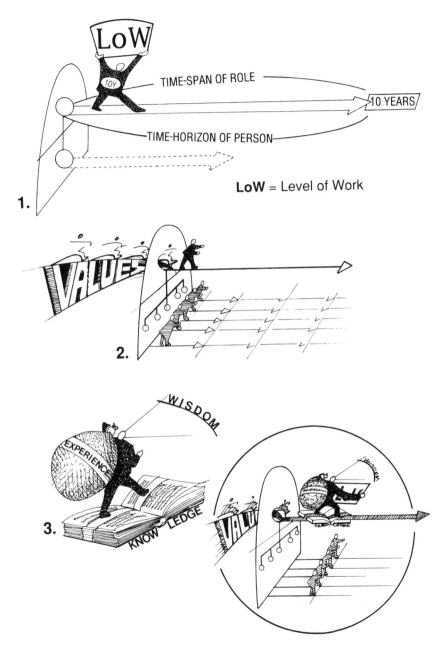

Figure 1.10 Conditions of leadership: psychological conditions

Conditions of Leadership: Organizational Conditions

When we turn to the organizational conditions that are essential for effective leadership, we can remove the last vestiges of mystery that surround the nature of leadership.

In particular, this demystification of leadership will shift the focus of attention away from the current excessive preoccupation with the psychological traits and styles that are supposed (incorrectly, we believe) to be what leadership is about. It is this current focus upon psychological characteristics and style that leads to the unfortunate attempts within companies to change the personalities of individuals, or to maintain procedures aimed at getting "a correct balance" of personalities in working groups such as a manager's group of subordinates or an *ad hoc* project task force. Our analysis and experience would suggest that such practices are at best likely to be counterproductive in the medium and longer term, however much they may give people a nice, fuzzy, warm feeling in the short term.

We shall adopt an approach that says that neither effective leadership nor effective leadership development is possible unless the organizational conditions are right. We shall argue that, in the case of managerial leadership, the organizational conditions have never been gotten even approximately right; they are universally primitive. We shall argue further that, until and unless the organizational conditions are gotten right, no progress will be made in the field of executive leadership. It is, moreover, our conclusion that attempts to improve leadership by psychologically changing our "leaders" serve mainly as placebos or band-aids which, however well-intentioned they may be, nevertheless obscure the grossly undermining effects of the widespread organizational shortcomings and destructive defects.

Because we are dealing in this book only with leadership in managerial (executive) roles and role relationships, we shall confine our attention to this type of organization. The same kind of analysis would have to be carried through for others, such as military organizations, political organizations, families, churches, universities, and schools.

The main organizational issues that we shall cover throughout this book are as follows.

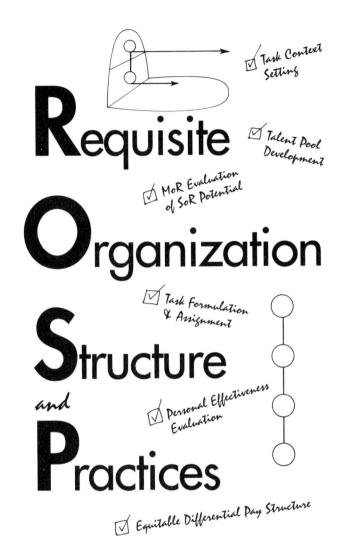

Requisite ☑ Task Context Setting

☑ Talent Pool Development

☑ MoR Evaluation of SoR Potential

Organization

☑ Task Formulation & Assignment

Structure

and

☑ Personal Effectiveness Evaluation

Practices

☑ Equitable Differential Pay Structure

Figure 1.11 Conditions of leadership: organizational conditions

- What constitutes "right" organization, or, as we shall formulate it, "requisite organization"?[1]
- How to use "clear articulation of mission" and resulting functions to structure role relationships correctly.
- Requisite structuring of organizational stratification (layers), to ensure that managers are sufficiently greater in level of capability than their subordinates to be able to exercise effective leadership.

- The establishment of planning processes in relation to direction-setting.
- Creating information and communication processes at the right level of complexity for each layer of organization.
- Requisite managerial leadership practices (see figure 1.11) with respect to:

  - Selection and induction.
  - Context setting and assigning of tasks.
  - Regular evaluation of personal effectiveness of subordinates, and coaching.
  - Assessment of current and future potential of subordinates-once-removed by managers-once-removed (MoRs/SoRs), mentoring, and career development.
  - Senior executive talent pool development and succession planning.
  - Education, training, and leadership development.

Unto the Breach

> Once more unto the breach, dear friends, once more;
> Or close the wall up with our English dead.
> In peace there's nothing so becomes a man
> As modest stillness and humility;
> But when the blast of war blows in our ears,
> Then imitate the action of the tiger:
> Stiffen the sinews, summon up the blood,
> Disguise fair nature with hard favour'd rage;
> Then lend the eye a terrible aspect;
>
> (Shakespeare: *Henry V*, III. i. 1–9)

All the issues we have raised in this chapter are magnified, and so can be seen more clearly, when men command and lead other men into battle and killing is at issue and life and death are at stake. Charisma and mass-produced razzle-dazzle style will be of no avail; they will be handicaps. What will be needed are properly selected commanders who are exercising their own genuine personalities and are fully trained in a finely tuned combat organizational system.

And that organizational system must be such as to function effectively in the relative calm of peacetime and to be able to transform instantaneously so as to function just as effectively under the wildly disorientating and stress-laden conditions of modern warfare.

First and foremost, every commander must not only possess the necessary ability to handle complexity to match the level of complexity in the situation (these concepts will be fully explicated later) but also must be seen, and clearly seen, to have that capability.

There is no way in which a commander can gain personally earned authority from soldiers in combat unless they have full confidence that that commander knows what he is doing. They must know, in short, that their commander is a winner and can bring them all through on top. This capability includes cognitive capability, knowledge of battle, physical war fighting skills, and wisdom in understanding not only his own men but also the minds of his opposition.

Along with these capabilities goes the paramount importance of values – values strongly held and expressed unequivocally and consistently in word and deed. The senior command must exude the values of the nation and cascade those values right down through every echelon to the bottom. These values include, among other traditional military values, the absolute commitment to victory and total caring for the well-being of subordinates.

Requisite organizational structure is the absolute foundation for effective military leadership. Clearly structured echelons and units are essential for commanders of units at every echelon to be able to move readily and rapidly and to deploy fire power. This dependence upon organization is why the military have been intensely preoccupied with continual experimentation in organization from the times of the very earliest great armies.

And we shall see, also, why requisite practices by commanders in requisite roles take on such an immense importance. Planning, information, communication, clear operation orders and follow-up must be perfected to the nth degree for combat. And in peacetime, talent pool development, human resources assessment and planning, continual appraisal of effectiveness accompanied by coaching, and combat training, are among the factors essential for the sustainment of a peacetime military continuously at the combat-ready.

All the above points readily translate into the managerial situation (see figure 1.12). The emphasis lies not upon the charismatic leader and style but upon the competent commander-leader in a sound organization, just as it should lie upon the competent managerial leader working in a sound managerial organization.

Figure 1.12   Unto the breach

General Leadership Responsibility

Our focus is upon the leadership process in roles that carry leadership accountability, in particular managerial and other executive roles. There is a general issue of leadership, however, that we must mention, one that transcends all role relationships regardless of whether or not they carry established leadership accountability. That issue is the broad social responsibility carried by any one of us to try to exercise leadership in any situation in which we find ourselves involved and that we think requires people to move in the same direction, and where we think we have whatever special knowledge or ability the situation demands.

We would draw attention to the fact that we are here using

the notion of leadership responsibility, in contrast to leadership accountability. The distinction is an important one.

By leadership "accountability" we refer to a relationship with others in which our exercise of that leadership will be appraised by a specified person or persons who have the authority to call us to account for how well or how badly we have done.

By leadership "responsibility" (or indeed any responsibility), however, the matter of how we conduct ourselves lies between each one of us and our own social conscience, our personal sense of what we ought to do under given circumstances where we feel that something or other should be done. What we do will influence what others think about us, how they regard us. But nobody carries the authority to call us to account (so long, of course, as we do not act illegally).

Examples of this general leadership responsibility are commonplace. Take the case of a public accident of some kind, in which one of the crowd feels that he or she has special knowledge of what should be done under the circumstances until official police and para-medics arrive, and so steps forward and tries to establish the personally earned authority to get the bystanders to take whatever concerted action he or she thinks is necessary. Such situations can arise under many circumstances other than catastrophes, such as pulling friends together at an outing, in which there is a need for someone to step forward spontaneously and take the lead.

We have introduced this topic of general leadership responsibilities for two reasons. The first is to show how deeply leadership notions are embedded in the most general issues of social conscience, social morality, and the general social good. The second is to show the relevance of this general leadership responsibility for all roles in the executive organizations we shall be considering.

General leadership responsibility must apply even where a person's role does not carry leadership accountability. Thus, for example, subordinates must strive to carry leadership responsibility even toward their managers whenever they consider it to be for everyone's good for them to do so. That is to say, they must take initiative in bringing forward their arguments as strongly as possible where they think their manager is taking a wrong direction (see figure 1.13) – dropping the matter, of course, if the manager does not in the end agree.

Figure 1.13 General leadership responsibility

The point is that managers and anyone in a role with leadership accountability need to be assured that their people will pursue this general responsibility when they think it necessary. Without that assurance, managers would be deprived of an important source of information about their circumstances. It is part of the effective exercise of managerial leadership to ensure that subordinates do discharge their general leadership responsibilities to the manager, to one another, and to others in other parts of the organization.

The effective and sensible discharge of general leadership responsibility is one sign of a healthy collaborative organization.

Note

1 This theme is elaborated in Jaques (1989) *Requisite Organization*.

2

Human Nature at Work

We have argued in the previous chapter why leadership and leaders do not exist on their own, with their own special competencies. Leadership accountability occurs in some but not all roles and relationships. Effective leadership depends first and foremost upon competence in role. The particular roles we are concerned with are managerial roles and manager–subordinate relationships. The issues in managerial leadership thus boil down to what is the nature of the competence necessary for doing managerial work and how can this work be done in such a way that subordinates will work willingly and effectively with the manager and with each other in order to go along together in the direction set.

Leadership and Competence

The unique significance of competence in role in managerial leadership shows in the fact that by far the most important factor in the successful functioning of any company is the match between the level of capability of the corporate CEO (and, secondarily, of the CEO's subordinate executive vice-presidents, EVPs) and the level of work called for in the CEO's role. We cannot emphasize this point enough. When a CEO is not quite up to the level of work in his or her role, there is an almost universal tendency to deny it, or at least not to discuss it, or to hide the problem under a rug, or to look the other way. Conversely, when the CEO has competence to burn, relative to the level of work in his or her role, and the corporation is thriving, his or her personality, or some special values, or unusual integrity, or some particular factor associated with leadership, will be stressed, and the fact of an unusually high level of pure native competence for the CEO role will be underplayed or only partially recognized.

If a corporation is doing very well over the long haul, look to the competence of the CEO as the most likely overriding cause. It is not a function of market circumstances or other lucky break "out there," since those factors can be relied upon only in the short term. A highly competent CEO takes advantage of changing market conditions, creates opportunities out of new situations and new technologies and sustains a team of competent subordinates in a rich talent pool.

In the same vein, if a corporation has been doing badly over the long haul, look to the CEO as having a level of competence (LoC) lower than that required by the level of work (LoW) in the CEO role. We use the abbreviation LoC < LoW to refer to situations where the capability of the person is less than the level of work in the role. The seriousness of any such disparity is, in a way, self-evident. Its full consequence, however, tends to be obscured, or difficult to get our hands on, because up until now we have not had the concepts that allow us to make a clear distinction between level of capability and level of work.

The seriousness of this LoC < LoW disparity is that it is becoming increasingly widespread today, especially in our larger organizations. The shortfall is at the top. It is characteristic of far too many of our large-scale organizations in industry, in commerce, and especially in public service. It causes a deterioration in quality of work and competitiveness.

In competitive industry and commerce, it leads to business contraction and to takeovers and buy-outs and subsequently to the failure of many LBOs (leveraged buy outs) where the management cannot muster any greater talent than they had before. In public service, where the scale of business does not contract because it is maintained by taxation, quality simply falls and we get a continuing mediocre service.

These shortcomings are often put down to a failure of "leadership," with its not being too clear just what is meant by leadership. Our argument is that in order to get effective leadership and excellence at the top, there is one essential condition that must be met, namely, competence at a level required by the work. We shall thus specify in this chapter what we mean by competence, and in the next chapter what we mean by level of work.

Who are the Great "Leaders"?

There are studies and biographies galore down through the ages seeking to explain the particular characteristics of great leaders. Although such characteristics have been picked over and over, there is no clear evidence of any particularly consistent personality qualities that stand out as true even for most, if not all, of these greats. But the central significance of raw native competence tends not to be systematically taken into account.

A popular conclusion these days is that it is the values of the great leaders that characterize them; especially, a valuing of their people, and, in the case of industry, their customers or their suppliers. Or they have great integrity; or are trustworthy; or they are totally committed to the task; and so on and on. The trouble with such analyses, however, is that most people who are not singular leaders nevertheless possess the supposedly significant personality qualities. And many people who are recognized as great leaders do not necessarily possess them in any unusual amount.

There is a catch somewhere. Something is wrong. Indeed, the catch is in the idea of the great "leader." We have argued that there is no such thing as free-standing "leaders." There are great military commanders, great industrial entrepreneurs, great presidents, great political representatives, but there are not great leaders *per se*.

Moreover, once we reformulate the matter from the notion of the "leader" to the full concept of the particular role – military command, political representative, entrepreneurial CEO – within which leadership accountability was also discharged, the problem of what constitutes the great "leader" becomes readily resolvable. They are all people with enormous capability in role. In terms that we shall describe, they all had ability to burn, ability way above that absolutely required by the level of work in their roles (see figure 2.1).

Thus, Napoleon was not just a military commander: he had the capability necessary to be political head of France, to create the French administrative system, to operate in almost superhuman manner. Charles de Gaulle was the same, as were MacArthur and Washington. Ho Chi Minh was a good example of what can happen when an individual of enormous competence becomes head of a small nation.

General De Puy has put this issue of "leadership" versus

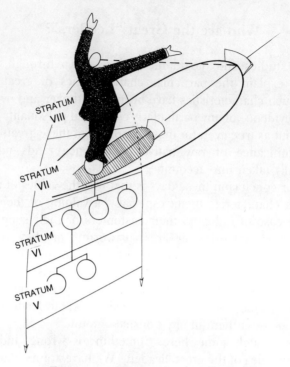

Figure 2.1   Who are the great "leaders"?

outstanding competence in role very clearly and vividly in his description of General MacArthur in Korea:

In the summer of 1950 US Eighth Army was penned into the Pusan Perimeter in Korea. It was not a shining moment in the history of American arms. Then, in the face of skepticism on the part of his advisers – subordinates and superiors – General of the Army Douglas MacArthur launched a sweeping amphibious left hook to Inchon. N Corps, led by Marines, went on to Seoul, cut the main supply route of the North Korean army and collapsed the invasion.

Inchon was an incandescent moment and a smashing victory, which sprang solely from the mind of the top commander. The experiences of a lifetime, the lonely thoughts of a superior mind and the demands of the crisis at hand combined inside General MacArthur's head to produce a stroke of genius – a concept of operations so powerful and unexpected that it carried the day, the battle and that first campaign of a long and disagreeable war.

(William E. De Puy, Gen. US Army ret., *Army*, August 1988, pp. 29–30)

Now was this great leadership? Only in part. It was first and foremost great combat commandership. The command leadership was there as a workmanlike part of the total packet, since MacArthur with some difficulty certainly succeeded in getting the Eighth Army to move along together with him. Otherwise, the victory could not have been won. And they did not follow because of his personality: both his senior commanders and his subordinates followed because of their confidence in his vast competence as commander. It is the competence as commander that is the prime issue.

As far as leadership is concerned, we must concentrate on the role in which leadership is but one part of the total accountability being discharged. When we do this, the "great leaders" turn out to be those individuals with super levels of competence; that is to say, with levels of competence well beyond that required by the level of work in the role as established.

In order to elaborate this proposition, we shall turn to a consideration of the nature of work and of level of work, and of the nature of the human competence required in carrying out that work, as the foundations of our analysis of managerial organization and managerial leadership.

The Nature of Work and Tasks

The capability we are trying to understand is the capability to do work. In order to understand work itself, it is useful to note that there are two major kinds of human behavior: musing or reverie, which is behavior without a goal, and goal-directed behavior, which is what work is. Both are important, but we are concerned in this book only with goal-directed behavior, that is to say, with work and with work that is tied in with leadership accountability.

Work is directly associated with goal-directed behavior or, in other terms, with the carrying out of tasks. A task is an assignment in which we have to produce a given output within a given time, and we have to do it with the method and with the financial, physical and organizational resources that we have been given, and we also have to conform to the ruling policies, regulations and procedures.

In short, a task is an assignment to achieve a given goal (or a what-by-when) with allocated resources and methods and within prescribed limits. In managerial hierarchies, tasks are assigned by a person's manager or by others (including the person) acting for the manager.

The work concerns the discretion and judgment that the person has to use in carrying out tasks. In order to do the work, it is necessary to value doing it, to bring to it the skilled application of the necessary knowledge, and to act with wisdom, in order to exercise (and here is the real work) the necessary discretion and judgment in making decisions in order to attain the goal.

Work is thus about good judgment and decision-making (see figure 2.2). It is not about doing what we already know so well that we can do it automatically without thinking, such as carrying out lists of calculations. Any computer can do that.

Work is about pondering, wondering, uncertainty, choosing to do this rather than that at critical decision points, starting with choosing one pathway rather than another within the general method specified to be used, and continuing to use judgment in overcoming obstacles until the goal is reached. No computer can make such choices, because it is not the computers that really choose!

Figure 2.2   The nature of work

The point about working is that we have to find our way through a continually changing complex of variables that constitute the information we have to be able to take into account. Thus, suppose we are trying to sell a new product to an established customer: we have to take into account the customer's needs, the buyer's outlook, what our competitors are offering, how best to make a first approach, what arguments to use, possible price discounts, and so on. Or suppose we are trying to get a production order completed: we have to take into account our work load, the state of our job tools, the skill levels of our labor, the availability and the quality of raw materials or components, and so on. Or suppose we are working to acquire a new subsidiary company: we have to take into account its balance sheet value, its position in the market, our own capital situation, cash-flow implications, enhanced market thrust, condition of capital equipment, relations with banks, and on and on and on.

It does not require a great stretch of the imagination to recognize that, for example, in the third of the above instances, not only will vastly more variables be encountered on the way than in the first two but also each of the variables will in itself be more abstract, more conceptual, more general, more intricately woven, more difficult to perceive and get into perspective, and more changeable.

In working we have to deal with these multiplicities of variables. The greater the number of the variables, the more ambiguous the variables, the more rapidly changing the variables, and the more the variables are intertwined so that they have to be teased apart in order to be dealt with, so the more complex does the task seem to be, and the more difficult is the work to be done in carrying it out.

In short, work is the use of discretion and judgment in making decisions in order to proceed towards a goal (i.e. to carry out a task).

As we proceed with our work, we encounter many variables or unanticipated factors in the situation and we have to deal with them. Those variables constitute the information embedded in the task, and therefore the complexity of the task. Now this may be academically interesting, but what does it have to do with hierarchical leadership? The answer is simple: plenty! The more complex the task, the more difficult is the work and the greater is the competence required to handle it, hence the starting point for effective hierarchical leadership. Subordinates are intensely aware of whether and how well their managers handle the complexity of their situation in general and of their own tasks in particular.

If a manager can handle the complexity, and handle it well, the manager will win much personally earned authority, and the subordinates will be reassured and will be more willing to go along together and expend their own full competence with enthusiasm in the direction set. Moreover, this enthusiasm is reinforced by the fact that the competent manager will be able to set an effective context at an appropriate level of complexity for the subordinates to work within.

An effective managerial leader must not only be capable of handling the complexity in his or her own role but also be able to be seen to be doing so. Effective managerial leadership absolutely depends upon the confidence of subordinates in the ability of the manager to do his or her own work effectively. Without that confidence no trust is possible. Without mutual confidence and trust, no one is going to lead anyone anywhere.

The Importance of having a "Big Enough" Manager

Anyone who has ever been employed in a managerial hierarchy will at some time or other have had a manager who was not sufficiently greater in capability than the person concerned, to give effective managerial leadership. Such a manager cannot set adequate context; gets involved in too much detail; breathes down the subordinate's neck; seems to be more comfortable doing work that the subordinate ought to be doing; does not add any value; is inclined to take all the credit for what goes well, and to blame the subordinate for everything that goes wrong. The experience is unpleasant, and morale-breaking. It is the exact opposite of what managerial leadership ought to be. It is, unfortunately, so common as almost to be the rule rather than the exception. Its widespread occurrence is a major social disease.

Even worse is to have a manager whose level of capability is below that of the subordinate. This circumstance also occurs much more frequently than might be thought possible. It is nothing short of a disastrous producer of stress and conflict. It is a powerful testament to the toughness and constructiveness of human nature that we are able to get any work done at all in our managerial hierarchies, so common is the disruptive state of affairs we are describing.

These difficulties arise mainly from organizational shortcomings. There are no commonly available sound principles for arranging the structure of organizational layers, or for specifying the levels of competence necessary for filling managerial and subordinate roles. The result is that we ordinarily have too many layers, and our selection, appointment and promotion processes are so full of shortcomings that it is by luck rather than by design that we get optimum manager–subordinate role relationships with incumbents of the right levels of competence.

In view of these severe organizational difficulties, the present-day tendency to see organizational problems in terms of psychologically determined personality conflicts is most unfortunate, because it obscures the organizational sources of most conflict, pointing the finger at individuals rather than at the organizational morass that lies at the heart of the problem. A useful principle is that no difficulties arising between individuals in these organizations is to be seen as arising from personality difficulties, unless and until it has been clearly established that the organizational context is requisite!

By contrast, we may have had the experience of working for a manager whose level of capability was sufficiently greater than our own to enable him or her to set clear context and assignments, to be helpful when problems arose, and to be self-assured enough to get on with his or her work while leaving the subordinates to get on with theirs. What a refreshing experience that can be, however infrequently it might occur. There is nothing wrong with the managerial hierarchy when such conditions exist. With effective value-adding managerial leadership, the managerial hierarchy can be a most creative and humanly satisfying institution, one that uplifts the human spirit and contributes to the good society.

Our experience thus points to an absolute condition for achieving decisive, humanly constructive managerial leadership: the managerial leader must be a quantum step higher in capability than his or her immediate subordinates. But how big must that quantum step be? What is the nature of this capability that seems to be of such importance? And how can we organize to ensure this condition?

We propose to address these questions in the next few sections under the heading of cognitive processing and complexity. This subject is probably the single most important topic in the book. Unfortunately the material is new and will be unfamiliar. It is also inherently difficult, since it involves a change in frame of reference from the current, more familiar ways of looking at human competence. With this word of warning, therefore, we now turn to the subject of human competence and cognitive processing. This will lead us into the basic groundwork of requisite organizational structuring and evaluation of individual potential that is crucial to the establishment and sustainment of total systems of effective managerial leadership.

Leadership Competence is a Function of Role Competence

We have emphasized that there are no such things as free-standing leaders or leadership. Managers, commanders, parents, and teachers, if they were to be competent in role, would by definition have to be competent at role leadership because their roles specifically call for effective leadership behavior in relation to subordinates, children, and pupils. The leadership component of these roles calls for the setting of direction for subordinates, children, and pupils, and for getting their willing and enthusiastic collaboration to go along with the direction-setter and with each other. It is a flat contradiction in terms to have a competent manager, commander, parent, or teacher who is not effective with the leadership accountability that is an integral part of those roles.

Leadership competence, therefore, is a matter fundamentally of competence in the specific role that carries the leadership account- ability. What do we mean by competence in role? What are its elements? What is it composed of? Can it be developed? To answer these questions, we shall need a few precise definitions. They are among the most important ideas in the book.

In order to sort out these definitions, we shall have to sort out two problems. The first problem is that of terminology. There are many terms for what we want to talk about; namely, competence, capability, capacity, ability. We shall use them interchangeably but will couch our definitions in terms of *capability* for doing work.

The second problem arises because most of us think mainly in terms of two aspects when we consider a person's capability; namely, a person's actual or present capability, and that person's potential or future capability. We propose, however, to show that there are three different aspects to be sorted out: a person's current actual capability, plus two kinds of potential – the person's current potential (as distinguished from current actual), and that person's future potential. We shall use the following definitions.

Current Actual Capability is the capability to do a particular kind of work at a given level; for example, to operate a lathe, to manage a sales organization, to design new products. The level of a person's capability to do some particular kind of work will depend not only upon that person's current cognitive power (see the formula on p. 46) but also upon how much he or she values that kind of work, and whether or not he or she has had the training and experience (accumulating the skilled knowledge) necessary to do the work (see figure 2.3). Thus, someone who does not value giving leadership to subordinates is unlikely to have high capability for work in a managerial role as compared to working as an individual contributor, doing work in which he or she is keenly

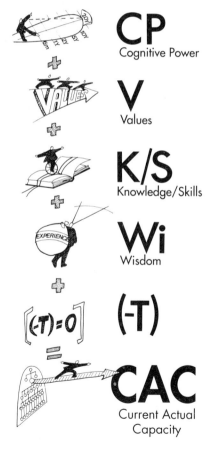

CP Cognitive Power

V Values

K/S Knowledge/Skills

Wi Wisdom

(-T) $[(-T)=0]$

CAC Current Actual Capacity

Figure 2.3 Leadership competence is a function of role competence interested and for which he or she has the necessary skilled knowledge. This concept can be expressed as a formula as follows:

$$\text{Current Actual Capacity (CAC)} = f \text{ CP. V. K/S. Wi. (-T)}$$

CP = Cognitive power (cognitive-complexity, or the innate mental ability to organize information).
V = Values (interest, priorities).
K/S = Skilled use of relevant knowledge.
Wi = Wisdom about people and things.
(-T) = "Minus T", or the absence of serious personality (temperamental) defects.

Current Potential Capability is the maximum level at which a person could currently work given optimum opportunities and conditions provided that the work is of deep inherent value for the person, even though he or she has not had past opportunity to acquire the necessary skilled knowledge.

We shall show that a person's current potential capability (CPC) is determined by that person's cognitive power alone. The significance of a person's CPC is that it is the critical judgment for determining at what level a person ought to have the opportunity to be employed, regardless of gender, color, etc., and for talent pool mapping and career development.

The significance of the difference between current actual capability and current potential capability can be illustrated in the case of individuals who were disadvantaged in educational and employment opportunities, and who do not have the necessary skilled knowledge for anything other than unskilled work. Their current actual capability does not, however, necessarily accurately portray their current potential were they given the opportunity to make up for their lack of education and occupational experience. We shall show not only that sound career and talent pool development depends upon the assessment of the potential capability of individuals (an obvious point), but also how to assess that potential (a less obvious point) and rapidly overcome the deficiencies in skilled knowledge.

Future Potential Capability is the maximum level at which a person will be capable of working, say, at 5, 10, or 15 years into the future.

We shall show not only how future potential is determined by the maturation of cognitive power, but also how to predict it.

What about the generally assumed importance of personality factors in managerial leadership? We have already indicated at various points that anyone who values occupying a particular role which carries leadership accountability (that is to say, who genuinely and strongly wants that role) will be successful in carrying the leadership component so long as he or she has the necessary competence to carry the role itself. That person need not have any particular personality traits that are supposed to be specific to the "leadership" requirements of the role.

Thus, we would argue that if a person has the competence to handle the role of general manager of an engineering components factory, or of a sales force, or of a research department, and that person enjoys and relishes that role of general manager, then he or she will be able to exercise the leadership accountability in the role in relation to his or her subordinates just as effectively as another person with the same level of competence, regardless of the possession of any particular personality traits or characteristics – so long as none of them is of a quality to disturb working relationships with others. A thousand different people under such circumstances will "lead" in a thousand different ways with a thousand different styles and all will be effective, so long as none is socially debilitated by psychopathology. This enormously wide range of so-called "leadership styles" is what is found in practice and no special style has been proved to be better than any other.

The conclusion that we shall offer is that effective leadership demands four straightforward and basic conditions. First, a person must have the necessary competence to carry the particular role, including strongly valuing it. Second, that person must be free from any severely debilitating psychological characteristics that interfere with interpersonal relationships. Third, the organizational conditions must be requisite, including both requisite organizational structure and specified managerial leadership practices. Fourth, each person must be encouraged to use his or her own natural style; namely, to allow the full and free expression of his or her own natural self. It is necessary, in short, to be able to "be oneself."

It will be apparent that by role competence for managerial leadership we do not mean this or that list of traits or personality qualities which has been gleaned from interviews in which successful "leaders" state what they think is important, or built up from a psychological analysis of personality traits of those "leaders." What we are after is an analysis of the factors required for competence in work, based upon a coherent and consistent set of principles.

We shall turn first, therefore, to a description of the cognitive processes in people, and of how cognitive complexity grows and matures in individuals. We shall show that cognitive complexity comes in the same kind of discontinuous step functions as does task complexity. Then we shall describe why effective managerial leadership can occur only when managers are one category higher in cognitive complexity than their subordinates. Moreover we shall demonstrate how this approach can lay a foundation for the early identification of high-potential managerial leaders and for the development of a sound corporate talent pool.

Following our analysis of cognitive processes, we shall explain why we are replacing notions of motivation by the concept of values, and will describe the precise way in which we are using the words "knowledge," "skills," and "wisdom." Finally we shall describe how we propose to take personality (temperamental) characteristics into account.

Cognitive Processes and Cognitive Power (CP)

The concept of cognitive processing is one of the most central ideas in this book. It lies at the heart of any possibility of understanding the nature of competence in work. It has to do with the particular characteristics of the mental processing in individuals that is required for handling and organizing information. This processing enables the individual to deal with information complexity: when a person's cognitive processing is up to the complexity, he or she is comfortable; when the information is too complex, information overload occurs; and when the person's cognitive processing could handle greater complexity, boredom and frustration result.

Cognitive processes are the mental processes by means of which a person is able to organize information to make it available for doing work.

We have defined complexity in terms of the number, ambiguity, rate of change, and interweaving of variables involved in a problem. Task complexity thus has to do with the amount and quality of information that must be processed in the course of carrying out any task, and understanding this reality provides a useful insight into the nature of the maximum potential capability in the individual. The ability of individuals to handle complexity in doing work is reflected in how they manipulate and organize variables: some people seem to be able to gather up and deal with huge quantities of variables all at once, some with medium amounts, and some with very few.

It will be evident that, regardless of the necessary values, knowledge, skill, and wisdom for a particular type of work, there will always be a ceiling on the number of variables – the amount of information – that a given person can carry; that is to say, there is a maximum level of complexity that any person can cope with. Just as the mental processes that determine the level of complexity that a person can carry are called the cognitive processes, so we shall use the phrase "cognitive power" as defined here:

Cognitive power is the potential strength of cognitive processes in a person and is therefore the maximum level of task complexity that someone can handle at any given point in his or her development.

Our cognitive power, therefore, refers to the maximum number of variables we could deal with, the maximum amount of information we could process in a given period of time. When we can learn to count true pieces of information (and we are engaged in that search now), we will have an objective measure of cognitive power. By the very nature of things, problems come in an enormously wide range of degrees of complexity. For example, in sweeping a floor there are only a few variables to be taken into account, such as where to start and how vigorously to sweep. All are directly observable, not changing, and not nested and tangled up within each other.

At the other extreme, to direct a program of putting a man on the moon contains an uncountable number of variables: the state of the surface of the moon, its movement and position, the art of rocketry, the art of computers and control systems, human physiology, selection and training of astronauts, and so on. Each of these variables is a shifting and changing conglomeration of entangled elements, new knowledge is appearing, many factors are at best incompletely known, and all are interwoven in a great tangled skein whose pattern keeps changing.

In between, tasks and their problems may range in complexity from the relatively straightforward writing of a routine computer program to competing for a major contract (with all the difficulties of assessing client needs and outlooks and of best-guessing what the competitors might be offering), or building a new factory and getting it into production, or buying a new company.

Just as we find that the greater a person's cognitive power the

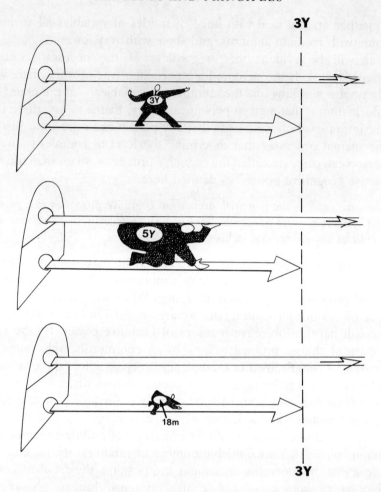

Figure 2.4 Cognitive processes and cognitive power (CP)

greater is the mass of information that can be coped with, so we find that the greater the person's cognitive power the longer is that person's working time outreach or, as we shall call it, "time-horizon" (see figure 2.4).

Time-horizon is the longest period into the future within which a person is capable of organizing and carrying through given tasks or projects, handling problems as they arise on the way, and reaching the eventual goal.

Some people can work up to a maximum outreach of a day or so, others up to some weeks, others months, and still others years; we emphasize that we are fixing on the longest. The longest tasks of any kind that a person can cope with gives a direct indication of that person's cognitive complexity, or cognitive power. We shall show later how cognitive power and time-horizon increase in a regular and predictable maturation pattern throughout life.

We are purposely going into a fair amount of detail on the theme of handling complexity. That is because handling complexity is at the heart of the competence to deal with problems. And, as we have argued, how well or how badly managers handle their problems is in turn at the heart of not only the way in which they are regarded by their subordinates but also the strength of their managerial leadership. Subordinates will go along willingly and enthusiastically with nearly any manager whom they judge to have a firm grip on day-to-day events within a clear vision of the future. As we have also indicated, to understand complexity is crucial for understanding that specific pattern of organization layering that is essential for effective managerial leadership. Let us pursue further this last theme by examining the four types of cognitive processing.

The Four Cognitive Processes

At this point we come to one of the key elements underlying the basic structure of the managerial hierarchy. It sets the most critical condition for effective managerial leadership. This element lies in the fact that one of the most striking things about cognitive processes is that not only do they come in greater and lesser degrees of complexity, but the increase in complexity from small to great does not proceed smoothly. It occurs in a series of discontinuous steps. Each of these steps is characterized by a change in the very nature or state of the cognitive process, just as materials change in state from crystalline to liquid to vapor as they are heated. We shall thus refer to these different steps as states or types of cognitive process.

In the rest of this chapter, in order to elaborate on this stepwise discontinuity in the nature of cognitive processes, we shall first describe the fundamental four types of cognitive process that have been discovered. Then we shall show how these four types reappear as we move to higher and higher levels of information complexity.

Here are the four types of cognitive process (see also figure 2.5).

Assertive processing   Organizes information and pulls it together in the form of direct associations and assertions relevant to the immediate situation.

Cumulative processing   Reasons by accumulating possibly significant pieces of information and organizing them in relation to each other so as to be able to combine them into a conclusion and decision.

Serial processing   Reasons by putting information together in a linear serial form in some logical sequence (e.g. a progressive

COGNITIVE PROCESSES

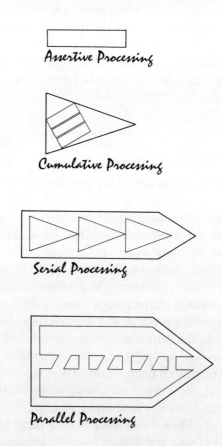

Figure 2.5   The four cognitive processes

story, or algorithm, or logic/decision tree) as a cause and effect series of events connected through time leading to envisaged consequences, and possibly to predicted future courses of events.

Parallel processing Reasons by organizing information into a number of separate serial processes, and then deals with the information in each of those processes in parallel with each other, making relationships between the processes themselves as found relevant; that is to say, showing how the processes impact upon each other.

A fundamental point is that as we mature we progress through developmental stages, moving from one type of cognitive processing to the next more complex type of process as we move from one stage to the next. We shall show in later sections how this maturation proceeds throughout the whole of one's life. Suffice it to say, for the moment, that at any stage of our development, we will use predominantly that cognitive process to which we have matured.

The Worlds People Live in: Orders of Information Complexity

We have described how cognitive processes change in state as their complexity increases, much as materials change in state with changes in their temperature. Unfortunately, however, the changes in complexity of our mental processes are not as simple as the changes in state that occur in material things. The changes in state of our mental processes are not determined by our cognitive processes alone. They are determined by a combination of a particular cognitive process and the complexity of the information a person is processing. Let us explain what we mean by the complexity of information.

There is a sense in which we all live in the same world. This world is the objective world of "everything that exists out there in its own right." This objective world is, of course, infinite and unknowable – the world of data. But what anyone of us actually knows is limited to what we can make sense of at any given moment, and that depends upon how much of the vast array of data available to us we can manage to make sense of.

The way in which we make sense of data and turn them into

information is by encompassing them in language. We literally wrap them around with words. It is a truism that if we cannot say it we cannot see it. In other words, the world anyone of us actually occupies in any meaningful sense is the world that is made up of the data we have managed to transform into information and words. In that sense, we ourselves determine the size of the world we live in, by the amounts of data from the infinite stockpile around us that we can turn into useful information.

The question is: how do we turn this vast world of data into a world of usable information from which we can extract what we need in order to solve problems and do our work? The answer to this question is that there are four ways in which we can do it. These four ways constitute what we shall call the "four orders of complexity of information." These four orders are as follows.

A First order complexity: Concrete things   The first order world is that of specific things that can be pointed to: "This one here" or "That one over there." An example of a task would be: "I take this pot, put this water in it, take an egg, put it in the water, put the pot on the stove, I light the gas and boil the egg."

It will be clear that a person can deal only with small numbers of variables at this level of concreteness.

It is the concrete world of childhood up to late adolescence for many people, such as the "juniors" in industry and commerce, and the young 18–21 year-old enlisted soldiers in the military.

The variables are clear and unambiguous, they are not tangled together, and they are relatively unchanging.

B Second order complexity: First level abstraction of verbal variables Concrete things are chunked into verbal information as used in the everyday world of ordinary discourse. We deal with each other in verbal terms without having to point to the specific concrete things that we may have in mind.

This order of information complexity allows us to discuss our work, and to issue instructions to others in a manner that makes it possible to run factories, to do designs of new products, to discuss orders with customers, to record data and get out financial accounts, to maintain information systems, and all the activities necessary to manage each and every level of a business unit.

An example of work within this second order would be to market a regional waste disposal service, using a newly patented method. The variables that would have to be dealt with include: an analysis of potential customers and the market, recruiting staff, generating sales promotion work. These variables can all be broken down into myriad concrete things and actions, all of which interweave in complex patterns. They have to be handled by chunking them together into useful categories so as to be able to see the woods and not get lost in the trees.

C   Third order complexity: Second level abstraction of concepts   Ordinary second order language is chunked into the more complex conceptual order of information as used in the conceptual world of the corporation, of the corporate CEO and EVPs.

The factors at work in corporate problems are vast in number; they are very ambiguous, continually changing, and inextricably tangled together. They must be chunked into concepts such as balance sheet values, international competitor systems, third world development, European Community 1992, the Pacific basin, Japan and the new Far East competition, FOREX (foreign exchange), political economic circumstances in specific countries, treasury policies, raw material resources.

We cannot readily go from concepts like these directly to concrete things; for example, balance sheet values pull together a wide range of recorded accounting categories and assumptions, which in turn can be translated into the specifics of a very large array of concrete items of expenditure, revenue, assets and liabilities.

D   Fourth order complexity: Third level abstraction of universals   Third order concepts are chunked into the universal ideas and language that are required for handling the problems of whole societies, social movements, ideologies and philosophies.

The variables are of a complexity well above that required for handling the problems of corporate life. It may be apparent that universal ideas encompass a large number of concepts, each of which in turn can be referred directly to large numbers of concrete things in the immediate perceptual world.

This analysis would suggest that the worlds that different people live in could be quite different (see figure 2.6). And of course that is the case. Ten people placed in the same situation and faced with a common problem will certainly "see" ten different sets of important

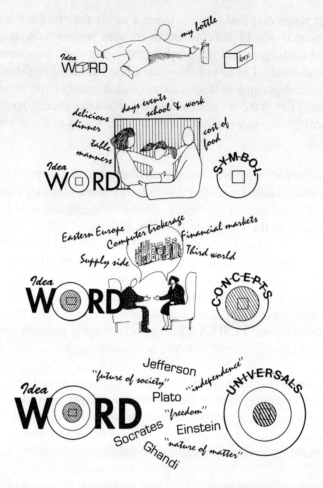

Figure 2.6 The worlds people live in: orders of information complexity

features. But those ten different sets of information will not only differ in content, they could also differ very markedly in the amount of information they will be able to distill from observing and thinking about the situation. They will differ sharply in the actual amount they are able to see and to take into account. A person whose cognitive capability has matured to the point where he or she is working with third order complexity conceptual information will be able to see and to process something of the order of ten to hundreds of times the amount of data that a person working with first order complexity concrete information can see and process in the same period of time.

That is why people capable of working at so-called high levels are commonly described as being able to handle masses of detail rapidly and in an orderly and useful way.

The Categories of Potential Capability (Quintaves)

Let us briefly review the previous two sections.

Cognitive processes are the mental processes by means of which a person is able to organize information to make it available for doing work. There are four cognitive processes: assertive, cumulative, serial, and parallel and they are increasingly complex, going from assertive to parallel.

Orders of information complexity are the increasingly complex chunks of data in the external world which we must take in and give name to and use to inform our cognitive processing to solve problems. These four orders of information complexity are:

A First order complexity: Concrete things
B Second order complexity: First level of abstraction
C Third order complexity: Second level of abstraction
D Fourth order complexity: Third level of abstraction

The significance of distinguishing the four cognitive processes from the orders of information complexity is that, as we mature, we not only move from less to more complex cognitive processes but we also move up in the orders of information complexity that we can handle. Thus, in childhood, we work with first order complexity. We move from assertive processing (pre-verbal) through cumulative processing (early language), through serial processing (determined temper tantrums) to parallel processing (full socialization based on the ability to relate one's own goals and strivings to an understanding of the different and possibly conflicting strivings of others).

Then the whole process is repeated when, in adolescence or early adulthood, we move into the second order complexity world. First of all we use assertive processing, then mature to cumulative processing, then to serial processing (fewer people mature to this level), and then to parallel processing (still fewer people). And then some very few people, those with the capability to work at the higher corporate levels, will shift into the third order complexity world by first using assertive processing. Very few people will move up through all four processes. The very rarest person will then move into the great complexity of the fourth order, third level abstraction world.

Thus, we get a series of repetitions (recursion) of the four cognitive processes in each of the four worlds of information complexity.[1] Different individuals will mature to different levels of complexity at different stages in their lives. We can express these levels of complexity by combining the four cognitive processes and the four orders of complexity of information. We shall use the term "category" of potential capability to refer to a particular cognitive process within a given order of information complexity. Thus, for example, category B–3 would refer to an individual who is serial processing with second order complexity verbal ideas and language, or category C–2 would refer to an individual who is cumulative processing with third order complexity conceptual ideas and language.

We are now in a position to describe how to evaluate the current potential capability (CPC) of individuals. The category of potential capability in which a person is operating shows in his or her problem-solving behavior. It can be observed in everyday life when that person is fully engaged in engrossed discussion and argument. By an "engrossed" discussion or argument we mean one in which individuals are heavily personally and emotionally involved; they care about, and are trying hard to convince each other of, the rightness of their own point of view. Look not for stereotyped, uninvolved comment but rather for arguments mustered in the heat of battle.

Individuals characteristically manifest one of the four different methods of organizing their arguments: assertive processing, cumulative processing, serial processing or parallel processing (see figure 2.7). We know that it is possible to learn by practice to observe these processes. We know also that it is possible to teach managerial leaders how to observe them as a help in judging the potential of subordinates-once-removed.

Here are some examples of how information is organized in the course of engrossed discussion and argument. We have selected material from a number of discussions on euthanasia with people whose category of complexity we have had the opportunity to evaluate. We have chosen this topic because it is an issue everyone can understand. Our object is to provide the kinds of illustration that will enable our readers to translate the ideas into examples in their own work situation.[2] Precisely the same processes can be observed whenever people are engaged in argument or in intense discussion

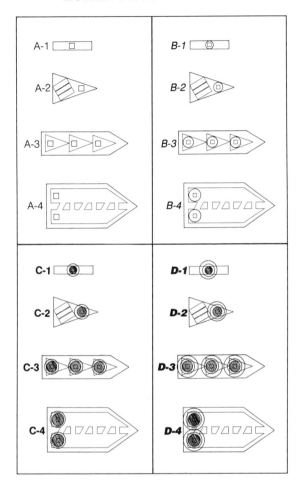

Figure 2.7 The categories of potential capability (quintaves)

upon some intense topic at work. In approaching an understanding of these cognitive processes, it may be helpful to refer back to pp. 54–5 for explanations of the four orders of information complexity (A,B,C, or D).

Category B–1 Assertive processing: unsupported verbal assertions People may argue by unconnected strings of assertions, using ordinary verbal language. "Well, it's wrong isn't it? People shouldn't be allowed to kill themselves." Or, "You don't know what you're talking about." Or

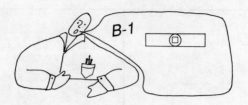

Figure 2.8a   Illustration B-1

"People have their rights, you know." Or simply, "No, no I do not agree with it." (See figure 2.8a.)

Category B-2   Cumulative processing: arguments supported by accumulated data   Here a person states a view or views but, in contrast to the category B-1 type of arguing by a series of bald assertions, the argument proceeds by bringing one or several supportive reasons to bear upon the stated views or opinions or conclusions. "I've often

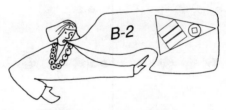

Figure 2.8b   Illustration B-2

thought about it, and it seems to me that euthanasia is wrong because after all no-one should take a life, even their own. And there's no use arguing that we kill people in wars, or use the electric chair, because that's a different matter – it's a social thing, and not just the decision of one person." (See figure 2.8b.)

Category B-3   Serial processing: arguments organized as a logical series of events   The individual at category B-3 now reasons continually by organizing his or her information and arguments in sequence, in which one thing leads to another, or may have been led on to from another in the past. There are repeated references to earlier and later, to what happened or will happen, to what went on, is going on and will ensue in consequence, and so on. In the following example, we are taken sequentially through what can happen to patients. The speaker continued his mode of argument at length, with many serial examples. "My experience has been that it's a bad idea. I've been a social worker and I've personally dealt with many people who didn't want to live any longer. And many of them had good reason not to –

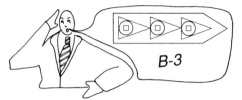

Figure 2.8c   Illustration B-3

illness especially, but other reasons as well. But what would happen would be – with a lot of them anyhow – that they would change over a period of time and then they would be glad they had stayed alive. Like this patient who was depressed over a crippling physical illness when she came into the hospital, and wanted to die. That was a year ago. Then she began to get better and life began to look better even though her physical debility hadn't changed. Six months ago she decided she wanted to live. Then a few months ago she went home. And now she's getting on with her life even though it will continue to be very rough." He continued in subsequent discussion to evoke further contributions, all in terms of serially described episodes. (See figure 2.8c.)

Category B–4   Parallel processing of several lines of argument   This next person carefully outlined two different sequences, her two "paths," and then related them. She pursued each path at length and then took aspects from each, by relating them, to arrive at her own conception of "limited euthanasia" which she elaborated. "You have to be careful when you argue for or against euthanasia. One consequence when you follow down the path in favor of it is that you risk weakening our concerns for human life – and that's serious. I've seen it happen to

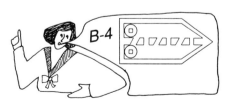

Figure 2.8d   Illustration B-4

some people over the past few years. They got interested in euthanasia and they became a bit callous. You can see how in a few more years they would lose concern for human life. [Someone interrupts, argues for a moment.] Now just wait a minute. I have still another argument to make. It's about what happens if you don't provide for euthanasia. It's just that I've been able to follow the arguments over the past few years – since we've become more able to keep really unconscious people alive. In the past ten years our doctors have increasingly had to make decisions about discontinuing life support in some cases. But I can tell you about incidents in the past few years when they got into trouble for doing so, and now many of them are afraid of being sued. It's obvious that if we go on down that path we'll be in trouble. When I think about it, neither the path of legalization nor of non-legalization can be right. We need some kind of limited euthanasia." She then proceeded to try to work out an in-between argument. (See figure 2.8d.)

Category C–1   Conceptually formulated assertions   This person turned to the use of third order complexity ideas (principle of primacy of life, the kind of society we want, etc.). He repeated the references to principle in different ways several times during the discussion, prefaced by comments such as, "Look, let me get back to the principle I was trying to put forward," after which he grounded his statements with concrete examples of what he was talking about. In short, he had real concepts in mind, but was not able to articulate them and to support them by relating them to each other and

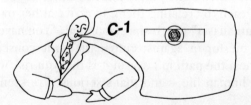

Figure 2.8e   Illustration C-1

explaining in conceptual terms how they worked together. The statement about freedom is another simple assertion. "You know, all this stuff you're arguing about is all very well. But I think it misses the point. It's too specific. The issue is bigger than that. We have to look at euthanasia for what it is. It's a matter of how we in our society are going to sustain our belief in the absolute primacy of the life of each and every individual. That principle is indivisible. It's greater than the freedom of the individual. For after all, what's freedom for if you're not alive? There are real underlying principles here. I'm sorry I'm not enough of a philosopher or a lawyer to argue them properly. But you know, what we're talking about lies at the heart of what kind of society we want to have – and I'm here to tell you that I want one in which the principle of the life of the individual is paramount." He continued his argument by a series of strong assertions, reaching for conceptually based supportive arguments, but not quite able to articulate them either to his own or to anyone else's satisfaction. (See figure 2.8e.)

Category C–2 Arguments supported by accumulated conceptual information in which the concepts are actually related to each other Here the person not only argued with general principles and concepts but also played the concept of individual rights against the rights of society and ended up by possibly extending his concept of euthanasia, a topic he elaborated later on in the discussion. Thus, as in category B–2, he was able to bring supportive arguments together, except that

Figure 2.8f Illustration C-2

he was capable of using third order complexity information in the form of conceptual ideas and language. "I agree with Tom's argument about the primacy of life but I'm surprised at his conclusion. The way I see it is that the life of the individual is absolutely crucial – in the sense that no one has the right to take anyone else's life – except for war, I guess. But even in war, no one has actually decreed that a particular individual's life should be taken. And I'm against capital punishment. But that's a social issue – it's about the individual's rights in society. Euthanasia is not a social issue. At least I don't see it that way. It's a personal issue. I know it involves other people, otherwise we are talking about suicide. But the decision rests with the person . . . and that's in line with my view of the matter. But wait a minute, I might be inconsistent there! What if the person is permanently disabled . . . a living vegetable? Then society does have to take over. But no. That's consistent with my conception. For that's that other concept of the rights or wrongs of removal of life support. And if you call that euthanasia too, you change the concept, don't you? Yes, that's right.' (See figure 2.8f.)

Category C–3 Serial processing: conceptual arguments organized as conceptualized alternative sequences, leading to alternative strategies This person argued serially, as, for example, in putting third order conceptual information together into sequentially organized strategic statements. He specified the values concepts he was concerned about and progressed to linking values about euthanasia to a range of economic and other values issues and broader social and ethical developments. He was able to elaborate these conceptual arguments in subsequent discussion, and continued his emphasis upon movements in values from one generation to the next. But he did not connect his various strategies and parallel-process them in relation to

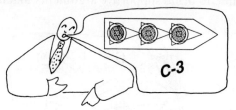

Figure 2.8g   Illustration C–3

each other. "When you come to problems in society as big as euthanasia, you have to take a broad cut at the problem and you have to give very serious consideration to possible alternatives. I'm against it myself, not necessarily in its own right but because of where on the whole I think it would lead society – its broad social consequences. You see, I think that a lot of our social values were overturned in the 1960s – with Woodstock and all that – and I think a positive attitude to euthanasia is in the same category. We took . . . or at least our young people did . . . a frankly loose attitude to drugs, sex, work. They changed the ethical outlook – I think for the worse. And now here we are with one great values problem on our plate. That's what really counts. Are we to go on with soft *laissez-faire* values – the Republicans call them liberal . . . but I don't want to get into party politics – or are we to return to our earlier moral standards of self control? You will gather that I think we need to strengthen self-control in America – or we face grave consequences down the road, in the next generation. We need a national ethical strategy in that direction. I can't say that I can see all its elements. But we have to find ways of working towards getting everyone to work – to get economic security better distributed – to strengthen family ties – and then we'll be able to get euthanasia into perspective where it would really feel wrong to think that way. It's all part of a total social development; a question of where you want the country to go." (See figure 2.8g.)

These case examples are brief versions of longer discussions. The material did not come out in the form of single unbroken statements. They were broken up by argument, interruption, angry criticism, and all the things that might be expected in heated discussions. The point is that none of the arguments was a polished or coherent, previously thought-out or formulated statement. They were all fashioned piece by piece as the discussion progressed, with everyone engaged in thinking on their feet. Under such circumstances it is possible to see how people's cognitive processes got to work.

One can observe these patterns in many areas of daily life: in heavy policy arguments, or arguments about best plans or decisions, or in free-ranging discussions. But one has to learn to listen at right-angles to the discussion. That is to say, to listen not for the content of what people are saying but for the order of complexity of the ideas they are using, and to how they are mustering their arguments – the category of complexity they are using – within the broad order. Listening at meetings, watching TV discussion and argument programs or searching interviews helps one to become familiar with these patterns.

We shall show later how familiarity with these concepts can become the backbone for the development of a managerial leadership talent pool.

Hollow Language and Ideas

There is one difficulty in all these descriptions that must be taken into account. It is a difficulty that cannot be overcome in this book, since we are not writing a treatise on the psychology of reasoning. (One of the authors – Jaques – is currently doing this in a book he is preparing on the nature of human capability.)

The difficulty has to do with recognizing the difference between solid language and ideas, and hollow language and ideas. It is the difference between using "mere words" and using words with substantial meaning. Another way of putting the same point is the difference between an "academic" argument, in the pejorative sense of academic, and an argument based upon real experience.

Thus, anyone can argue about such abstract ideas as freedom, truth, the sanctity of the person, ethics, beauty, democracy, national policy, the people, humanity, fairness and justice. Professors do it all the time; and indeed can write books about books about books on these subjects. Such argumentation can be of interest in its own right. But it is not what we are getting at with respect to understanding the complexity of people's ideas and language in problem-solving work. In the case of an academic, it would be a matter of noting not the cross-referencing to the ideas of others but how he or she musters his or her own ideas in arguing an abstract issue, including how the ideas of others are organized into the argument.

The test of hollow versus solid language and ideas lies in the extent to which the language and ideas are grounded and exemplified in a person's own practical experience (see figure 2.9). When solid language is being used, a person will uniformly not only illustrate more general ideas by reference to specific illustrations but will also relate general ideas to one another via these personally owned concrete examples. Here is an illustration. It is a discussion between a manager, whom we shall call Bill, and two specialists in compensation, Marcia and Russ, one of whom has been brought up on books and established procedures and "knows" them inside out. The other has studied the same books and procedures but has been able also to pull together and organize personal experiences resulting from direct contact with operators and staff in the workplace as they discussed and argued their own views and demands with respect to pay.

RUSS: "The way I see it, we've got to be objective about our measurements. Our system lets us be objective because we get points ratings on the three most critical factors in a job. And the ratings are made by people on the job who really know it – and their ratings are checked by experts who measure the job separately. Then they can all get together and adjust

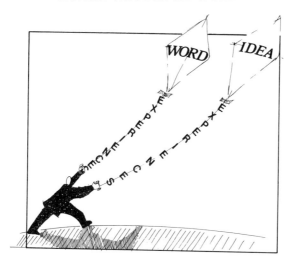

Figure 2.9 Hollow language and ideas

their measurements so as to iron out any of the inconsistencies that may occur in their ratings."

BILL: "Oh I see. You get an objective measure because they
(the manager) check their ratings against each other. That's very interesting."

MARCIA: "But surely that's not objective measurement? All you have are some subjective ratings."

RUSS: "Oh yes it is. You don't seem to understand. Our system is a real system of objective measurement

	because our experts are very experienced and are able to make comparisons with jobs they know. It's very clear to us that our system is objective."
MARCIA:	"Well, you may call it objective measurement but I don't. You don't have an objectively defined instrument like a thermometer or an ohmeter. I don't mean that it has to be a physical instrument. But surely you have to have a well-defined instrument that everyone can use in the same way, so everyone who has learned to use it can get the same answer. Your ratings aren't like that at all."
RUSS:	"Well, I don't see why it isn't measurement. We end up with numbers the same as any other measurement."
MARCIA:	"I know you do. But just because you get numbers, that doesn't make for objective measurement. Objective means that different people can share an objective instrument. And a points rating procedure for job evaluation is no more an objective procedure than is a rating process for determining beauty in a beauty contest. They're both completely subjective."

The differences in approach between Russ and Marcia are very substantial. Russ appears to be presenting his description in terms of the third order concept of "objective measurement." But it quickly becomes clear that it is merely a phrase for him. There is no content in the way he uses the phrase. He does not see any distinction between objective measurement and subjective rating.

Marcia, by contrast, can deal with both the concepts of objective and of measurement. She concretizes them by relating them to objective instruments, such as thermometers, as compared with subjective ratings, such as beauty, and shows that she really does understand the meaning of an objectively shareable instrument. Thus, Marcia is able to move to the very specific and concrete in illustration, and to the general conceptual form in relating the concepts of objective and measurement to each other.

This example is but a small illustration of our point and was elaborated much more fully and extensively in the argument between Russ and Marcia.

Values and "Motivation," or Why People do Things

The second factor to be taken into account in understanding the nature of a person's actual capability is that of his or her values. Thus, for example, a point that is very commonly made about CEOs who are regarded as outstanding business leaders is that they are intensely devoted to their work and get pleasure from being workaholics. They are said to be that way because of the inherent value to them of being able to do the work itself, rather than because of the great economic and status recognition that they might obtain. The way in which this quality is described, it would seem to be regarded as a special personality characteristic possessed by those particular CEOs.

Our view is substantially different. Our experience would suggest that everyone will put their best effort into doing whatever they value. The more the activity is valued, the more they will express energy, imagination, initiative, proactivity (and down through the many items in the many lists of so-called executive and "leadership" competencies). And if there is one thing that most people value intensely, it is the opportunity to have work, at a level consistent with their full potential capability, that is of interest to them. It is this condition that CEOs of companies by and large have the opportunity to create for themselves (that is, unless constricted by the board). Such opportunities for valued work at full capability and interest is enormously stimulating. We have all had the experience at some time in some aspect of our lives, and will know the great satisfaction to be obtained.

We here enter into the realm of what is commonly known as motivation. However, we are going to translate the issue from motivation to values, because motivation with respect to work is too heavily tarred with the idea that people need to be stimulated by external incentives if they are to do anything. We shall argue that people are spontaneously energetic with respect to things that interest them. The issue is not to encourage output by incentives but to provide conditions in which the work itself has its inherent value and allows the individual to release and direct his or her energy and imagination into the work.

Regardless of our view, people in roles that carry leadership accountability must be crystal clear about what they themselves think others are about; that is, their assumptions about human nature and why we do things. People are intensely sensitive about the outlook and attitudes towards them of those in managerial leadership roles. Their concerns are: "Do they care about us?"; "Do they regard us as 'only bodies,' mere counters to fill slots and to be moved hither and yon?"; "Do they think of us as pigeons, needing to behave so that we will be rewarded before we will work, or fight, or move or do anything?"; "Do they believe we are all fundamentally lazy and slothful, and needing to be continually prodded?" (See figure 2.10.)

Unfortunately, such negative attitudes towards other people at work are universal. Everybody has them to some degree. The only questions are: towards whom, and to what degree? It is useful to search our own souls, to listen to our own spontaneous outbursts and to discover who our own choices are as candidates for this negative view of human "motivation." Someone's view, for example, about why people work will often show up sharply in that person's opinions about what people should get paid for. A very common viewpoint is that we need to pay people incentive payments if they are really to work hard and creatively (see figure 2.11).

Figure 2.10 Values and "motivation," or why people do things

Figure 2.11 Incentive payments: pigeon theory conditioning

The view that we shall adopt – and it is crucial for managerial leadership – runs completely counter to this common view of people in their work. Our view is that we work hard not only because we have to or because we are given incentives to do so but, given half a chance and proper conditions, because we want to. The ordinary view is: "I like my work but, of course, everyone else is work-shy." This is not true. The opportunity for work that stretches one's capabilities, enabling us to learn and grow, is an aspect of effective managerial leadership that is enormously valued by everyone. Such opportunities release and redirect our natural flow of energy and initiative.

This view might be termed "natural initiative theory." According to this view, it is the prime duty of good managerial leadership to provide the conditions that release people's full and enthusiastic initiative and creativeness into their work. It is these conditions that our book is about.

Our advice is to put away incentives, bonuses, and other pigeon theory conditioning approaches, and get on with ensuring the conditions for effective managers to recognize good work, encourage it, pay fairly for it, and provide managerial leadership that lets everyone get on with their work. The problem is to arrange the organization structures and insist on the managerial practices that are requisite, that is, conforming to the properties of hierarchical organizations and human nature.

The Importance of Values

From this point of view, the core of what has been called motivation is to value something. If we value something we will go after it. So we do not need a concept of motives and motivation but we do need a clear concept of values. Values range from generic to specific. Generic values are usually referred to as our philosophy or ethical position; e.g. we value fair treatment. Specific values are the things that we will currently give priority to, seek to satisfy, spend our energy pursuing. The more intensely it is valued the more strongly will a goal be pursued.

By formulating motivation in terms of our values, we lay a basis for sound top-level corporate leadership. If the CEO can establish over-arching corporate values and philosophies which are nested within basic societal values and which meet people's own generic values, he or she can get the whole organization working effectively in the same broad direction. That is an enormous gain, as we shall see under corporate organizational leadership in Chapter 10.

The question of a person's values in relation to that person's current actual work capability, therefore, is of the greatest importance for managerial leadership. Our proposition is that to be an effective managerial leader a person must really value the opportunity to work with subordinates and value being able to unleash their enthusiastic and effective collaboration. Get the values right and factors such as style and personality will fall into line.

This issue of values is of particular significance in separating out those who really do value being managers and those who prefer to work as individual contributors (see figure 2.12). The tendency today is to accord the greatest value, and to provide advancement to higher levels, to those who take the managerial route. We thus influence creative individual contributors to become uncreative managerial leaders by taking up work they do not value. The provision of opportunities at high levels for individual contributors to do the work they value can get the corporation's innovative work done. It can also ensure that people have managers who value and enjoy managing and giving managerial leadership.

Our advice would thus be to avoid the artificial solutions that many companies use when they do not have confidence in their managerial organizations and leadership to support creative work; these include

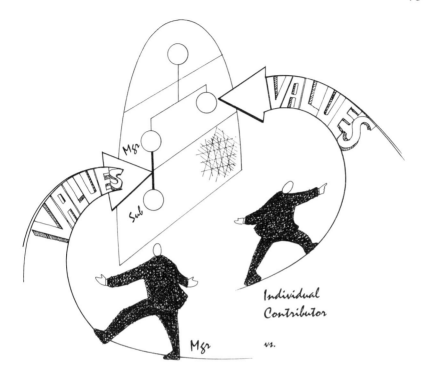

Figure 2.12 The importance of values

setting up skunk works, or encouraging employees with innovative ideas to set up in business for themselves and then buying their developments back from them when they are successful. What is the alternative? Sustain effective conditions for managerial leadership, including compensation that is equitable for the level of work; set up properly organized *ad hoc* project task forces (see Chapter 8) where necessary, at a level, however high up, that accurately reflects the complexity of the project; and ensure the appointment of competent managerial leaders who are not only one category of cognitive capability above the heads of project team individual contributors but who also value the managerial leadership work in its own right.

It is our values that move us, bind us together, push us apart, and generally make the world go round.

Knowledge and Skills

The third factor determining a person's actual work capability is that of knowledge. If every time we tackled a problem we had to start afresh as though we had never dealt with a problem like that before, we should never get anywhere. The fact is that we do learn – from our experience, from teaching, and from practice. We store our learning in the forms of knowledge and of skill in the use and application of that knowledge.

We have found it valuable in understanding managerial leadership to use the notions of knowledge and skill in a special, more limited way than they are commonly used. We propose to confine their meaning as follows.

By knowledge, we refer to objective facts, including procedures, which can be stated in words, formulae, models, or other symbols that one can learn, in the sense of being able to pass examinations about them, and which with practice one can use without thinking.

By skill, we refer to the application of facts and procedures that have been learned through practice to the point where they can be used without thinking, for example, solving simultaneous equations or riding a bicycle.

One of the reasons for our wanting to be so precise and explicit with regard to knowledge and skill is that we want to get away from the common notion that there are "leadership skills" than can be stated and taught. Such skills are often talked about in terms of communication skills, or listening skills, or sensitivity skills, which can somehow be learned in our bones or our muscles, so that we will automatically go through certain actions that will enhance our leadership competence which has to do with our relations with others.

We are going down a different road in our approach to managerial leadership development. We are arguing that the key issue is to set the conditions necessary for effective managerial work, and we can now describe those conditions a bit more sharply. Thus, for example, it is necessary to have a requisite organizational structure, with layers wide enough and few enough to call for managers who are one category in cognitive complexity above their immediate subordinates and who are working at a level of task complexity that is also one category higher. And it is necessary to have established a range of requisite managerial practices for managers to carry out, which can be taught and which the managers can, with practice, learn to use without having to think about it (see figure 2.13). Once these conditions have been established, managerial leaders will be needed who can do the necessary managerial work. Such managerial leaders will have to have the necessary cognitive complexity for their roles, and will have to value managerial leadership and the necessary working relationships with subordinates, as we have described in the previous two sections.

Figure 2.13   Knowledge and skills

Of course, in addition, we can see that they will need to have a fair amount of straightforward knowledge – knowledge about the structure and their role in it and knowledge about the managerial practices. Fortunately, once these features are formulated (as we shall be doing presently), they can be learned by teaching and practice so that they can be used without having to think very much about them. A company can be sure that it has established sound managerial leadership precisely when and only when it can be sure that every one of its managers carries out the practices we shall describe, automatically and consistently, whenever the need arises. That is how knowledge is used.

Thus, education in managerial leadership should be approached not in terms of the inevitable vagaries of "leadership skills" but instead by learning standard practices that have been formulated for clear understanding and teaching. Given sufficient teaching and training to learn these practices, managerial leaders will be able to discharge their leadership accountabilities without thinking too much about it, so long as they will just be their own natural selves (and are not emotionally disturbed to a degree that renders them incompetent to carry satisfactory interpersonal relationships).

Being clear about knowledge is a matter of no mean importance when it comes to the development of good managerial leadership. Our knowledge provides the verbal framework within which we organize and set context for our work. It enables us to set context for subordinates as the prime act in managerial leadership. Knowledge and its appropriate skilled use enable us to organize our field of work so that our non-verbal cognitive process can all the more readily handle the complexity of that field.

Wisdom

There is another significant aspect of capability for effective managerial leadership which everyone knows about but which is difficult to capture in words. It is often referred to as wisdom, and that is the term we shall use. Wisdom has to do with the soundness of a person's judgment about the ways of the world, about what people are like and how they are likely to react. Wisdom becomes increasingly important at the higher levels in the organization. As someone moves up in the organization, he or she must deal with greater numbers of other people and his or her actions may affect a greater number of people. That person uses wisdom in anticipating how certain actions may affect individuals and groups and how they may respond.

Wisdom is a crucial component in the discharge of managerial leadership accountability. It is the sense that any effective managerial leader must have about the ordinary day-to-day variations that occur in the state of mind of subordinates and in their prime current needs; what is sometimes called sensitivity or empathy. We are referring here not to any rare or special personality characteristics but just to the understanding that most people expect from each other. There are, however, degrees of such understanding, and these differences can affect to some extent the overall managerial leadership competence of different individuals.

Wisdom expresses itself in tact, and the presence of an ample supply will contribute to the effective internal functioning of an organization, and to smoother relationships with customers, investors, legislators, and other key groups outside. Wisdom adds spice to managerial leadership.

Experience can be a great teacher, and it teaches many different things. We all add more or less to our storehouse of knowledge. Equally, it is difficult, in the course of everyday experience, not to learn new skills, improve existing ones, or become skilled in ways we are not even aware of. But there is one area in which experience seems to be a great teacher for some but to have little or no impact on others; that area is the acquiring of wisdom.

The acquiring of wisdom is one of the areas that shows that action without sound theory and concepts can be counter-productive. Concepts, theories and ideas are used continuously in everyday life. They determine what we see and what we learn from our experience. Unsound theories distort our experience, narrow our vision, and leave us none the wiser about the effects of our action on others (see figure 2.14). Action without sound theory is folly.

Wisdom can be developed in people. Its development can be reinforced and enhanced, especially by good mentoring by a more senior person. We shall consider these mentoring processes in Chapter 9, and discuss there why good mentoring requires the experience, maturity and outlook of a manager who is two cognitive categories higher (what we call the manager-once-removed, MoR, as compared with the immediate manager). Some people do have difficulty in using their experience to gain wisdom but attention to this issue given by a wise MoR can have a considerable impact on most people and a very dramatic impact on some.

In managerial leadership, the confidence of subordinates in a manager is markedly influenced by how wise the manager is in his or her understanding of people. Such confidence is not limited to the manager's wisdom as shown in relation to themselves but to how it is shown in relation to people more generally, such as clients or customers, colleagues, and higher managers. Perhaps the extreme instance of the need for wisdom is in a combat commander's sensing of how an opposing commander is likely to act in the circumstances of a battle; the subordinates are certainly interested in that. In a less

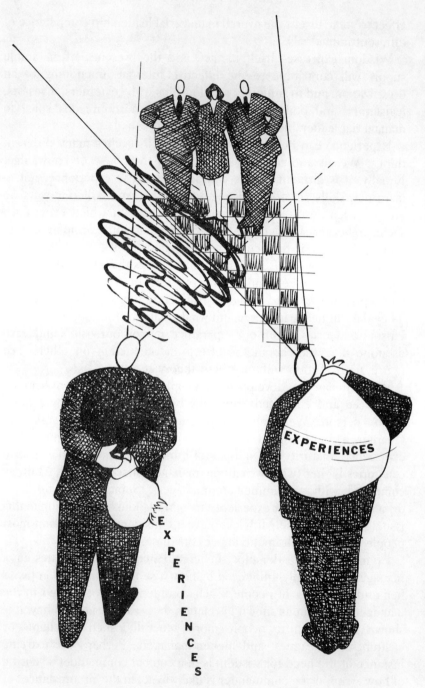

Figure 2.14 Wisdom

exigent way, this applies in all situations and the accent is on the notion of sensing, of having a "nose" for the situation because the person has a sense of the ways of the world.

One special direction for the expression of wisdom lies in an understanding of how tight to hold the reins of discipline under given circumstances – to sense when to tighten the reins and when to loosen them. Subordinates can vary like the weather in the amount of constraint needed to help them to toe the line. Financial, technological, and other problems can also influence how much constraint is necessary over given periods. Subordinates appreciate just the "right" amount of constraint, and the wise application and release of constraint gives the maximum of real freedom.

T and Minus T (-T): "Personality, Temperament, and Style"

All the foregoing might be fine, but where does personality fit into our analysis of the nature of managerial leadership competence? The general wisdom is that what is called "personality" plays an important part in leadership. By "personality" is commonly meant those enduring qualities of a person that are used to describe what a person is really like underneath.

The descriptions of personality in this sense are enormously varied. Leadership experts have constructed many different lists of what they call leadership qualities or traits by picking various clusters of such personality variables. They have three aims. One is to find just that profile that will identify the good leader, and to use it for leadership assessment. A second is to identify the key traits to focus upon in developing "leaders." The third is to try to develop teams made up of members who between them possess "all" the necessary traits.

In our view this focus upon personality qualities or traits is misguided. The main point is that the particular pattern of qualities that constitutes emotional make-up has little effect upon that person's in-role leadership work, unless these qualities are at unacceptable or abnormal extremes and the individual lacks the self-control to keep from disturbing his or her work and working relationships with others. An important characteristic of the qualities that go into what is called personality make-up (or emotional make-up) is that they do have limits, or extremes, beyond which their expression becomes unacceptable.

On the acceptable side of that limit, there is an infinite range of possible behaviors. Thus, for example, a person may be reflective in a million different ways. But when reflectiveness goes over the boundary into inability to make up one's mind, that is not acceptable. The same applies to optimism as against critical rashness; or aggression as against violence; or tenacity as against mere stubbornness; or critical evaluation as against paranoid suspicion.

In the English language, there are over 2,500 personality variables which are possessed to greater or lesser degree by everyone, and expressed more or less strongly depending upon the situation. They include: sensible, reliable, responsive, intuitive, sympathetic, tough-minded, tender-hearted, intense, cordial, hearty, happy, stimulating, caring, thorough, dispassionate, imaginative, discriminating, loyal, candid, sincere, eager, demonstrative, detached, unruffled, optimistic, honest, unbiased, realistic, shrewd, credible, skeptical, keen, diligent, trustworthy, truthful, enthusiastic, just, fair, serious, open-minded, decisive, adaptable, stable, brave.

This huge range of commonly occurring characteristics combines in infinitely varied patterns to give the great richness of differences in personality make-up, all of which may be consistent with effective managerial leadership, and none of which is likely to be better or worse.

On the other hand, there is another, equally long list, any one element of which could disqualify a person from effective managerial leadership. These characteristics are what we call minus T (-T), and can be illustrated by the following few examples: obsessive, joyless, hopeless, pitiable, obtuse, heartless, frigid, slapdash, opinionated, unctuous, maudlin, frenzied, destructive, anti-social, misanthropic, inhibited, priggish, envious, gluttonous, irascible, soulless, careless, fanatical, bigoted, petty, guilt-ridden, compulsive, depressive, paranoid, schizoid, timid, dishonest, untrustworthy. These characteristics are not simply matters of degree in a person; they either are or they are not disruptive of work and working relationships. They ought to be readily detectable by managers and managers-once-removed (see figure 2.15).

Our argument is that personality variables figure in managerial leadership in a negative rather than a positive way. A person's emotional make-up must not contain elements that are so abnormal

Figure 2.15 T and minus T (-T): "personality, temperament, and style"

and so out of control as to damage his or her effectiveness in role and in working relationships with others to an unacceptable degree.

It is the duty of the manager to judge whether or not a subordinate's behavior might on balance have moved across the boundary into an unacceptable degree of loss of effectiveness. It is further the duty of the manager to discuss such a judgment with the subordinate as part of on-going personal effectiveness appraisal and coaching. It is also the duty of the manager to assist a subordinate who wishes to seek professional help. It is certainly not the duty of the manager to attempt to change the subordinate or, as we shall see in a moment, to adapt his or her own behavior to the subordinate's emotional shortcomings.

One common problem is that managers themselves may become inhibited by (-T), in the form of excessive, guilt-driven anxiety about making such judgments about subordinates. Similarly, managers-once-removed may have the same feelings about making judgments of potential capability. It can be a useful part of managerial training to help managers to become aware of the widespread existence of this kind of emotionally driven reticence in this important area of managerial leadership.

Self-control and Requisite Behavior

There is one absolutely fundamental issue that must be established with respect to managerial hierarchies. It has to do with the amount of self-control and capability that a manager is entitled to expect from subordinates.

To illustrate the point we can use the salesperson–purchaser relationship by way of comparison and contrast. When a salesperson deals with a client he or she has to accept that client's "personality," values, level of capability, mode of behavior, as given. The art is to find ways of selling to different clients, taking into account the vast array of behaviors they may exhibit. It is not for the salesperson to complain about a client's behavior, or values, or lack of knowledge. If, in the final analysis, they are entirely unacceptable to the salesperson then he or she must retire from the field without a sale. The salesperson is not accountable for clients' outputs or decisions and has no authority with respect to their behavior.

In similar vein, political representatives must accept the behavior of the individual constituents who elect them, even though they may try to influence the behavior of their constituents as a whole.

Parents and children are an interesting case. Using the contrast we made earlier between accountability and responsibility, parents cannot be held accountable for the behavior of their children (except for grossly destructive behavior), but they are certainly expected to have a strong sense of personal responsibility for that behavior. It might indeed be in the best interests of society were the parents to be charged with greater accountability for providing leadership to their children with respect to societal values.

But managerial hierarchies are not seller–buyer situations, nor political representative institutions, nor families; managers are not salespersons to their subordinates, nor are they their elected representatives, nor are they like their parents. This point needs to be made, because any and every type of analogy is used to try to describe managerial leadership; in particular are those analogies which try to persuade managers that if only they can get to understand the psychology of their subordinates they will be better able to exercise effective leadership and to "motivate" them. Instead, it should be made clear at every level of the managerial hierarchy that it is simply not acceptable for individuals to behave in ways that are disruptive to their own working relationships with others or to relationships between others. In short, every individual can be required to leave his or her psychopathology at home (see figure 2.16).

The meaning of this approach is that a range of reasonable behavior is assumed, managers are entitled to expect such behavior from subordinates and must, of course, conform to these limits of behavior themselves. In the managerial situation, therefore, the managerial leader is entitled to expect a reasonable quality of interpersonal behavior from subordinates. It is therefore not incumbent upon the manager to adapt his or her behavior to the idiosyncrasies of the subordinate.

Many people would disagree with this view. They would argue that it is precisely by understanding and attending to the special emotional needs and personal styles of each individual that a "leader" can best motivate each follower. But that can result in the "difficult" personalities getting special attention as compared with their more collaborative colleagues, who gradually become fed up with the imbalance in treatment. That is not what managerial hierarchies should be about.

Indeed, we shall show that sound managerial leadership is about learning how to carry out a pattern of requisite practices within a requisite structure; and within those practices, allowing the spontaneous play of ordinary self-control and wisdom in the full expression of the richness of individual personalities in everyday interaction.

Maturation of Potential Capability

We shall refer to maturation of potential capability rather than maturation or development of capability *per se*. This is because, as compared with the other components of capability, namely values, knowledge/skill, wisdom and (-T), it is the growth of potential capability as reflected in cognitive complexity that holds a special interest for us in career and talent pool development.

The first point of special interest is that, as we have shown on p. 49,

Role Relation	Cognitive Power	Values	Knowledge	Skills	Wisdom	Temperament	(-T)
Manager to Subordinate	Take into account in selection and task assignment.	Take into account in selection and task assignment. Teach.	Take into account in selection and task assignment. Teach.	Take into account in selection and task assignment. Train.	Take into account in selection. Role model. Coach.	Require self-controlled behavior (i.e. subordinate is accountable for own self-control). Point to deficiencies.	Not acceptable. Assist subordinate to get outside professional help.
Manager-once-Removed to Subordinate-once-Removed	Evaluate for career development and for talent pool.	Evaluate and mentor. Role model.	Teach or arrange for teaching for future development.	Train as necessary.	Mentor.	Require self-controlled behavior (i.e. subordinate is accountable for own self-control). Point to deficiencies. Mentor.	Mentor. Assist SoR to get outside professional help.
Military Commander to Subordinate	Take into account in selection and task assignment.	Influence towards Army values. Role model.	Require minimum and teach.	Require minimum and train.	Coach.	Require self-control and mold and counsel towards it.	Counsel, and refer to available military services.

Salesperson to Buyer	Take into account and adapt.	Take into account and adapt.	Take into account and adapt.	Take into account and adapt.	Take into account and adapt.	Take into account and adapt.	Take into account and accept.
Political Representative to Constituent	Adapt communication to level of group.	Take into account and influence.	Communicate to teach.		Communicate political wisdom.		
Husband and Wife	Share.	Share and discuss.	Share and Discuss.	Mutual help.	Mutual help.	Sensitive understanding.	Mutual help.
Parent to Child	Take into account for education etc.	Transmit. Role model.	Teach.	Train.	Mentor.	Influence towards self-control.	Get professional help.
School Teacher to Pupil	Take into account for teaching.	Take into account and influence towards societal values. Role model.	Teach.	Train.	Role model.	Influence towards self-control.	Requires professional help. Advise parents.

Fig. 2.16 Self-control and requisite behavior

cognitive complexity determines the maximum potential capability of a person at a given time. By a method which we shall illustrate, a person's future potential capability can be evaluated. None of the other components of capability indicates a person's maximum potential.

The second point is that cognitive complexity (and its expression in time-horizon), unlike the other components of capability, grows by true maturation; that is to say, it grows in a regular and predictable manner towards full maturation in old age. It is this maturation process that makes possible the evaluation of where a person is going in potential capability, and where that person's potential is likely to be in, say, 3, 5, or 10 years' time.

By contrast, none of the other components of capability develops by predictable maturation. The development of knowledge and skills depends upon experience, education, and training opportunities. Values change or not depending upon experience and influence. Wisdom may or may not increase. Personality (temperamental, emotional) characteristics tend to endure, unless modified by significant experience or by therapy. And even when emotional changes do occur, they do not do so in accord with any regular and predictable maturational pattern.

Figure 2.17 (Potential Progress Data Sheet) shows how cognitive complexity (quantified in terms of a person's time-horizon) matures throughout life.

The horizontal scale shows age. The vertical scale shows potential capability in time-horizon, the longest time-span (level of work) at which a person could work given the necessary values, K/S, Wi, and absence of (-T).

The vertical scale is also arranged in organizational strata, with time-span boundaries corresponding to the time-horizons, showing the organizational level at which a person of a given time-horizon would have the potential to work, given the opportunity and necessary background.

The curved bands on the chart show the patterns of maturational growth of individuals in cognitive capability. These bands group people by mode, that is to say, by the highest stratum at which they could work when their potential was fully matured. In other words, this is the highest level of work they would ever be capable of doing if they valued it, had obtained the necessary knowledge, skills and wisdom, and were not troubled by emotional disturbance.

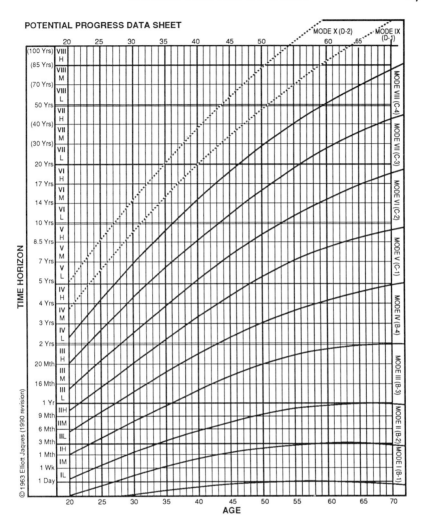

Figure 2.17 Maturation of potential capability

Let us take a couple of examples. A person with the potential to work at mid-stratum–III (III M) at age 30 would have the potential to work at mid-stratum–IV (IV M) at age 45 and would eventually mature in potential to stratum–V. It is possible to work backwards as well: a senior executive who demonstrated the capability and potential to work at low-stratum–VII (VII L) at age 55, would have had the potential to work at high-stratum–IV (IV H) at age 30.

There are two features of these maturation bands that are worth noting. First, the greater our cognitive potential, the faster will be our rate of maturation and the longer in life will our potential continue to mature. Thus, most senior executives with capability to work at stratum–VII and stratum–VI in full adulthood will not reach their full potential during their lifetime. By contrast, people in mode–I tend to reach full maturity in potential between 50 and 60 years of age.

Second, the progression bands imply that people actually change in the nature of the cognitive processes they use, as they pass from one stratum of complexity to the next. Thus, as a person matures across the stratum–III/IV boundary into stratum–IV, he or she will change in method of cognitive functioning from serial processing to parallel processing.

These changes are readily observable if a person is studied just as he or she is maturing across a boundary. For example, James Parker, at age 37, had steadily matured to the top of stratum–III. He began to find himself changing away from his practice of holding firmly to getting just that right pathway to a particular goal, to what he experienced as a more "flexible approach" in which he was reaching towards the putting together of several interlocking projects, all to be processed in relation to one another. He felt that his world had suddenly expanded to a new and more open perspective.

Once it is possible to locate any one of these qualitative change points in a person's life and outlook, it is almost certain that this datum will provide the key to finding the maturation band within which that person is maturing. We shall show in Chapter 10 how these maturation bands can be used for the development of a practical model of the corporate managerial leadership talent pool.

Individual Development

In the previous section we described the maturation of cognitive capability. Because it is a true maturational process, there is little that can be done to speed up its growth or to slow it down. It is constitutionally in-built and matures at its own natural rate unless it is interfered with by some kind of massive deprivation. If this should occur in the early years, it will show up as crippled rather than as slowed-down in progress. Thus, under ordinary circumstances, our potential capability will mature at a steady and predictable rate from childhood into old age.

The art of facilitating the managerial leadership development of individuals, therefore, is to take note of the rate of growth of their potential and to try to provide work opportunities which are consistent with their potential. In addition, they should be given the opportunity to consider their values, to gain the necessary skilled knowledge, to fortify their wisdom, and to take the necessary steps to get rid of any seriously abnormal quirks they might have.

Helping subordinates with the consideration of values, with the development of skilled knowledge and wisdom, and with the elimination of minus T is one of the most important activities in gaining personally earned authority in managerial leadership roles. There are five major practices for doing so: coaching, teaching, training, mentoring, and counseling (see figure 2.18). Here is how we propose to use these terms.

Coaching is the process through which a manager helps subordinates to understand the full range of their roles and then points out the subordinates' strengths and weaknesses. (Weaknesses could include the fact that any given subordinate's personal make-up is affecting others adversely.) Coaching should be an integral part of a manager's regular review of a subordinate's personal effectiveness. It is an important influence on values and wisdom. It should add, to a greater or lesser degree, to a subordinate's knowledge.

Teaching is the imparting of knowledge to individuals by lectures, discussions and practice. Teaching is not specific to any particular role.

Training is a process of helping individuals to develop or enhance their skill in the use of knowledge through practice, either on the job or in a learning simulation. Skill enables individuals to use their knowledge in problem-solving activities without having to think, thus freeing up discretion and judgment capabilities.

Mentoring is the process by which a manager-once-removed (MoR) helps a subordinate-once-removed (SoR) to understand his or her potential and how that potential might be applied to achieve as full a career growth in the organization as possible. Mentoring includes helping SoRs to become smart in "the ways of the world" and hence develop sound judgment and wisdom.

Counseling relates to circumstances when someone asks for advice with a personal problem, either internal to the individual or as a result of external circumstances. Managers can give counsel in general terms, for example, "What someone else I know did with such a problem was this . . .," or, "You

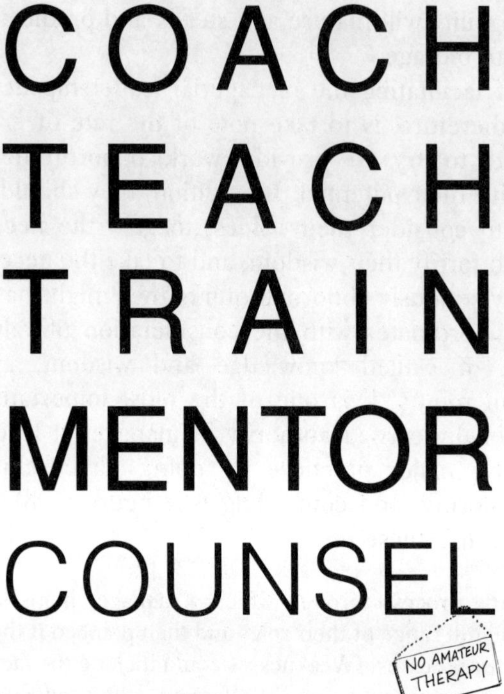

COACH
TEACH
TRAIN
MENTOR
COUNSEL

NO AMATEUR THERAPY

Figure 2.18   Individual development

might like to think about the possibility of . . .," but should otherwise refer individuals for professional help if more is required.

Notes

1 Jaques has referred to these repetitions as "quintaves" because they are like the "octaves" of music that are made of seven tones in which the first tone is not only the start of the octave but also the top of the lower octave. Assertive processing not only starts each quintave but is also the top of the lower quintave in ways that we need not pursue here.

2 This material is taken from a systematic research by Jaques and Cason, to be published. The research showed clearly the strong relationship between our categories of mental processing and level of work in roles.

3

Role Complexity and Task Complexity

In order to understand the nature of truly effective organizational structure, it is essential to understand the nature of the tasks we seek to get done by means of the organization. The complexity of a task lies in the complexity of the data and variables that have to be handled in carrying out the task – the number, ambiguity, rate of change, and degree of interweaving of those variables. It may thus be seen that the difficulty in any task centers upon the complexity of the variables encountered in trying to carry it out. The more complex the variables, the more difficult are the problems to be solved and the more difficult the task.

An interesting finding has been that just as there are four different types of cognitive process, so also are there four (and only four) types of task complexity and the nature of the complexity is very similar for both tasks and cognitive process. This finding is not so surprising if you consider that our cognitive processes must relate to the character of complexity in the world if we are to survive. It does seem as though nature has seen to it that our mental processes are organized in such a fashion as to deal with the way in which complexity confronts us in the problems we meet in the real world.

The Four Types of Task Complexity

The four types of task complexity that have been found to exist can be described in terms of the minimum that has to be done to cope with the variables that are encountered in solving problems related to the task (see figure 3.1).

> *Direct action and immediate situational response*   Problems can be dealt with as they are encountered.

TASK TYPES

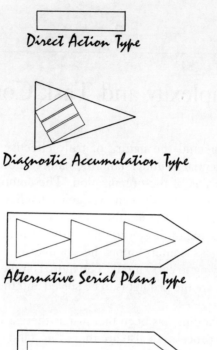

Direct Action Type

Diagnostic Accumulation Type

Alternative Serial Plans Type

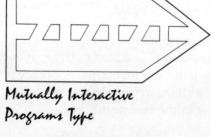

Mutually Interactive
Programs Type

Figure 3.1   The four types of task complexity

Diagnostic accumulation   Problems have to be anticipated and resolved by sorting out and accumulating significant information and putting it together to anticipate problems and overcome difficulties.

Alternative serial plans   Possible ways of carrying out a task have to be devised and evaluated, and one of the alternatives chosen and planned. That plan is then followed, always with the possibility of changing to an alternative plan if major difficulties are encountered.

Mutually interactive programs   The task requires that numbers of interactive, serially planned projects be undertaken, and adjusted to each other with regard to resources and timing as the work proceeds, so as to keep the total program on target.

Categories of Task Complexity

In addition to the four types of task complexity (as was the case with the four cognitive processes), the four orders of information complexity (A, B, C, and D) have to be taken into account. For example, a task that has to do with anticipating difficulties which are likely to be encountered in using a spoon to eat a bowl of soup (cumulative processing of first order complexity of information [A] in a concrete world) will be substantially less complex than the task of anticipating difficulties which are likely to be encountered by a detective in solving a crime (cumulative processing of second order complexity of information [B] in a verbal symbolic world).

Thus (as was the case for the categories of cognitive complexity), we shall combine each of the four orders of information complexity with the four types of task complexity, giving the same range of categories of task complexity running from category A–1 to A–4, B–1 to B–4, C–1 to C–4, and D–1 to D–4. But we shall limit our considerations to B–1 to B–4 and C–1 to C–3, since these cover the world of managerial leadership in stratum–I to stratum–VII, upon which we are focused.[1]

Second Order Categories of Task Complexity

The following are illustrations of the nature of task complexity in tasks to be found at stratum–I to stratum–IV.

Category B–1 task complexity (stratum–I): Direct action in immediate situation   These are the kinds of task found at shop- and office-floor level. The task requires a person to proceed along a prescribed linear pathway to a goal, getting continual feedback in order to proceed. As problems are encountered, the person has to use practical judgment to decide what is wrong and then has to apply previously learned methods for overcoming the obstacles. If these methods are unsuccessful, the person reports back to his or her manager.

Examples of such tasks would be: type this memorandum, coping with words which are difficult to read; drill holes with this jack hammer, and get around big rocks in the ground which are in the way of the drill.

Category B–2 task complexity (stratum–II): Diagnostic accumulation These are the kinds of tasks found at first line managerial level. An individual must be able to note things that might indicate potential problems and obstacles, accumulate such potentially significant data, and initiate actions to prevent or overcome such predicted problems as may be identified.

Examples would be: design a new jig for this machining process, working out the design as the job proceeds, accumulating data on how various parts are most likely to fit together so that the whole will work well; use good detective procedures to accumulate the evidence necessary to find a hit-and-run driver.

Category B–3 task complexity (stratum–III): Alternative serial plans Increasingly complex situations require alternative plans to be constructed before starting out, one to be chosen and serially progressed to completion, with possible change to another alternative if necessary.

For example, a person in a computer company heads a team of four programmers on a project to create a program that will make it possible to translate material from one computer language to another. She constructs three possible paths to the goal: the first would be sure but would take much too long, the second would be excellent if it worked but would lead to an expensive project failure if it did not, the third is relatively sound and could most likely be completed in the time available although it might be slow and might create uncertainty in the early stages. She opts for the third.

Category B–4 task complexity (stratum–IV): Mutually interactive programs These are problems still more complex because they comprise a number of interacting programs which have to be planned and progressed in relation to each other, and controlled by transfer of resources between them and by adjustment of resources and schedules so as to keep the overall program on target. Trade-offs must be made between tasks in order to make progress along the composite route to the goal.

For example, a designer and developer of new venture products for a large corporation (who has four assistants to help her) has to construct and pursue simultaneously a number of development paths: a developing design of the product and product applications, an in-depth analysis of potential international markets, the making and testing of models of the new product, and a sustained commercial analysis of its potential business value to the corporation. A balanced focusing of attention upon each of them in relation to the others is essential yet difficult; the designer may require to change any of the pathways at any time and, in doing so, she will have to adjust each of the others, all in relation to one another.

Third Order Categories of Complexity: Corporate Strategic Levels

Here are some examples of the basic categories which show up in the conceptual order of ideas and language, second order of abstraction (category C–1, C–2, and C–3). At this broad order of complexity, we move into what life is like in the corporate strategic world.

Category C–1 task complexity (stratum–V): Situational response These are the kinds of task faced by presidents of strategic business units in large corporations. Practical on-the-spot judgment must be used to deal with a field of ambiguous conceptual variables, and to make decisions envisaging the second and third order consequences of those decisions.

For example, a business unit president is driving half-a-dozen critical tasks to achieve a 7-year plan, and must continually pick up the important areas of impact and the likely consequences of changes and events: on customer attitudes, on competition and policies, on world commodity prices, on legislation, on third world countries, on tariffs, on technology, on his own R&D programs, on interest and foreign exchange rates, on availability and cost of capital, on cash flow, etc. In order to do so, he maintains a continuous "what-if" analysis of business priorities to sharpen his judgments of consequences and of what has to be done at any given time. He must rely upon situational responses and direct action, as he steers the business in the surrounding environment, to keep his profits at a reasonable level while maintaining customer goodwill, high morale among his own people, and the survival of the business with a growing balance sheet value.

Category C–2 task complexity (stratum–VI): Diagnostic accumulation This is the level of corporate executive vice-presidents who must build up a picture of likely critical events world-wide, using international networking to accumulate information about potentially significant developments that could affect the corporation and its business units. In order to take sound actions, they must anticipate changes so as to forestall adverse events and to help to sustain a friendly environment for corporate trade.

Thus, for example, an executive vice-president, overseeing six full-scale P&L account business units, sustains a world-wide network of information sources and picks out changes which may constitute unexpected threats or opportunities for any of his business units. He applies pressure to influence this environment, by such means as sponsoring or encouraging particular pieces of research in given universities or research associations, and meeting with political and government leaders and with senior executives of large customers. By means of accumulating significant conceptual information, and within corporate capital expenditure policies, he decides whether and when to make changes in the major resourcing of the business units, taking into account other corporate priority demands.

Category C–3 task complexity (stratum–VII): Alternative strategies This is the level of corporate CEOs working out strategic alternatives for world-wide operation, using complex conceptual information concerned with culture, values, and the business of nations and international trade.

For example, a corporate chairman and CEO is expanding his company, developing two additional executive vice-president roles as a base for growing between 5 and 7 new business units. Some of these are already partially grown within the company but are in need of capital infusions to enable them to grow into true P&L account subsidiaries, some are to be developed to capitalize upon new products in new fields, and some are to be added by the acquisition of new small companies with interesting products and outstanding young potential talent – a double gain. He has worked out a number of alternative strategic paths, has obtained support for them from the board and his senior subordinates, and is currently pursuing one of them that calls for penetration into related fields both at home and abroad. It is a program that is planned to see the corporation well into the twenty-first century.

Time-span and the Measured Level of Work in a Role

It might be useful if we reiterated at this point why we are devoting so much attention to the issue of task complexity and categories of task complexity. It is because we shall show that these categories, or steps in task complexity, are at the very heart of the requirements for the sound structuring of the managerial hierarchy. They tell us just what the correct number of managerial layers ought to be: one layer for each category of task complexity. And because, as we have described, each category of task complexity has a corresponding category of cognitive complexity in human beings, it becomes possible to reap the great benefits that come from being able to match complexity in work with complexity in people, in the same organizational layer. That match, as we shall see, gives a profoundly important basis for achieving managerial competence and effective managerial leadership relationships between managers and subordinates.

It will be self-evident that the higher up one goes in a managerial hierarchy, the more complex and difficult the most difficult tasks become. We might ask, therefore, what is the complexity not simply of one task but of a role? The answer to that question is that the complexity of a role is, at a minimum, the equivalent of the most complex tasks to be found in the role. However, it may be more complex than that because of the pattern of interweaving of the individual tasks, which is difficult to quantify in its own right. We shall have to look elsewhere for a method of measurement.

In order to solve this problem of measuring the complexity of a role and to strengthen our analysis and development of these ideas, we wish to add one more general idea to the mixture. It is based upon the interesting finding that the level of work in any role can be measured by what Jaques has called the "time-span of discretion" of that role (see figure 3.2). By level of work we mean what is often referred to as

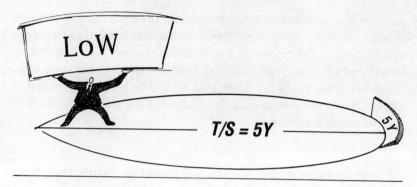

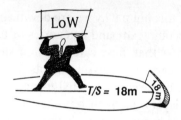

LoW = Level of Work

Figure 3.2   Time-span and the measured level of work in a role

the weight of responsibility of a position, or the size of the position, the quality that people try (but fail) to get at by so-called job evaluation procedures.

This finding, confirmed in projects in many kinds of hierarchical organization, in many parts of the world, over more than 30 years, is that the level of work (weight of responsibility) experienced in a role corresponds uniquely with the time-span of that role. That is to say, the longer the time-span of a role the greater is the felt level of work. But even more significantly, roles with the same time-span are experienced as being the same size, or weight, regardless of type of occupation, and regardless of the various other factors built into job-evaluation schemes.

What is this so-called time-span?

Time-span stems from the fact that the work in any role comes in the form of tasks. Whenever any task is assigned, it has a target completion time; that is, the maximum time that the person has been allotted in which to complete it. This maximum target completion time is not always made explicit, but it is inevitably always there. Otherwise, the carrying out of the task cannot be planned.

The consistent finding has been that those tasks that have the longest target completion times in a role have a peculiar significance for us. Those are the times within which all of our work has to be planned and so the time-span of the role is measured in terms of these longest tasks in the role.

Thus, a manager may have many tasks targeted for completion in a week, a month, several months, a year, 18 months, and so on. But if his or her longest task is, say, a major development project to improve production methods, which is targeted to be carried out over 2 years, then the current time-span of the role is 2 years. This measure is objective, because it is derived from actual (real, objectively observable) target completion times set or agreed by the immediate manager.

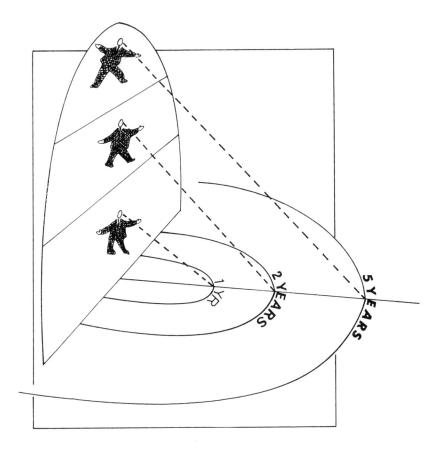

Figure 3.3a Time-span and the boundaries between categories of task complexity

Time-span and the Boundaries between Categories of Task Complexity

Time-span measurement has a wide range of applications but its significance for our present purpose is that the maximum complexity of task that will be found in any given role depends upon the measured time-span of the role. Thus, for example, tasks of category B–3 complexity will be found in roles above 1-year time-span but not below, or tasks of B–4 complexity in roles above 2 years' time-span, but not below. The full findings are shown in figure 3.3b (see also figure 3.3a).

Time-span range	Stratum of role	Maximum complexity of task to be found within the range
	VIII	C–4
50 years		
	VII	C–3
20 years		
	VI	C–2
10 years		
	V	C–1
5 years		
	IV	B–4
2 years		
	III	B–3
1 year		
	II	B–2
3 months		
	I	B–1
1 day		

Figure 3.3b Time-span and the maximum complexity of task within the range

There would appear to be a series of discontinuous steps in organizational layers which corresponds to the discontinuities in categories of task complexity and, by the same token, to discontinuities in categories of cognitive complexity. The concept of time-horizon of the individual, mentioned in the previous chapter, is thus explained. A person's time-horizon is a statement of the longest role time-span that that person can handle, and thus corresponds also to the maximum task complexity that the person can deal with. We shall illustrate in the following chapters the practical value of these concepts for an understanding of managerial leadership and for the development of managerial leaders.

Note

1 Stratum–VIII roles, requiring C–4 cognitive capability, are to be found at the top of the super-corporations such as General Electric, General Motors, Ford, Exxon, and IBM. These super-corporations are made up of stratum–VII divisions, each of which is the size of an ordinary stratum–VII corporation.

4

Basic Concepts of Organizational Structure

We have emphasized that effective managerial leadership cannot be bought on the cheap. It can be achieved only by a special series of steps, each one of which must be gained before we can move on to the next. But if we do invest in these steps, the rewards are great not only economically, competitively, and socially, but also in terms of deep personal satisfaction.

The sequence (from top to bottom) is from mission, to functional alignment and structure, to requisite managerial practices including sound selection, and finally on to managerial leadership and the winning of personally earned authority in one's own way and with one's own style.

Under "mission" we include the broad objectives of the corporation, along with the CEO's long-term vision. In the case of a large corporation, that vision would be the overarching, 25-year strategic goal. The 25-year vision gives the context for the development and carrying through of strategic options. The vision can be modified as circumstances dictate but should be reviewed at least annually.

For example, the mission of a large computer corporation was to provide any and all kinds of systems, equipment, and services in the broad area of information, word- and data-processing, and communications, as a world-wide multi-national. The long-term vision set by the CEO was to complete by the year 2020 the establishment of the company's multi-national network, and to extend their range of systems into world leadership in the satellite communication field.

The mission and vision determine the working functions that are required from the organization. It is these functions that must be distributed effectively through the organization not only at the right stratum but also properly aligned in relation to each other at each stratum and between strata (see figure 4.1). A full description of functional alignment by type of function and organizational stratum will be found in Section 9 of Jaques (1989).

Once mission and vision and the resulting functions are clear, it becomes possible to consider an appropriate organizational structure. Structure is critical for managerial leadership for two very fundamental reasons. First, the structure establishes the roles that determine the

Figure 4.1 The cascading road to managerial leadership

types and level of the people who will be needed. Second, it establishes the role relationships and thereby the working relationships between people. These factors taken together set the basic conditions for getting better or worse managerial leadership working relations. It is necessary to have the right roles, and to have people with the necessary capability to carry out those roles. We shall elaborate and illustrate this theme.

Given a requisite structure, we have the necessary basis for establishing the requisite managerial practices. The rest of the book will be devoted to describing these practices. It will be seen that they can be formulated sufficiently clearly to be able to be taught, and thus to become part of the ordinary everyday knowledge of each and every manager. It will become apparent that these practices must be carried out consistently and effectively if a managerial leader is to win personally earned authority.

Given the above conditions, we will show that anyone who has the necessary capability to carry his or her managerial role, and who, having been taught the requisite practices, does carry them out consistently and competently, and who is not handicapped by extreme qualities of personality (-T) which undermine working relationships with others, will be able effectively to discharge leadership accountability and get subordinates to go along willingly and enthusiastically in the direction set. Some managers will achieve moderately better results and some moderately less, but all will be well within the range of more than good enough.

What is Organizational Structure?

All social relationships take place in a social structure. Some people would like to deny this fact. It seems to make them uncomfortable. They feel unnecessarily constrained. It seems to take their freedom away. But structure is there whether we like it or not. There is no such thing as an interaction between people which does not occur within some structure. If relationships were totally unstructured, people would not know what to do, how to act. They would be confused.

It is the social structure which is known to the parties to a relationship that sets the limits and basic roles within which we behave towards each other. Even casual contacts, such as buying a newspaper, or standing in an elevator, take place within strict limits which are structured by law and by culture and which we have to learn and know in order to live comfortably with others.

This fact of the existence of a structure which provides the context for all social interactions by setting limits to them is especially important for leadership. It explains why it is so necessary to understand leadership within the context of the particular roles within

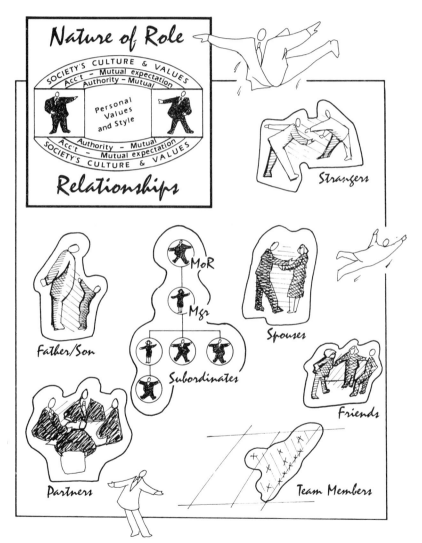

Figure 4.2   What is organizational structure?

which it is carried. The roles set the limits and expectations on the behavior that is required if we are going to be able not only to work effectively with people but also, more specifically, to encourage them to move along together with us and with others with initiative and effectiveness, in order to help to get to what are experienced as common goals, "our" goals.

How, then, are we to look at organizational structure? Structure lies in the pattern of relationships among the roles in any organization, large or small. The pattern of mother, father, child roles in the family is an example: the pattern varies in different cultures, but the particular structure in any family can always be found. However, the pattern of roles (structure) in families is patently different from the pattern of roles in managerial hierarchies, in a political party, in a church, in a school-room, or in a university.

If it is the case that it is the pattern of role relationships that defines organizational structure, we must then examine what role relationships are about. The roles in a relationship are vested with two main properties: accountability and authority (see figure 4.2). Knowing what each person is accountable for in a relationship, and with what authority each has been vested with respect to the other or others, is the absolute foundation of effective human relationships of any kind. Unclarity about what is required of each person simply by virtue of his or her role in the situation, and equally about what each person is authorized to require each other person to consider or to do, is a recipe for disorder and for strained and uncertain personal relationships. In contrast, clarity lays a foundation for effective interaction.

In saying that clarity about role-vested accountability and authority lays the foundation for effective human interaction, we mean just that. Without such clarity, human interaction is strained. But having the foundation alone is not enough. We need to build not just any old accountability and authority into the roles, but the proper kinds of accountability and authority. What constitutes proper (or as we prefer to term it, requisite) accountability and authority for any given role in relation to others is a big question, and one that is certainly central to managerial leadership. We shall address it in some detail.

Why Structure Comes First: Who "Leads" Whom?

We have shown that leadership has to do with a special form of accountability in some role relationships, but certainly not in all of them. We have also shown that there are profound differences in the nature of these role relationships. But a central fact is that leadership accountability, and authority, are specified by role. That is to say, who leads whom is determined by the roles that people occupy (except for the very general leadership responsibility, defined on pp. 32–3, that involves anyone and everyone).

Thus, a clear managerial structure must come first if effective managerial leadership is to have any chance of occurring (see figure 4.3). That is why matrix organization, for example, is disruptive of

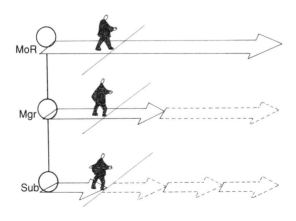

Figure 4.3 Why structure comes first: who "leads" whom?

effective managerial leadership. With the matrix, most people are explicitly stated to be accountable to two or more "bosses." But that evades the issue, because the real question is not to whom we are accountable but who is held accountable for our work. It is only the person who is held accountable for our work who can requisitely be held accountable for setting our direction and getting us to move enthusiastically along with our colleagues in the direction set; that is to say, for discharging leadership. A matrix of people cannot be held accountable for giving vigorous and creative leadership to anyone. The resulting loss of incisiveness is grievous.

A second reason why structure must come first is that structure determines the degree to which it is possible to change the persons who occupy the roles in the relationships. Thus, for example, if a father's actual competence as assessed by cognitive capability is less than that of his 14-year old son, he is not going to be as effective in his exercise of parental leadership as he would be if his cognitive capability were greater. Family life is full of such surprises. But there is nothing to be done. The father is the father, and the son is the son, and that is that.

By contrast with the family, there is a flexibility in the filling of managerial roles which matters a great deal. The question of which actual persons shall be managerial leaders and which persons they shall exercise managerial leadership towards, is a matter of who occupies the relevant roles, for the time being anyhow. We can change our managerial leaders if they do not exercise effective leadership. And changed they ought to be, since, as we said earlier on, there can be no room for the notion that there is any such thing as someone who is a "good manager" who just does not happen to be a very "good leader."

Thus, the managerial hierarchy gives an extraordinary opportunity to attain and maintain outstanding managerial leadership, so long as our sequence is observed: mission followed by structure followed by requisite managerial practices followed by sound selection and education, such that the requisite managerial practices become second nature to every manager, followed by tight appraisal by every manager of his or her subordinates' effectiveness as managerial leaders, and by the replacement of those who do not meet the necessary standards.

Structure must be gotten right because it sets the roles and role relationships that specify not only the people who are needed but also how they will behave towards one another. There is no activity that is more psychologically constructive.

The Heart of Organizational Structure for Managerial Leadership

Central to managerial organizations is the meaning and structure of the hierarchical layering, since hierarchical layering is fundamentally what these organizations are about. This method of layering is a true human discovery, such as fire or the wheel. The best evidence is that it happened in China about 3,000 years ago. It was a major event in the transition from the family/tribal type of society to the more dispersed type of society that we take for granted. It has become the most widespread type of organization in industrially developed societies: the USA has more manager–subordinate role relationships (about 150 million) than it has husband–wife relationships (about 45 million).

The hierarchical layering stems from the manager–subordinate role relationship, which is precisely and exclusively what organizational layers are about. Those in one layer are in roles in which they may delegate work to those, called subordinates, in the layer immediately below; and they can be held accountable (by someone in the next layer up) for the output of those subordinates.

These rather simple and obvious points need to be explicitly stated, because they give a rather less obvious answer to the question that has vexed so many for so long, namely, how many layers of organization should any company have? The answer is: just that number of layers which will provide for effective managerial leadership relationships between managers and subordinates in roles in adjacent layers, starting with the topmost role as established by the mission.

That, at least, is the superficial answer. The more substantial answer that underlies it – and this is the central proposition of our argument about the necessary conditions for managerial leadership – is that the layering must be such as to encompass successive categories of task complexity and of cognitive complexity within each stratum of organization. We introduced this notion in the previous chapter in our introduction of the time-span concept. Let us now elaborate that argument (see figure 4.4).

We have indicated that only eight categories of cognitive complexity

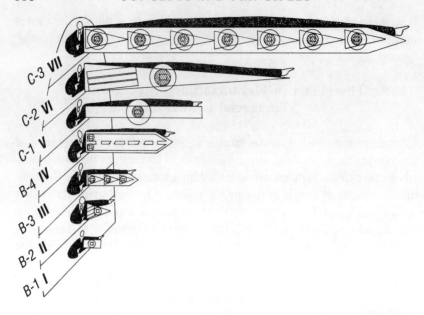

Figure 4.4 The heart of organizational structure for managerial leadership

are used in managerial hierarchies. The categories are those we labelled category B–1 to B–4 and category C–1 to C–4. Category B–1 is the level of cognitive capability which is called for at shop- and office-floor complexity level; category C–3 is the level of cognitive capability which is needed at the level of complexity of work that is required in CEO roles in large corporations; and category C–4 applies to the very highest level, to the capability that is required in CEOs of the super-corporations. According to our proposition, therefore, even the very largest super-corporations ought to be able to be structured with a maximum of eight layers, down to and including the shop and office floor: categories B–1 to B–4 plus C–1 to C–4.

By the same token, a smaller company, or department within a company, whose role of CEO or of departmental head contains work of maximum complexity at, say, category C–1, would require five layers or strata, including the top and the shop and office floor (i.e., categories B–1, B–2, B–3, B–4, and C–1).

Thus, we are linking the practical requirements of managerial structure to the absolute requirements of the category of capability that is needed in a manager in order to be able to exercise managerial leadership in relation to immediate subordinates; i.e. not charisma, not personality traits, but raw cognitive complexity, sheer competence.

These propositions have been strongly and strikingly borne out by consistent and clear-cut evidence, accumulated over the past 30 years, of the existence in all managerial hierarchies of a universal underlying pattern of true managerial strata, which gives a truer picture of who the real managers are than does the manifest organization chart. Disjunction between this universal underlying pattern of layers (how many there really ought to be) and the number in existence on the organization chart (there are nearly always many more) is one of the main sources of negative bureaucratic practices, mediocrity, and ineffectual managerial leadership.

Hierarchical Layering and the "Real Boss"

Here is how the universal underlying pattern of real hierarchical managerial layers was uncovered, and found to coincide with the basic categories of task and cognitive complexity. It is necessary first to specify the nature of a true manager–subordinate relationship. Having done so, we shall recall the means of measuring the level of work in a role, which we alluded to earlier, in terms of what is called time-span of that role. Then we shall put these two sets of data together in order to present our findings about systematic managerial layering.

Let us begin, then, by defining a managerial role in terms of three critical factors:

First, every manager must be held accountable not only for the work of subordinates but also for adding value to their work – that is crucial; second, he or she must also be held accountable for sustaining a team of subordinates who are capable of doing their work; and third, he or she must set direction for subordinates and get them willingly to work along with him or her to move in that direction, that is to say, he or she must carry leadership accountability.

In order to make the carrying of such accountability possible, it is essential to ensure that every manager has at least the minimal authority requirements of his or her role. That authority must comprise at least: the right of veto on any applicant to join the team whom he or she judges to be below minimum standards in working ability; the right to decide about the tasks to be assigned to subordinates; the right to decide (not recommend) the performance appraisal for each subordinate, and also the merit award for each one within policy; and finally, the right to decide, after due process, that a particular subordinate whom he or she judges to have become unable to do the work shall no longer be a member of his or her team.

Merely defining the basic nature of the managerial role, while important in its own right, gives only one feature of what a managerial layer is about. It does not indicate how wide a managerial layer should be and how much higher a manager must be above a subordinate in level of work and accountability. Fortunately a second development occurred that supplied the missing piece of the puzzle.

This second development was Jaques's unexpected and startling discovery, described in Chapter 3, that the level of work in any role can be objectively measured (instead of using subjective job evaluation ratings) in terms of the target completion times (as set by the manager) of the longest assignments (tasks, projects, programs) in that role. The longer the target completion time of the longest tasks or programs, the heavier the weight of responsibility is felt to be. He called this measure the time-span of the role. It has been found, for example, in all types of managerial organization in many different countries over the past 35 years that people in roles at the same time-span not only experience the same weight of responsibility but also state the same level of pay as fair, regardless of their occupation or actual pay! Our time-span range runs from one day at the bottom to over 20 years at the top, at the large corporation, with felt-fair pay (in 1989 terms) ranging from $15,000 to over $1 million per year.[1]

Armed with the above definition of a manager, and his time-span measuring instrument, Jaques then came upon the following strongly confirmed finding about layering in managerial hierarchies: the boundaries between successive managerial layers occur at certain specific time-spans, just as ice changes to water and water to steam at certain specific temperatures.

Here is an illustration. Figure 4.5a shows the organizational structure of part of a department. P is the designated manager of Q, Q of R, and R of S. The approximate time-spans of these roles are shown. It will be noted that P is above 5 years, and Q, R, and S are between 2 years and 5 years. Here is how it really worked. Despite the managerial roles shown in figure 4.5a, Q, R, and S all described P as their "real" manager as shown in figure 4.5b. R and S complained that Q and R respectively were "far too close" and "breathing down my neck." No value was being added. They were in the way. It was a

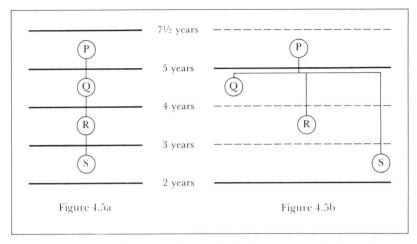

Figure 4.5a Departmental organizational structure as designated
Figure 4.5b Departmental organizational structure as perceived

typical bureaucratic muddle, with too many layers. In addition, Q and R admitted to finding it exceedingly difficult to manage R and S: the latter seemed to do better if Q and R treated them as colleagues and left them alone.

In short, there appeared to be cut-off points at 5-years' and 2-years' time-span (as at 0°C and 100°C) such that it needed a manager in the layer above 5-years' time-span to be able to be a real manager to any subordinates in roles in the layer between 2 years and 5 years (see figure 4.6). This finding has been confirmed time and again.

But that is not all. Equivalent firm boundaries of real managerial layers were found to exist at time-spans of 3 months, 1 year, 2 years, 5 years, 10 years (and 20 years), as illustrated in figure 4.7. This regularity, which has so far appeared consistently in over 100 projects, points to the existence of a structure in depth, composed of true managerial layers with boundaries measured in time-span as illustrated. When there are more layers than these, trouble will ensue.

The Big Finding about Hierarchy

Now we come to a finding that is absolutely crucial for setting the scene if we are to attain even a semblance of effective managerial

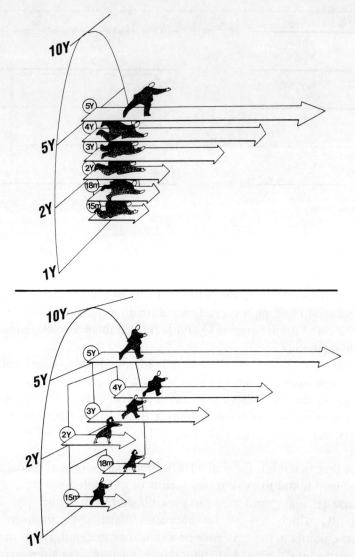

Figure 4.6   Hierarchical layering and the "real boss"

leadership. The finding is that the universal underlying pattern of true managerial strata, which we have just described, coincides precisely with the categories of task and cognitive complexity that we described in Chapters 2 and 3. Let us elaborate this fundamental proposition.

The finding (and we alluded to it at the end of Chapter 3) is that the time-span range of 1 day to 3 months, which provides for the layer of non-managerial roles at organizational stratum–I (the first organization layer), also happens to coincide in observed reality with the existence of tasks whose maximum complexity is category B–1 (direct action in immediate situation). It also happens to coincide with the need for the roles within this time-span range to be filled by people with time-horizons between 1 day and 3 months, a range that encompasses the B–1 assertive processing category of cognitive complexity. In short, the true organizational layer at stratum–I coincides with category B–1 in task and cognitive complexity.

If we then move to stratum–II, time-span range 3 months to 1 year, the first managerial layer, we find that it coincides with the appearance of roles with tasks of maximum B–2 complexity (diagnostic accumulation), and successful incumbents of category B–2 cognitive complexity (cumulative processing). It would appear that a person must be able to function at least at category B–2 level of cognitive complexity in order to be competent to discharge managerial leadership accountability in relation to individuals of category B–1 cognitive complexity. Or to put it more descriptively, it takes a cumulative processor to give managerial leadership to an assertive processor.

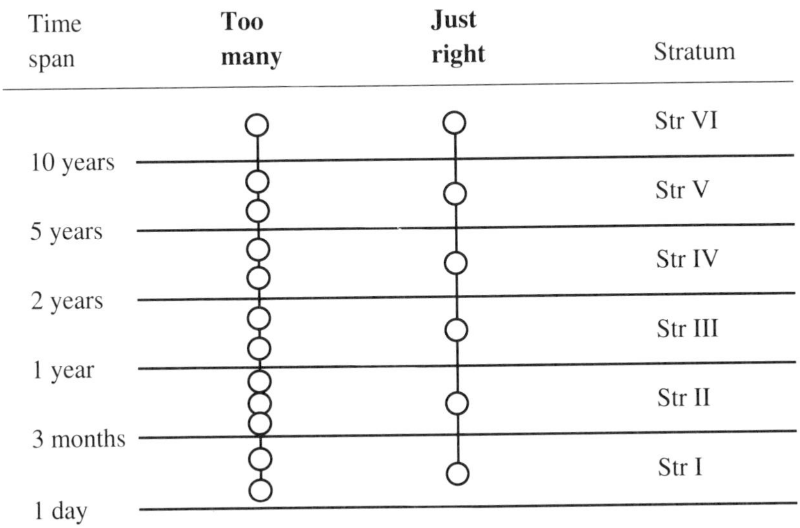

Fig. 4.7 The underlying structure of organizational layers

And so it goes right up to the top. Stratum–III coincides with category B–3 task and cognitive complexity, while stratum–VII corporation roles, with time-spans over 20 years, coincide with category C–3 task and cognitive complexity/serial processing of international strategies, at third order of conceptual language and ideas. And it requires a serial processor to lead cumulative processors, a parallel processor to lead serial processors, and a third order assertive processor to lead second order parallel processors.

In short, evidence has accumulated rapidly in project work, over a period of three years, that the requisite organizational layers, and the categories of task and cognitive complexity, and the requirements of effective managerial leadership, all coincide. They are isomorphic with one another.

The perfection of the match is a fascinating phenomenon which, on reflection, is not in the least surprising. Its significance, however, is far-reaching. It means that at long last we have a sound explanation for the emergence and tenacious hold of hierarchical organizations as a means for getting work done. This form of organization is a reflection and expression of the hierarchical property both of work tasks and of cognitive working capability in human beings.

It means, further, that there is one, and only one, correct system of organizational layers, which we are calling "strata." Using this particular system of layers, or strata, makes it possible to bring the organizational hierarchy into full correspondence with the basic nature of task complexity and human nature, with one layer of organization for each category of task complexity and of human capability. We shall show that the correspondence is fundamental for getting the necessary conditions for managerial leadership.

Span of Control and Leadership

If there is a universal underlying pattern of organizational strata, then why has it not been used universally? One contributing factor is that we organize into levels for pay and status rather than for getting our work done. Another contributing factor is the incorrect view of what an appropriate span of control ought to be.

There is more nonsense centering around the topic of span of control than around nearly any other subject in the whole field of organization and management. The current wisdom holds that to have somewhere between 3 and 6 subordinates is about right for any manager to be effective (see figure 4.8). That is an idea that has no basis in theory or fact. It was formulated on the basis of no evidence by a management expert named Graicunas in the 1920s. It has been around ever since, probably because it satisfies the desire for easy-to-apply rules of thumb which need no thought.

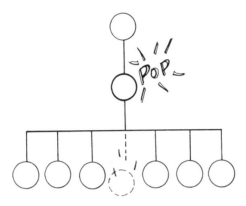

Figure 4.8   Span of control and leadership

This notion has had a widespread and devastating effect. It has done more to produce too many levels of organization than any other factor except our pay and grading systems. There is plenty of experience to show that, depending upon the circumstances, a manager can cope with between 1 and 70 immediate subordinates and can maintain effective mutual-knowledge conditions and inter-personal leadership. Span of control decreases as the variability of the conditions and the absences of the manager increase. It is possible to get by with up to perhaps 10 to 20 immediate subordinates at middle levels, and less at corporate levels. Up to 50 or more is possible under routinized technologies, such as a standardized production line or a typing pool, where the manager has no scheduling or technical problems, does not have to go to any meetings, and can spend his or her time overseeing subordinates.

The trouble with the "rule of six" is that every time a manager has more than six subordinates they are likely to agitate to have "the promotion opportunity" established; namely, a managerial role between the manager and some of the subordinates. Abracadabra, another level or layer of organization appears!

Having too small spans of control produces excessive numbers of
levels and encourages "delegation disease." It has led in military
thinking to the all too easy but unfortunate arithmetic formula that
3 soldiers plus 1 NCO equals 1 section, 4 sections equals 1 squad of
16, 4 squads equals 1 platoon of 64, and 4 platoons equals 1 company
of 256. The result of this kind of organizational kindergarten
arithmetic is that military companies, the true first-line command
entities, are far too large. They should be no more than 70. In special
forces they are a mere handful.

The same kind of thinking is widespread. There is a great need to
break out of this mold. We will not be able to get the necessary
foundation for truly effective creativity-releasing managerial leadership
until we do.

Complexity and Organizational Magnitude

In addition to immediate span of control, there is the further question
of how large can any given multi-level unit of hierarchical organization
be and still retain the conditions for effective managerial leadership?
This question has not been satisfactorily answered, nor even
satisfactorily addressed, despite the fact that it is a major issue for
organizational development, and for the effectiveness of leadership
which depends upon this organizational development.

The span of control question is usually considered only in terms of
how many subordinates a manager should have, but it is more
complex than that. For example: how big should a factory be? What is
the optimum size for a total sales organization or for a strategic
business unit? How big can a corporation be?

It may seem strange, but the maximum size of an organization
should be set exclusively by the requirements of managerial
leadership. Although technology, markets, and other factors can
reduce the size below the maximum, the top limit is set by human
leadership consideration only and not by these other factors. The
alternative would be that we could simply say that a manager could
have as many immediate subordinates as the fancy takes, without any
intermediate managers: say, a small section of 20, a production unit of
200, a whole factory of 1,000 or 2,000, a strategic business unit of
5,000 or 10,000. It does not really matter, does it? Of course it does.
Everyone "knows," for instance, that it is not possible to have a

factory of 3,000 with only one manager and one subordinate layer. "But why?" "Because that's too many people." Still the questions arise: "But why, and what is too many people?"

The only organizations that have considered these questions systematically are military organizations. The questions were explicitly argued, for instance, by the Imperial Roman armies in the first century AD, in terms of optimum size for their centuries, manciples, cohorts, small legions, and large legions. The same questions of scale continue to be argued today in relation to the optimum size for squads, platoons, companies, battalions, brigades, divisions, and corps.

The reason why military organizations have had to be specially concerned with these matters, as compared with businesses which can continue to allow the issues to be more obscure, is that combat organization has to be mobile. It must be possible to pick up units of various size, along with their commanders, and move them about, rapidly, continuously and over long distances and difficult terrain. It

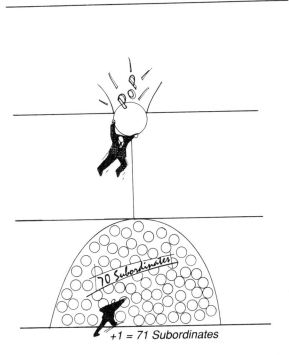

Figure 4.9 Complexity and organizational magnitude

must be possible to reconstitute them rapidly. Thus, the ratio of commanders to troops must be just right. If the units are too small, the commanders will be bumping into each other; if they are too large, the troops will be bereft of an adequate command leadership cadre in the confused disarray of the battlefield.

The problems are the same in business organizations, but they are less painfully obvious. None the less, wrong-sized units are great energy drains and they certainly do not help to establish the best conditions for hierarchical leadership.

The real point about numbers has to do with complexity. If there is an increase in the number of subordinates of a manager, then the complexity of that manager's role is inevitably increased. But if the numbers go on increasing, there comes a point where any further increase not only expands the complexity but also shifts it up one category of task complexity. That is to say, there are certain boundaries in numbers of subordinates beyond which it is not possible to go without shifting upwards the stratum of the role itself (see figure 4.9).

Maximum Unit Sizes for Effective Managerial Leadership

Here is our working answer to the question of the numbers of people it is possible to have in units of given numbers of organizational strata. Some of the answers are based on principles developed over the past 40 years, and some are based on simple practical experience over the same period. Remember, we are concentrating upon the specific question of the maximum numbers of people towards whom it is possible to exercise effective hierarchical leadership from various organizational strata.

It is of the greatest importance to understand that all of the unit sizes which we shall propose are based upon the maximum number of subordinates a managerial leader could handle effectively if that manager had little else to do other than to attend to those subordinates and to what they were doing. But under most circumstances where work is not routinized, as in most managerial, technical, and professional work, the numbers are going to be anywhere from slightly to substantially less than the maximum. They may be down to as few as one, two or three subordinates in the case of individual contributors at any level, such as designers, who may need to have the direct assistance of only a few people.

In short, we are describing where the natural steps in task complexity from one category of complexity to the next higher category occur solely as a response to increases in the numbers of subordinates. It is these boundaries that establish the maximum numbers of people in units which are consistent with the minimum requirements of good managerial leadership (see figure 4.10).

Two-Stratum immediate manager-subordinate units These are what we shall term "mutual knowledge units" (MKUs), which are made up of managers and their immediate subordinates, and which occur at each and every level in the organization. The upper limit is 70 subordinates. This limit derives from the principle that immediate managerial leadership requires that managers and subordinates should be able mutually to know one another. This is so that the manager can know the subordinates' personal strengths and weaknesses, can be able to judge their personal effectiveness, can coach, and can do all the other things that effective managerial leaders must do, from one category higher in cognitive complexity. Where the manager is pulled away by meetings or travel and has many of his or her own tasks to do, then the maximum possible number of subordinates will be considerably less; perhaps up to a maximum of 15 to 20 at middle management levels.

Three-Stratum mutual recognition units (MRUs) We shall call these units MRUs because, with up to a maximum of 250–300 people, it is possible to fulfil the basic principle that the manager-once-removed (MoR) and all of his or her subordinates, i.e. both the intermediate managers and all of the subordinates-once-removed (SoRs), must be able to know one another well enough to recognize each other. In other words, anonymity has not yet set in. There is substantial experience to show that with more than 300 people the mutual recognition quality gets lost. This principle of mutual recognition among all members of a unit is extremely important for organizational leadership (see figure 4.10). We shall describe in Chapter 8 how MRUs cascade down through the organization, providing the glue for constructive vertical cohesion.

There is no common language available for discussing units spanning four to eight levels of organization except in the military. In many armies they are called Brigade (stratum–IV), Division (stratum–V),

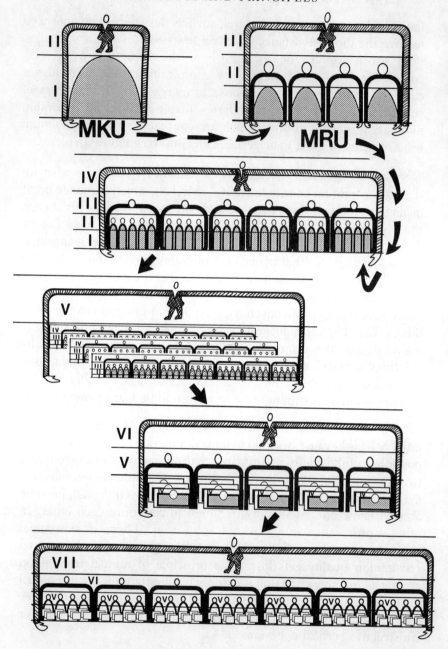

Figure 4.10   Maximum unit sizes for effective managerial leadership

Corps (stratum–VI), Army (stratum–VII), and Army Group (stratum–VIII). Here are the maximum numbers we find associated with these units:

Stratum–IV   up to 2,000
Stratum–V   up to 6,000
Stratum–VI   up to 30,000
Stratum–VII   up to 100,000
Stratum–VIII   up to 1 million and more.

As we mentioned above, these maximum figures are pretty rough but, give or take 20 percent, they are of substantial practical significance. They set the maximum limits at which the increasing complexity that is inherent solely in increasing numbers builds up to the breaking point and then moves across the boundary from one category of task complexity to the next higher category, thus calling for a manager at the next higher category of cognitive complexity. They can help to identify the maximum number of layers that there should be in any organization, a problem which exercises most companies. As we have mentioned, it is possible to have much smaller numbers than these, depending upon the inherent complexity of the work; for example, a very large property trading company whose CEO role was at stratum–VII task complexity had only 78 personnel, although appropriately organized in seven true layers.

Leadership in the Immediate Mutual Knowledge Unit (MKU)

To have effective managerial leadership, a manager must be in a role one stratum higher than immediate subordinates, must handle maximum task complexity one category higher, and must possess cognitive capability one category higher. It is these conditions that are necessary and make it possible for a managerial leader to exercise his or her vested authority, including direction and context setting, task assignment, providing performance information, appraising personal effectiveness, and coaching.

These aspects of role-vested authority have one important feature in common. They all require that the manager should be able to have a two-way, face-to-face relationship with each of his or her immediate subordinates. It must be two-way because the manager must be able to know and understand the strengths and weaknesses of the subordinates and the subordinates must know the manager well enough to be able to tell what to expect. In short, the conditions must allow for a mutual knowledge relationship between managers and subordinates. The immediate manager–subordinate group can thus be called a mutual knowledge unit, or MKU (see figure 4.11). It will be apparent that such a unit will also provide for conditions of mutual knowledge among the subordinates, an essential condition for effective team working.

If the conditions for an MKU do not exist, then a managerial leader not only will have difficulty exercising his or her vested authority but also will most certainly be unable to muster the personally earned authority needed for the kind of managerial leadership that engenders excitement and enthusiasm.

One of the worst barriers in the way of achieving true MKUs is that of having too many layers in the hierarchical structure. When the "real boss" is two or three false layers up, a two-way relationship

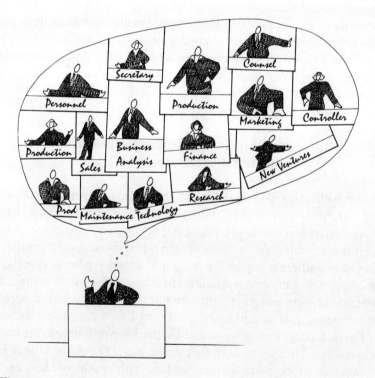

Figure 4.11   Leadership in the immediate mutual knowledge unit (MKU)

between true managers and their subordinates can take place only by an awkward bypassing. Dynamic managerial leadership is impossible under such circumstances. Another barrier is that of having too many immediate subordinates, an issue that we have discussed above.

Manager–subordinate teams are not the only kind of MKU. There are two other types that must be noted. They can play an important role. They are project teams (task forces) and supervisory sections, both of which we shall consider in relation to requisite practices.

Project teams or task forces These are teams of people who are brought together with a project team chief for a specific project with a targeted completion date, and who return to their home-base managers when the project is completed. Such teams can be useful for handling special development problems within the company, for example in production technology or in product development work. They are essential for those companies that sell services by providing teams of specialized talent to work for clients on discrete projects, as in, for example, construction services. The concept of matrix organization was developed to try to deal with project situations; it not only has proved inadequate for this purpose but also unfortunately has been extended to cover every kind of organizational requirement.

There are two kinds of project team. Those which are made up of the project team chief and attached experts who are at the same organizational stratum and cognitive category as the chief are called "colleague project teams;" those which are made up of experts from subordinate strata are called "subordinate project teams." In both cases, the chief is held accountable for the output and must exercise leadership accountability. His or her authority will be less than that of a full-scale accountable manager but the basic conditions of the mutual knowledge unit must be maintained. We shall detail the provisions of project team leadership accountability in Chapter 8.

Supervisory sections These are made up of parts of a first line manager's total team of subordinates. They are a quite special kind of MKU which can be employed only at shop- and office-floor level; that is to say, at stratum–I. These sections are a response to the problem encountered at stratum–I, where the bottom section of the population requires the continual availability of supervisory assistance in dealing with problems as they are encountered. We are here dealing with people who have just enough competence to work at the bottom half of stratum–I; for example, the still young and not fully matured 16–21 year old group of juniors, trainees or young soldiers. The way in which assistance can be made available to them, by providing a special intermediate role of supervisory assistant between the first line manager and the team members, but without adding a managerial layer, and the situations in which it is useful to do so, are described in the next paragraphs.

Supervisory Leadership Roles: First Line Managerial Units

A special circumstance which is crucial to managerial leadership exists at shop-floor and office-floor level. It arises because individuals at bottom level, the so-called unskilled and semi-skilled levels of capability, have some trouble in sustaining order in the progress of their work. They require the continual availability of a more experienced person to help them out of difficulties they may encounter, and to keep them going in the face of those difficulties.

These individuals require someone to help them in addition to their managerial leader. They need a managerial leader at stratum–II who has the category B–2 capability to determine their task type, to assess their personal effectiveness, to coach them, to recognize and award merit, but they also need continual on-the-spot attention to help to keep the work moving and to help when things go wrong.

This issue of capability interacts with another important factor at stratum–I in industrial, commercial, and military mass-production work. This stratum is the bottom level of work. It is the basic production level, and there are very strong economic reasons to keep production going 24 hours per day, 168 hours per week. That arrangement requires shift work.

With shift work there are two ways to break up the day: either by having a different manager with each shift or by having one manager throughout the full cycle. There are strong reasons of effectiveness for preferring the second option. One managerial leader controls the whole area. This advantage is startlingly clear in the military where one commander can maintain day and night control of the sector. However, there is a problem; the manager cannot be continuously on duty all the time. That problem is not serious if the people involved are high-skilled, self-supervising personnel who can take care of themselves so long as the manager sees them once every few days, for example, between shifts. Even with personnel who are not self-supervising, the problem can still be overcome by having a supervisory assistant on each shift. The supervisor must be given the task-assigning accountability for the duration of each shift. This should be within the task type set for each person by the manager. Then, as will be described fully in Chapter 7, the supervisor must be given the vested authority to make recommendations to the manager on all of the matters relating to the team members personally, about which the manager has the authority to decide. On this basis, the supervisor can be given leadership accountability for the duration of each shift (see figure 4.12).

This supervisory role will be familiar to those who have experience of military combat organization. It is the role of the team, squad (and

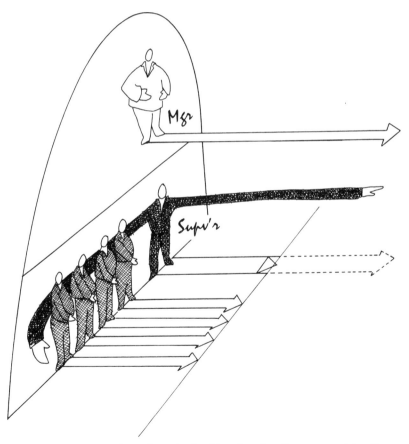

Figure 4.12 Supervisory leadership roles: first line managerial units

sometimes platoon) NCO. Such a person is required by the company commander to help to move whole sections in complex maneuvers and to exercise fire control under the confusing and disorganizing conditions of modern combat in which the men, if they do not have immediate supervisory help with immediate problems, may get shot. The problem is not so dramatic in industry and commerce, but it nevertheless requires that, under the circumstances where a manager has unskilled subordinates at the bottom half of category B–1, he or she shall be able to provide shift-to-shift, on-the-spot supervisory leadership for them.

Leadership in the Mutual Recognition Unit (MRU)

One of the routes to effective managerial leadership is to establish explicitly and clearly the key role of the manager-once-removed for whom we shall use the abbreviation MoR. We shall also use the abbreviation SoR to refer to a subordinate-once-removed. As can be seen from figure 4.13, it is the MoR who is inevitably in a position to observe the quality of working relationships of his or her own immediate subordinate manager with the SoRs of the MoR.

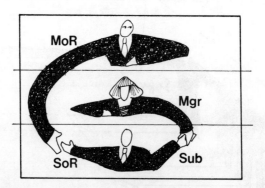

Figure 4.13   Leadership in the mutual recognition unit (MRU)

The fact that every manager who has managerial subordinates has in turn a manager-once-removed relationship with those managers' own immediate subordinates tends to be soft-pedalled, because it is regarded as bad for the MoR to have any contact with SoRs since it is generally held that this means bypassing the in-between manager.

Indeed, if the MoR goes directly to the SoRs to issue instructions, that is certainly dysfunctional.

But just because there are dangers of undesirable interference inherent in an MoR's having direct contact with SoRs in the everyday work situation, it does not mean that there are no proper MoR–SoR working relationships. There are in fact three duties that must be required of MoRs, which are absolutely fundamental aspects of the effective leadership in the organization. Their absence will undermine the total leadership effort. These three duties are, first, to oversee and appraise the qualities of managerial leadership of their immediately subordinate managers; second, to know their SoRs well enough personally to evaluate their current and future potential and to be accountable for mentoring them and for decisions about their career development; and third, to ensure that their managerial subordinates are applying roughly similar standards to their subordinates (that is to say, an equilibrating function).

With respect to overseeing the quality of managerial leadership, it is incumbent upon MoRs to oversee the manner in which each of their immediate managerial subordinates is exercising managerial leadership in relation to their own subordinates (the SoRs of the MoR). Are they carrying out the requisite practices consistently and well? Are they getting enthusiastic collaboration? Is morale high? Is there a good spirit within the team? Is each individual being treated fairly and justly without need for grievance about their treatment? Is there a good sense of cohesion and of working together?

The second duty is to judge the current and future potential of their SoRs, and to oversee their career development. We have discussed the nature of potential capability in Chapter 2, under the heading of cognitive power and of cognitive categories and how to recognize them. We shall have more to say about evaluation procedures in Chapter 9, on MoR leadership. It is obvious that evaluations of this kind cannot be made in thin air. MoRs must get to know their SoRs and be able to talk to them about these very sensitive judgments. This is an extremely important act of MoR leadership, which is probably most significant in achieving constructive longer-term commitment to the organization.

In addition to evaluation of potential, the MoR must be accountable for sitting down with each SoR and mentoring him or her with respect to how best to prepare for further progress in the company. If the SoR has unrealized potential because of shortage of knowledge, then the MoR should discuss possible educational programs or other means of providing the missing knowledge or practice; similarly, the MOR should suggest means of making up for other deficiencies. The SoR must share responsibility for his or her own career development.

The third duty, that of equilibration, can be illustrated in terms of ensuring that managerial subordinates do not become too soft-hearted or too tough-minded. Thus, the MoR must review the personal effectiveness appraisal and merit awards to ensure that none of his or her immediately subordinate managers is being unrealistically lenient and generous or too tough and mean.

Apart from these two activities of the MoR, which are individually directed to each of the SoRs, there is an organizational activity that is the fulcrum of the see-saw between individual interpersonal managerial leadership and organizational leadership. It is the MoR leadership of the three-stratum unit of MoR, intermediate managers, and SoRs. This unit is the mutual recognition unit that we described above. MRUs cascade down the organization in a series of overlapping trios (see figure 4.14). If the MRUs are organized correctly, they can be used to prevent the curse of feelings of anonymity from settling on the organization. If someone is a member of an MRU which is headed by

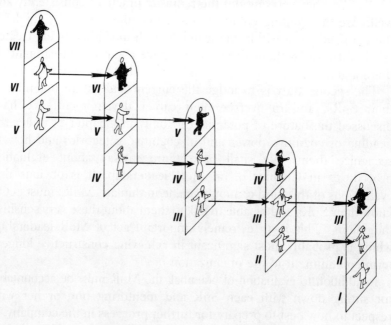

Figure 4.14   The cascading MRUs

an effective MoR, then that person is ensconced in a personalized unit which in turn is encompassed within the larger organization. It engenders a good feeling of involvement in the whole organization and of commitment to it.

How the MRU functions in relation to managerial leadership is treated in Chapter 9. It is one of the more interesting managerial leadership roles.

Organizational Structure and Organizational Leadership

We have so far focused our attention upon organization for interpersonal leadership: the face-to-face leadership of the immediate manager, the project team chief, and the supervisor, and their MKUs (mutual knowledge units); also the leadership of MoRs and their three-stratum mutual recognition units (MRUs). But interpersonal leadership is far from the whole story. There is, in addition, the leadership work of managers of four-, five-, six-, seven-, and even eight-stratum organizations, with respect to their total subordinate organizations.

We shall refer to the leadership work that is involved in the management of four-stratum and higher organizations as a whole as "organizational leadership."

By organizational leadership, we mean the work that managers can do in relation to their total subordinate organizations, so as to set a common over-arching direction for everyone from top to bottom, and to do so in such a way as to support their competent and willing collaboration in moving along together with their managers, who in turn will be moving in the broad direction set.

Organizational leadership thus provides the background or foundation for the more intensive interpersonal leadership within the nesting and overlapping MRUs, at each level of the organization from the corporate CEO to the first line managers and supervisors.

There are two main types of organizational leadership, each associated with a natural grouping of type of work and organization to be found in all managerial hierarchies. These groupings are as shown in figure 4.15.

The grouping that comprises stratum–III to stratum–I has already been discussed. It is the special case, of shop- and office-floor, of the

Str-VII Str-VI	Corporate organization	Strategic organizational leadership: culture values, vision	Up to multi-100,000s of people
10 years			
Str-V Str-IV	Unified business units or divisions	General organizational leadership: local culture	Up to 7,000 people
2 years			
Str-III Str-II Str-I	Operational Units (MRUs)	Interpersonal managerial and supervisory leadership	Up to 300 people
1 day			

Fig. 4.15 Types of organizational leadership

interpersonal manager-once-removed (MoR) leadership of the mutual recognition unit (MRU), that cascades down from the top and recurs at each stratum down to stratum–III.

It is the groupings that comprise stratum–V and stratum–IV, and stratum–VII and stratum–VI, that throw up the special features that we have labelled organizational leadership and will discuss in Chapter 10.

Stratum–V (with stratum–IV) is uniformly associated, for reasons that are as yet not entirely clear,[2] with the highest possible level of unified organization; that is to say, the level at which all the major business functions of an organization are present and whose interdependence the manager can control and co-ordinate.

In business organizations it is the largest scale of profit-and-loss business unit in which a president can regulate the interdependency between product development, production, and marketing/selling; or of a unified functional division such as a corporate research laboratory, or corporate finance services. Equivalent levels of unified organization associated with stratum–V, and with time-spans between 5 and 10 years, are the combat division in armies and the diocese in episcopal churches.

Stratum–VI and stratum–VII (and stratum–VIII super-corporations) are uniformly associated with the corporate levels of organization. It is the region of the corporate CEOs and their corporate EVPs who oversee the strategic groupings of business units and divisions through whose presidents the corporation gets its operating work done. The work at these highest organizational strata is commonly described as strategic, conceptual or "abstract" in nature, to express the shift to the third order complexity of language and ideas (see p. 55) that operates at these levels of organization.

As we shall describe in Chapter 10, organizational leadership in these two groupings is concerned respectively with the following matters. Stratum–VIII to stratum–VI corporate organization calls for strategic leadership, in which the objective aspects of corporate culture, including corporate vision and values, procedures and regulations, and key customs and practices, are articulated for everyone in the organization. Stratum–V and stratum–IV business unit or division calls for general leadership, in which the aspects of culture specific to the unit or division are articulated. Culture in this sense gives the expected or appropriate ways of doing things or taking initiative (see figure 4.16).

By working with the various aspects of culture, the organizational leader, whether at corporate or at business unit level, can seek to

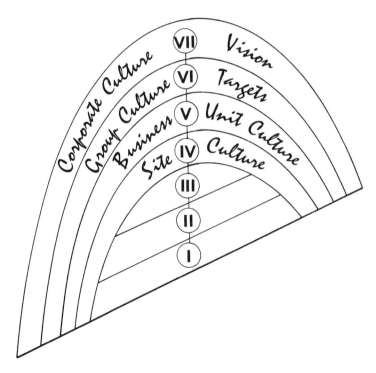

Figure 4.16 Organizational structure and organizational leadership

bring about and sustain the kinds of values and attitudes that he or she deems to be necessary. In particular, he or she can influence the way in which it feels to work in the company, from being restrictive, suspicious, and fearful to being open and trusting, and inducing enthusiasm, responsibility and initiative. Whatever the culture, it will certainly have a significant impact upon the effectiveness, competitiveness and morale of the organization.

Specialist Roles without Leadership Accountability

We have described the three types of role relationship in managerial hierarchies that carry leadership accountability; namely, manager–subordinate relationships, project team chief and attached team members, and supervisory assistants and supervisees. They all carry authority to assign tasks, and carry accountability for the outputs from those tasks. Because of the task assigning content, we call them "task-assigning role relationships," or TARRs.

But there is another major category of role relationships in these managerial organizations that do not carry leadership accountability. They arise from the various kinds of specialist roles that are set up to assist managers to get their work done. Such roles are often called staff, as against line, but that over-simplified distinction does not help very much. The kinds of role we have in mind include so-called staff officers, advisers, auditors, co-ordinators, service-givers, specialists, experts, individual contributors.

Regardless of the wide range of the functions in such roles, however, they have one feature in common that is of interest to us here, because it contrasts with leadership accountability and serves to sharpen our analysis and description of leadership accountability in both managerial, project chief and supervisory roles. The feature is that, on the one hand, they carry neither accountability nor authority to assign tasks to others, nor accountability for the outputs; but, on the other hand, they do carry accountability and authority to initiate tasks for specified others to carry out even though they cannot require them to do so. That is to say, they take part in "task-initiating role relationships," or TIRRs.

Thus, a general proposition is that managerial organizations carry two main types of role and role relationships which we can designate simply as TARRs and TIRRs. A central feature of this distinction is that those in TIRRs do not have accountability for whether or not those for whom they initiate tasks carry them out or, if so, do so willingly and enthusiastically. It is for those others to decide whether or not to respond.

The TIRRs have been described in detail in *Requisite Organization* (Jaques, 1989). They are presented there as comprising seven different authority components that may be found in non-managerial

Figure 4.17 Specialist roles without leadership accountability

roles or, more correctly, in non-TARRs: collateral, advisory, service-giving, monitoring, co-ordinating, auditing, and prescribing (see figure 4.17). Colleagues have the authority to seek mutual co-operation from each other. Advisers have the authority to present to specified others information that they think they ought to have. Service-givers must on request provide authorized services. In monitoring, a person must try to persuade another to take certain actions and, if not satisfied with the response, must report higher – as in some so-called staff officer roles. In co-ordinating, a person must get numbers of colleagues to agree to joint action or, as in monitoring, must report higher. In auditing, a person can instruct someone to stop doing something; that person must stop and if dissatisfied must report higher. And in prescribing, another person can be instructed to take certain actions and, if dissatisfied, to report higher afterwards – as in quality control of dangerous processes.

In none of these instances is there any leadership accountability, in either direction. The task initiator strives to get the other person to note something, or to do something, or to stop doing something. But the leadership accountability lies elsewhere. In the case of task initiators, it is their own managers who are accountable for ensuring that they do their task initiation work willingly and enthusiastically. And for the others, it is in turn for their own managers to ensure that they willingly collaborate with the efforts of task initiators to get them to do things.

It is important to note in this regard that the task initiator is not setting direction. Only the manager can do that. If there is disagreement between the task initiator and the recipient, then the matter must eventually be referred to their crossover-point manager to decide.

It is indeed dysfunctional for those with task-initiating accountability to assume the leadership mantle. That would be overstepping and would undoubtedly and understandably produce impatience and irritation rather than willing and effective collaboration.

In short, here is further support for the notion that not everyone should be trying to lead everyone else all the time if they can. Leadership accountability is a specific, limited, and extraordinarily important aspect of many roles, but not of all.

Interaction of Level of Capability and Level of Work: Case Studies

Let us conclude this and the previous two chapters by presenting six case illustrations of the close interaction between level of work in role and level of capability in person, and the consequences of that interaction for organization and for managerial leadership.

Alan

Alan had been promoted to become the executive vice-president of a stratum–VI division, employing 10,000 people in six strategic business units, that was part of a multi-national corporation. Prior to his promotion, Alan had for 5 years been the president of an overseas stratum–V business unit within his division, and had handled it very successfully. This business unit employed 3,000 people. Alan had a dry, self-controlled manner and was precise and slightly pedantic in approach – not what one would think of as charismatic. But he had had very effective relationships with his subordinates and with his manager, the corporate CEO, and was recognized as a sound and effective managerial leader whose subordinates had gone along with him with enthusiasm and commitment.

In view of his success as a business unit president, he had been promoted to the EVP role of the national division when his manager retired. The corporate CEO was not absolutely sure that Alan was ready for the post, but decided it was worth the risk. Alan assumed his new role in his own methodical way, and took the reins into his own hands. He seemed to know what he was doing. But over the ensuing two years the division ran into increasing difficulties.

The difficulties were at first attributed to a softening of the market over the same period, which had thrown competitors into similar difficulties. But gradually it became clear that Alan was not coping as well as he had seemed at first to be doing. He began complaining about his subordinates. Two of his best subordinates became frustrated and sought and were given transfers to other parts of the company. He replaced them with two people who, as it turned out, were below the competence required for their roles as established but whom, he argued, he could get to work effectively with him.

On one occasion he brought together all his subordinates and required them to discuss what they thought they were doing that was contributing to the company's problems. He became angry when, instead of criticizing themselves, they criticized him for keeping far too tight a grip on things, hanging on to details, and failing to set an adequately broad context within which they could work. They also believed that he was far too bureaucratic, setting increasingly constraining policies and regulations in order to get control; these reduced their sense of responsibility, and authority, and initiative to an unacceptable degree. They thought that he had deteriorated in his leadership qualities as compared with his effective leadership in his previous position. His personality seemed to have changed.

We describe this case because it is such a typical example of what happens when a person does not have the necessary competence for his or her role (see figure 4.18). One of us had the opportunity to work with Alan and his subordinates and manager, at their request. He was able to establish that Alan's previous stratum–V role had been at a level of complexity well within his competence to handle. The stratum–VI role to which he had been promoted, however, was

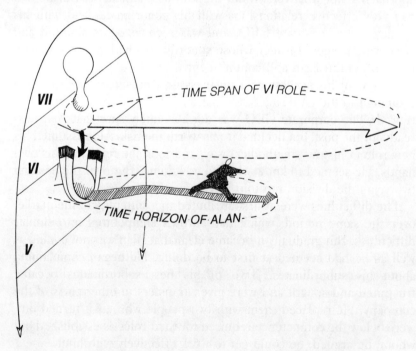

Figure 4.18 Interaction of level of capability and level of work: a case study

one full category of complexity above his own cognitive capability. Although it was likely that he would have matured to the necessary level of capability within a few years, it was nevertheless clear that he had been promoted too soon, on the basis of the corporation's sense of his future potential rather than of his current potential at that time.

Thus, Alan had been promoted to a role one category of complexity above his level of competence, and showed all the signs of that circumstance. The bureaucratic constriction, tightening of controls, blaming of subordinates, are all part of the usual symptoms. And so is the pushing out of competent subordinates (the two who sought transfer were both at the same level of competence as Alan) and their replacement by less competent but more "comfortable" subordinates (the two replacements were both at the next lower category of complexity). See figure 4.19.

Figure 4.19   Over-promotion: blaming and pushing out subordinates

It is this last effect, the gradual reduction in level of competence of the immediate subordinate team, that is the most serious outcome. The division begins to sink in scale, to match the competence of its CEO. Alan's division was in fact on the way to being shrunk from a stratum–VI division, made up of three strategic business units, to what would have itself become a stratum–V business unit; indeed, one of the three business units within the division was already on the brink of being closed.

In order to sort out the problem, Alan was transferred to head a stratum–V functional unit at his true level of competence. He did well and, within five years, had got back on track towards a role at stratum–VI division level. He is currently being considered once again for promotion. He is quite likely to succeed because, during the seven-year period described, his cognitive power has now matured across the boundary of the next higher cognitive category.

The point of this case is that it illustrates what appear to be changes in personality that occur when people are over-promoted and find themselves trying to cope with levels of task complexity which are one or more categories above their cognitive capabilities. They do not in fact lose their "leadership" capabilities. What they lose is any chance of being able to cope competently with the work requirements of their managerial role, and under those circumstances they cannot possibly exercise effective managerial leadership.

It is sad to watch how individuals in such circumstances twist and turn and maneuver, and become autocratic or *laissez-faire* or democratically groupish as they try to hang on to their status. But it is just as sad to see the adverse impact of these struggles upon the subordinates of such managers.

Worst of all is the fact that there are so many managerial leaders who are in the impossible position of being in the same category of complexity as their subordinates. That situation occurs every time that there are too many strata or layers in an organization. Every excess layer throws up one managerial leader who is out of his or her depth, since there are inevitably two (or more) managerial layers stuffed into one single stratum.

This case example illustrates the futility of attempting to improve managerial leadership under such circumstances by giving the people training, whether by methods aimed at individual personality, group dynamics, or personality matching, or by other methods. More training is not the issue. It is beside the point. It is necessary first of all to get a requisite organization with requisitely selected people.

Finally, however, it is also worth noting that our case illustrates the constructive resilience of human nature. It is remarkable what people can do, and what they can recover from, if and when effective managerial conditions and leadership enable them to occupy roles that are requisitely organized and well balanced with their capabilities.

Jonathan

Jonathan was promoted to a corporate staff role of general manager in which he had four stratum–III subordinates doing mainly direct output support work for him on policy development tasks.

Prior to Jonathan's arrival, the four subordinates, all of whom had high capability for their roles, had been given wide limits of discretion within which to work. They had been well respected by their manager, who had shared equally with them a very limited amount of office space. This manager had not only set sound context for them, within which he encouraged them to take initiative, but had also given them opportunities to give detailed reports to his manager, i.e. their manager-once-removed.

Jonathan put an immediate stop to these conditions. He used information as a weapon, and thus withheld context. He tightened the work limits to levels of work below the levels called for by their roles. He took over the largest of the two offices for himself, took the conference table with him, and left the four subordinates jammed into one small office with two typists, and with no access to the conference table. He frequently resorted to public verbal abuse of his subordinates, and took them to task for trivial departures from the most limited and rigid interpretation of rules and regulations. He was experienced as an arrogant martinet, who blamed subordinates for what went wrong, and took credit for things that went right. He was not pulled up by his immediate manager for his tyrannical behavior. At the first opportunity, each of his immediate subordinates got themselves transferred. He was left with much lower capability yes-men.

Jonathan is a case of minus T (-T), who has been allowed to get away with it in an organization that has difficulty in distinguishing between strong, firm managers and a marginal martinet. He probably could have been pulled into line by an effective managerial leader. Unfortunately his manager during the period described was himself becoming increasingly disaffected and eventually left. Jonathan's capability was demonstrated by his ability to carry a substantially higher level of work on his subsequent promotion, but his (-T) qualities prevented him from getting the role that he really wanted when he got his promotion.

Bill

Bill was a stratum–V corporate vice-president. He was sympathetic to everyone most of the time and tried to gain personally earned authority by pleasing people. But he was indecisive and vague in task assignment, for which he presented very little context.

When things were all right, and he was getting credit for his subordinates' work, he was gratefully supportive. But when things went wrong and he was in trouble, he would lose his temper with his subordinates and would use one of his support staff members to raise havoc with them. Everyone was pleased when he was transferred.

Bill is a clear-cut case of a person who did not have the level of capability required for his role. He was in the personnel field in an organization with low standards of capability for roles in that field. His transfer was to a role in a backwater, where he was able to mark time until he retired.

Vic

Vic was an outstanding machine tool designer who was capable of working at stratum–IV but was currently in a stratum–III role, assisted by a pair of stratum–II detail design subordinates. He was unable to get the promotion to stratum–IV that he realized he deserved, because the only stratum–IV position on offer to him was that of general manager of the 180-person design department. For many years he resisted offers to be promoted to this role because he did not value spending all of his time in managing as against doing his own design work.

Finally, however, in order to get more money, he gave in and accepted a "promotion" to the role of general manager of the design department. Although he had been an excellent manager to his direct output support subordinates (two people), he failed to exercise effective managerial leadership of the design department. A year later he asked to return to the design work that he really liked, and was very satisfied when he was given a stratum–IV position in which to do so.

Here is a straightforward case of the consequences of a company's overvaluing delegated direct output managerial work (see p. 158) and undervaluing the work of the individual contributor. Vic, as an individual contributor producing his own direct outputs (designs), was able to be an excellent managerial leader of the two or three subordinates who assisted him to do the work he valued, i.e. to produce the design outputs himself.

John and Stewart

John was president of the services division of a large corporation. When he took over the role, it was a stratum–IV position at 3-year time-span with 350 people. The growth in demand for this function led to its expansion over a period of 5 years, to 760 people and the assignment of 7- to 8-year critical tasks.

John was well liked and recognized as having an excellent "leadership personality." He was respected by his people, and they enjoyed working with him. He had been able to win considerable personally earned authority.

John gradually got into increasing trouble, however, as the role grew in level of work. He began to lose his managerial leadership effectiveness, despite the fact that his subordinates continued to like him as a person. They began to experience him as getting out of his depth, and his authority with them waned, although they continued to try to give him all the support they could.

Indeed, the immediate subordinates were worried that John would be transferred or retired early, because they feared the possibility that John's role would be given to Stewart, who was one of their colleagues. They did think that Stewart probably had the necessary capability, but they were put off by his rather cold and impersonal style, and doubted whether he could exercise effective "empathetic" leadership.

As things turned out, John took an early retirement and Stewart was promoted to replace him. In the four years that he has been president, Stewart has not changed in personality or "style." But gradually he has won the respect and confidence of his people, and has increased the productive effectiveness of his service by about 25 percent, as estimated by higher management. Nevertheless, the situation remains in which Stewart's subordinates, although they do not really like him very much, continue to work effectively for him.

In these two cases, John was a clear-cut category B–4 individual who got out of his depth when his stratum–IV role was gradually expanded to stratum–V. His strong valuing of managerial leadership work could not outweigh the shortfall in level of capability. Stewart, although a less warm person than John, was far from being minus T

(-T). He got on with his work in an effective manner, and readily earned the respect of his erstwhile colleagues.

David

David was a stratum–IV general manager of sales who was appointed to his position during a very strong seller's market. He had been endowed with great amounts of charisma. His sales subordinates went out of their way to perform well for him. He himself was recognized as a great salesman so long as the seller's market continued. He was well liked by customers and was always a welcome visitor at their offices.

David's charismatic personality appeared to work very well during the years of the seller's market. The work rolled in and everyone appeared to be happy. Even though some of David's subordinates were only too well aware that he really did not have a level of capability greater than their own, they were mesmerized by him and keen to make him look good.

This situation became strained, however, with a change in the market-place from a seller's to a buyer's market. David's inability to parallel process meant that he was not able to develop and execute the interaction of the multiple strategies that were necessary to sell in the tougher market. All of his subordinates became increasingly aware of this problem but his personal charisma was such that they did everything they could to prevent his downfall.

The effect of this support was to worsen the situation of work mix and resulting production problems, because David's sales subordinates put pressure on customers to get orders, regardless of how desirable the work might or might not be, which resulted in production problems. The situation became increasingly difficult as David's inability to keep control became more and more painfully apparent. He eventually resigned and his role was given to one of the stratum–IV factory general managers who gradually straightened out the problems.

David was a category B–3 capability individual in a stratum–IV role, who got away with it by means of his charisma, his ability to charm others. Looking back, it becomes evident that he was a serial processor in a role that required parallel processing. He was never able to pull together the various elements of his job, and certainly not able to pull them together with the work of his manufacturing and other general manager colleagues.

His case demonstrates how charisma is always counter-productive in the medium and long term. If he had not been so strongly supported by his subordinates and others, the CEO would never have been induced to keep him in role for so long, even in the seller's market.

Deploying Managerial Leadership to Win

We are now at the end of the presentation of our general approach to questions of leadership. In the next part of the book we shall be turning to a description of the practical procedures – the requisite practices, as we shall call them – to be required of all managerial leaders, and to be taught to them so that they may learn them as well as they know their own names and use them with equal facility without having to think about it. Before we make this changeover, we should like to summarize the central points that we have already emphasized several times and that are at the very heart of managerial leadership.

The major point is that effective managerial leadership depends first and foremost on competence in the managerial role. Competence demands that the managerial leader should be able to operate at a level of cognitive complexity that is consistent with the category of task complexity and level of work in the role and, by the same token, should value the role and have the necessary skilled knowledge and wisdom. Given this competence, managerial leaders must be in the next higher cognitive category than their subordinates, and the roles they occupy must also be one true organizational stratum and category of task complexity apart.

These conditions are absolute. It takes, for example, a category B–4 parallel processor to give effective managerial leadership to a category B–3 serial processor, and that is that. We do not know how to make the point more strongly, or we would. Working as a subordinate to a manager who is in the same category of cognitive process as oneself is enervating, uninspiring, frustrating, and eventually demoralizing. If he or she has "charisma," it only adds irritation to the mixture when the going gets tough.

The importance of investing in human competence cannot be

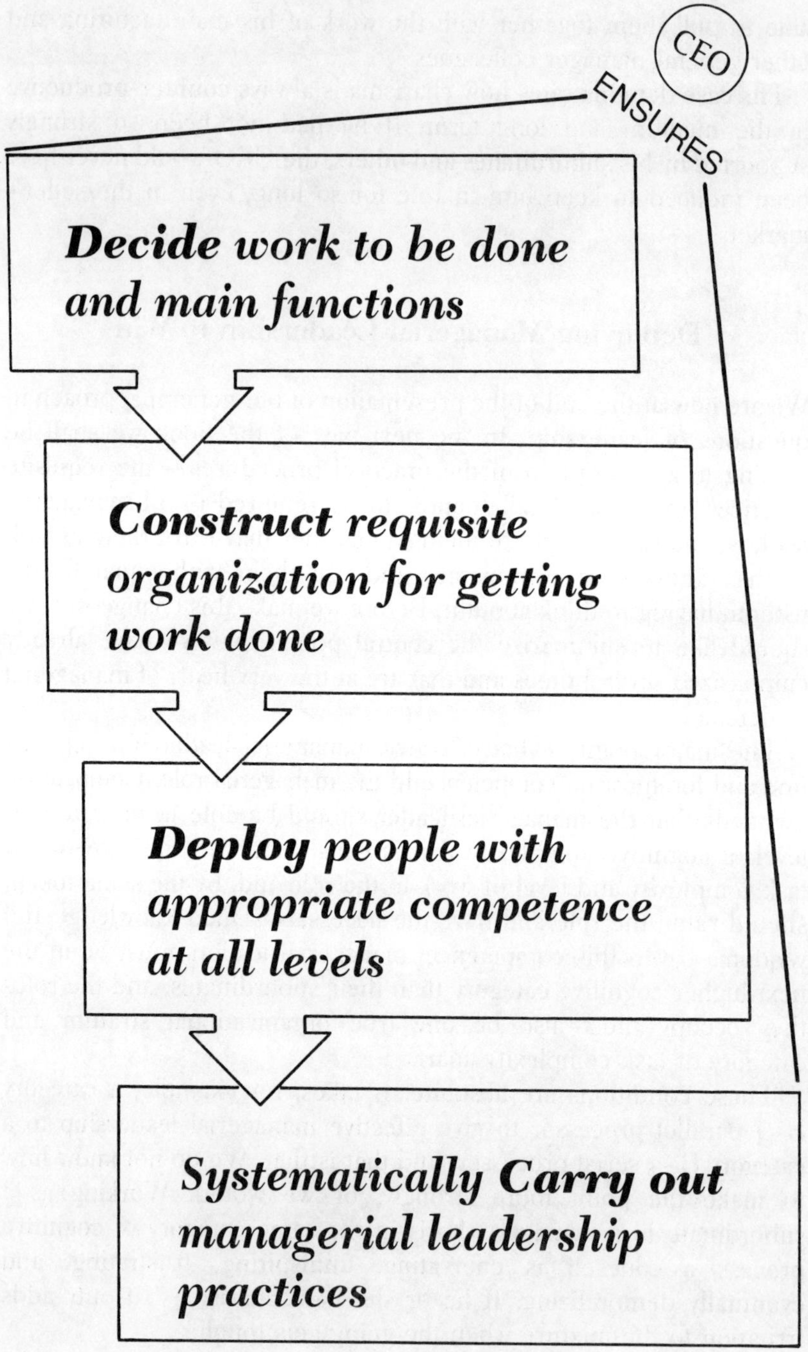

CEO
ENSURES

Decide work to be done and main functions

Construct requisite organization for getting work done

Deploy people with appropriate competence at all levels

Systematically **Carry out** managerial leadership practices

Figure 4.20 Deploying managerial leadership to win

underestimated. It is a familiar fact, for example, that the replacement of a corporate CEO by a successor of greater capability can transform the competitive fortunes of that company. Such a person quickly sets a wider context and begins to develop new strategies (see figure 4.20). A senior executive shuffle is put in motion, more or less urgently depending upon the circumstances, the net effect of which is to bring a higher level of competence, called "new blood," into the top echelons. The company gradually begins to compete more successfully.

By the same token, a company's fortunes will move observably in the opposite direction if there is a CEO replacement at a lower level of competence. This negative story has occurred in the history of the development of many, if not most, large corporations that were built by the giants of the business world; namely, there is a downturn in fortunes upon the retirement of the founder. It is like a positive or negative competence flow, akin to cash flow. As we suggested earlier, most public services and agencies tend to be mired in bureaucratic practices and mediocrity precisely because of the difficulties, for political reasons, of sustaining the necessary levels of competence at the top. Such a shortfall is reflected right down through every level of the organization to the bottom.

Our proposition is simple enough. While it is possible to refer to these manifestations as evidence of good leadership or of lack of leadership, such a formulation addresses the symptoms rather than the sources. A more useful approach is to build managerial hierarchies that match the work to be done, to deploy the necessary levels of human competence into those roles, and to ensure the great advantages of effective leadership by adding to the system the requisite managerial practices that we shall describe in Chapters 5 to 11.

Notes

1 Elliott Jaques, *Time-Span Handbook*, p. 148, and "Taking time seriously in evaluating jobs", p. 349.
2 See discussion in page pairs 27 and 28 of Jaques (1989).

PART II

Requisite Practices

Introduction

We now turn from our description of theoretical background to a presentation of the practices that are at the heart of managerial leadership. The essence of our story is that effective managerial leaders are managers who consistently and effectively carry out practices in their own natural manner in accord with their own personal natures. Every manager will carry them out differently. The critical issue is that every manager shall be held accountable for carrying them out, and shall do so, without equivocation.

It is simply no use talking about effective style or personality traits which are conducive to leadership when we do not hold our managers seriously to account for discharging even minimum managerial leadership practices of the kind that we shall describe in the following pages. What is needed are managers who strongly value getting subordinates to work together with them and with each other with the full effectiveness and enthusiasm necessary for the work, and who are sufficiently free from seriously debilitating emotional characteristics to be secure with the idea of being themselves. Then we need to ensure that they are held accountable for doing their ordinary leadership work, as an integral part of their role as manager.

A good example of the kind of difficulty likely to be encountered in getting these practices carried out is found in the area of personal effectiveness appraisal. Personal effectiveness appraisal is a procedure which everyone agrees that good managers should carry out as a continuous activity throughout the year. But few managers do carry it out, and even fewer are required to. It is said to be a psychologically difficult thing to do. The result is that managers do not make such appraisals regularly, everything gets piled up for annual merit review time, and that period becomes a nightmare.

What needs to be done to ensure that such a process is carried out regularly throughout the year by all managers? The answer is easy. It is to make it clear throughout the organization that all managers are in fact held accountable for personal effectiveness appraisal, and so every manager must require that each and every one of his or her managerial subordinates regularly discharges this accountability. Every manager must carry out the process in his or her individual manner by being his or her natural self. It is questionable whether any manager who is so seriously inhibited by guilt or other emotional hang-ups as to be unable to discharge this or any other prime accountability should remain a manager. It is questionable whether such a person values the work sufficiently to be able to carry it out effectively.

Difficulties arise to a greater or lesser extent in relation to every single requisite practice we shall describe: fair selection opportunity; on-going operational communication; coaching and mentoring; recognition of positive or negative effectiveness; evaluation of potential and career development; deselection and lay-off.

It will be patently clear that, in order for the accountability that we are describing to be discharged in the actuality of everyday practice, it is essential that all senior executives, including the CEO, should themselves carry them out consistently, and should hold their subordinates' feet to the fire to ensure that they also do so. But our thoughts run cold as we write these fateful words. They have been written so often before and in fact have been turned to pap by trite repetition. How is it possible to make our point, and to be taken seriously? Here is our best shot.

CEOs and senior executives should be debarred from talking about the need for improved leadership in their organizations, until and unless they have carried out the following five steps. They should have:

- Established a requisite organizational structure.
- Ensured that all appointed managers have the cognitive capacity appropriate to their roles (and subordinates at one category down), value sufficiently their managerial leadership duties, and are not affected by (-T).
- Settled in themselves to carry out all the necessary practices (which we shall describe), as an ordinary matter of everyday life, without even having to think about it.
- Ensured that every manager without exception throughout the

organization, from top to bottom, has been taught these practices and taught to understand their managerial accountabilities.

- Ensured that every manager is held accountable (by procedures which we shall describe) for actually doing what they are supposed to do.

Is this a tough solution? Not really, it is just the minimum necessary. Decisive, value-adding managerial leadership is worth its weight in gold, and is not to be bought for a mere pittance. It should come as no surprise that effective managerial leadership from the very topmost executives is indeed required to ensure organizational effectiveness. All we are trying to do is to give substance to what is actually required to be done to achieve outstanding managerial leadership. It will never be acquired by fads or personality tricks. We shall show not only how it can be acquired but also how it can be acquired in a properly institutionalized manner and thereby be sustainable into the future.

Democracy in the Workplace

Let us finally recall what we wrote in the Preface. The requisite managerial leadership practices that we shall describe accomplish everything and more that is being sought by those concerned, rightfully, while ensuring that the values of democratic free enterprise are fully expressed in the workplace. The reader will find the full panoply of participative opportunity, of fair and just treatment, of human dignity, of team working opportunities. But they are expressed within the managerial hierarchy, and not in place of it, so that effective managerial leadership is not undermined and destroyed but, quite the opposite, is strongly enhanced and enriched.

5

Task-Assigning Role Relationships (TARRs)

A prime act of managerial leadership in any managerial organization is to establish an effective and efficient work organization where the work gets done by competent individuals at just the right organizational strata necessary to deal with the inherent complexity of the work itself. These work systems involve the establishment of role relationships where one person can get work done by assigning tasks to others while still being held accountable for their outputs. These role relationships are called task-assigning role relationships (TARRs): one person assigns a task to another, requires that other to complete the task on time and to quality standard, and is held accountable by higher authority for the outcome.

These role relationships are described in greater detail in Jaques (1989). The following paragraphs are a summary of the authorities and accountabilities necessary for all task-assigning role relationships.

All roles where the role incumbent is held accountable for the output of others must carry with them a concurrent authority for assigning tasks to those others and include the following specific role relationships (see figure 5.1).

Manager–subordinate role relationship These relationships represent the foundation of any organization's work system. A manager is a person in a role who is held accountable not only for his or her own personal effectiveness but also for the output of his or her subordinates, for building and sustaining an effective team, and for getting his or her team to move in the common direction set, in an effective and collaborative way.

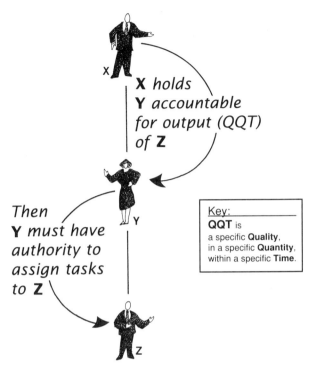

X holds
Y accountable
for output (QQT)
of **Z**

Then
Y *must have*
authority to
assign tasks
to **Z**

Key:
QQT is
a specific **Quality**,
in a specific **Quantity**,
within a specific **Time**.

Figure 5.1   Task-assigning role relationships (TARRs)

Supervisor–supervisee role relationship   The supervisors are the non-commissioned officers (NCOs) of industry; they are the prime assistants to the first line manager particularly when there is multi-shift work.

Supervisors provide the first line manager with help in situations where the work is broken into sub-sections or shifts. A supervisor is not the same as a manager because he or she has more limited accountabilities, i.e. accountability for output and for leadership on each shift but not for building and sustaining the team, this latter being the manager's task. These more limited accountabilities are matched by a more limited set of authorities, i.e. he or she can only recommend on veto of appointment; assign tasks within specified limits set by the manager; recommend on personal effectiveness appraisal; and recommend on deselection.

Project teams and task forces   A project team (task force) chief is accountable for the work of the team members only for the duration of a specific project and therefore has more limited accountability and authority than a manager, as described in this chapter.

These task-assigning role relationships are much too commonly thought of as one-way downward oriented relationships. They must be two-way. To be effective, managers, supervisors, and project team chiefs must be able to rely upon their team members to raise questions, to advise them, or to argue issues as appropriate, rather than merely to expect their subordinates to do what they are told in an unquestioning manner. Thus, we do not use the phrase "participative management" because it implies that there might be other kinds of appropriate managerial leadership that do not call for the active participation of team members.

The central issue is whether or not the quality of the relationship is such as to stifle or release effective interaction. There is no neutral position! Effective two-way interactions (all relationships) are always either improving or worsening. To the extent that they are improving, work will get done more effectively, subordinates will experience a secure sense of release, and the conditions for promoting collaboration amongst team members will have been strengthened.

Working Expectations in TARRs

To be effective, task-assigning role relationships must be built on some common expectations. Underlying every working relationship, it must be assumed that the individuals who are brought together by virtue of the roles they occupy must endeavor to work effectively with each other. This assumption does not mean that everyone has to like everyone else, but that everyone should be expected to try to help others with respect to the work to be done. When people work together they must be able to trust each other absolutely to discharge the accountabilities and authorities that are vested in their respective roles.

In particular, everyone in a task assigning role must be able to expect that the assigned output will be produced on time and to quality standard, unless he or she is notified differently by the subordinate. This assumption ensures that it is the accountable task assigner who must decide what to do if and when difficulties occur that make it impossible to meet targets with the assigned resources or,

Figure 5.2 Working expectations in TARRs

indeed, when circumstances make it possible to complete work more quickly than planned (see figure 5.2).

The above assumptions are important. They are basic, for example, to the work of Edwards Deming. They run counter, however, to many of the currently ruling assumptions, especially in shop-floor production work. Thus, payment-by-results incentive systems assume that it is a good thing for subordinates to produce more than targeted – they get a bonus. If they produce less, they get penalized by loss of pay. But what is not taken into account is the impact of the resulting unevenness in production flow on productivity, on planning, on the need for excess capacity, on stock inventories, and on delivery performance: it literally increases the process variance in a system.

There are equivalent dysfunctional assumptions about quality; namely, that workers produce as they please, managers inspect for quality and penalize subordinates for product rejects. The net effect of this way of thinking is that production systems must allow for low quality output (rejects) from the workers and therefore production numbers must be inflated to cover these rejects.

The requisite assumptions are that a manager must be able to assume that all subordinates will produce precisely what they have been assigned unless they inform their manager to the contrary. This assumption tends by and large to be taken for granted at all organizational levels above stratum–II. It is absolutely crucial to instill a similar type of expectation for work at stratum–I. Consistent quality will begin to occur when the first line manager stops thinking of his or her manual operators as people who cannot be held accountable. If operators are held clearly accountable for production relative to quality, quantity, and time, then final inspections can be held to a minimum. It is for the manager or supervisor to maintain sufficient contact with operators to be able to ask, "How are you doing? Do you have enough resources?" This kind of managerial and supervisory attention reduces the need for quality and production control departments, and substantially increases good quality output on time.

The systematic establishment of such an expectation is exactly what the current emphasis on quality is all about. But this approach is inconsistent with the current incentive ideology which pays people more if they produce more quickly. Incentive bonus systems are an outgrowth of the old cottage industry piece work production system where the employer literally paid by the piece, and the piece workers negotiated how many pieces they wanted to produce, and by when. Building and sustaining bonus work systems leads to expensive inventories and excessive scrap allowances and flies in the face of good planning. It contrasts adversely with the Japanese approach to quality, just-in-time inventory controls and the continuous attempt to reduce process variance to zero.

Individual Contributors as Managers

There is a difference between the managerial leadership situation where managers are delegating outputs to subordinates and the situation where an individual contributor is getting assistance from subordinates for his or her own direct output. The output delegating manager loses direct oversight and control of the delegated direct outputs (DDO) of subordinates, and must rely instead upon a combination of statistical feedback data enriched by personal observation. The individual contributor who is doing aided direct output (ADO) is also a manager, but has direct control over the subordinate's work, because the subordinate's output automatically comes back to the immediate manager to incorporate into his or her own direct output. Hence most of the requisite managerial leadership practices must be required of the individual contributor who has subordinates.

One immediate implication of this distinction, between managers who delegate work that goes directly to the customer from the subordinate and those who manage subordinates who hand their work up to their manager for his or her own use, is a redefinition of the idea of the individual contributor. Individual contributors are commonly thought of as individuals who do their own creative work (direct output) and who do not delegate work to others. That is to say, it is ordinarily considered that individual contributors do not need to be managerial leaders. It will be apparent, however, that being an independent contributor, while certainly inconsistent with being a manager who delegates direct outputs, is utterly consistent with being a managerial leader of subordinates who provide direct output support (DOS), and thus being accountable for their work and for building and sustaining an effective team (see figure 5.3).

This definition of the individual contributor role, and the fact that it might carry subordinate roles of the direct output support (DOS) category, has some very practical consequences for sustaining creative and innovative work in organizations. There are many departments, such as marketing and sales, information services, design, development, treasury, exploration, and acquisitions, where the direct output is produced by individual contributors at stratum–II to stratum–V and higher still, and where those individual contributors have direct output support subordinates assisting them.

In the absence of clarity, these individual contributors are trained to be "managers," and in the process they soon learn to "delegate" their projects and let their subordinates do the work as their own direct outputs. The effect is that the work gets done at too low a level and so suffers in scope and quality.

The lesson is to emphasize to such individual contributors the profound differences between themselves as aided direct output (ADO) managerial leaders and the more common and familiar delegated direct output (DDO) managerial leadership (which this book is mostly about), and to ensure that they continue doing their

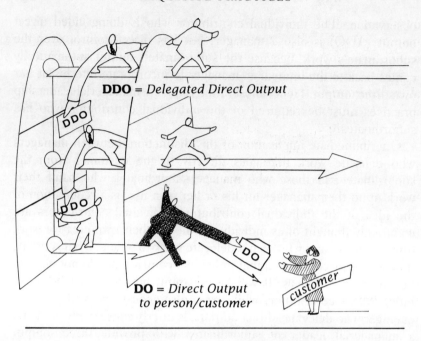

DDO = *Delegated Direct Output*

DO = *Direct Output to person/customer*

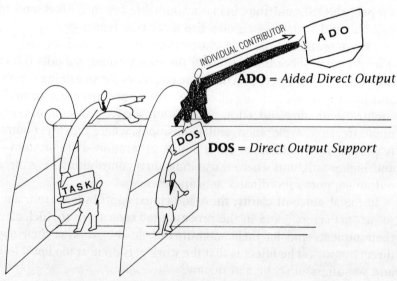

ADO = *Aided Direct Output*

DOS = *Direct Output Support*

Figure 5.3   Individual contributors as managers (ADO/DOS) vs. Manager-Subordinate DDO/DO own direct output work, however much direct output support they may be receiving from their subordinates. Only by making these distinctions can it be ensured that the final output of the work given to individual contributor specialists will reflect creative problem solving at the appropriate level.

Communication

Those individuals with task assigning authority and accountability must keep subordinates informed not only about their tasks but also about the context within which the tasks fit, and the subordinates' progress in task accomplishment. Task performance information is usually stated in terms of accounting data. Managers must keep their subordinates informed about major company policy shifts, current market conditions, significant personnel changes such as retirements, retrenchments or promotions, and a host of other related work environmental factors.

Subordinates, on their side, must keep their managers informed not only about their on-going progress but also about their ideas and insights, which might shape the task formulation process, and their advice regarding ways that the manager might wish to go about his or her own work more efficiently. How to achieve good communication has been a focal point for much management literature over many decades (see figure 5.4). The ensuing discussion will not attempt to summarize all or part of this vast literature. Rather, an additional dimension is offered; namely, that the best way to achieve effective two-way discussion is to communicate with people in a way that is consistent with their underlying cognitive capability.

If a manager communicates in too complex a fashion with a subordinate, that subordinate may not be able to take in the message. For example, a stratum–IV general manager may provide a stratum–III unit manager with control data in terms of variances, which is the way in which the general manager works with the information. Such data are of no use to a unit manager because, in order to use interrelated variance norms, it is necessary to be able to parallel process (category B–4). The unit manager needs his or her information to be given as accounting figures which refer to actual budget items such as labor cost trends by month or trends in the use of consumable supplies; that is to say, trend information that can be

Mgr   Subordinates

Figure 5.4   Communication

dealt with by serial processing (category B–3). Therefore, it is important for the general manager to transform the data he or she works with into serial form in order to have an effective discussion with subordinates.

In the other direction, a subordinate can create a situation of information overload by overwhelming his or her manager with too much or too detailed data, or not the right data, or can confuse matters by providing irrelevant or misleading data. Therefore, managers must communicate to subordinates what categories of data they need. The military refers to this process as specifying the essential elements of information (EEI). For a subordinate to provide essential elements of information, however, the subordinate must first have been given the context of the manager's work in understandable form and, within that context, the necessary categories of information which are needed as feedback from the subordinate. These processes, critical for effective communication, are discussed in detail below in Chapter 6, on task assignment.

Immediate Subordinate Teambuilding

One of the fundamental characteristics of a high performing organization is that the members of the organization routinely collaborate with each other. Building and sustaining this sense of collaboration is a prime managerial leadership accountability. A fundamental accountability of every manager is that he or she must build and sustain a team of subordinates capable of working together effectively. Thus, task-assigning role relationships (TARRs) are not limited to just one-on-one working relationships between a manager and his or her subordinates. All such relationships are also characterized by a concurrent relationship between the manager and all of his or her subordinates; that is to say, his or her whole team.

Teams, as we shall use the term, refer to managers and their immediate subordinates, supervisors and supervisees, and project team (task force) chiefs with project team members. Teambuilding thus is required of all managers, supervisors and project team chiefs who by virtue of their role are required to interact with their team members as a whole, as well as individually, in order to accomplish the goals for which the roles were established.

It may be noted that two different kinds of team are implied: the permanently established teams of managers and their subordinates, and of supervisors and supervisees; and the *ad hoc* teams which are set up to deal with one specific project and are dissolved when the project is completed – the kind of team that is so important for sustained continuous improvement work. We shall deal with these different types of team separately.

Since we shall be placing considerable emphasis upon team functioning, we must make it clear that we are not using the idea of teams in the way that has unfortunately become common in recent years; namely, that they take group decisions and are accountable as a group for their own work. Such teams are put forward as a replacement for the managerial hierarchy which is held to be disappearing because of the advent of the information age, or the post-entrepreneurial age, or the services age, or the post-industrial age. Such teams are referred to as semi-autonomous work groups, or self-management teams, which function without an appointed accountable manager, and are found in the form of quality circles and continuous improvement councils. Or, another more recent version, is the idea of teams which spontaneously group and re-group in response to the requirements of the common information they receive from a common data base.

The setting up of such teams is well intentioned in the sense of trying to increase working effectiveness. Unfortunately, because they are established in opposition to the managerial hierarchy with its managerial accountability, they undermine accountable managerial leadership and inevitably become seriously counter-productive in the medium and long term.

It will be clear from our whole approach that we believe that the managerial hierarchy is not only an extremely useful type of organization for getting work done but also the only type of organization available for bringing large numbers of people together in a unified work system. Requisitely structured and staffed with accountable, decisive, value-adding managerial leadership, the managerial hierarchy can be an extremely effective type of organization that can give great personal satisfaction to its employees at all levels.

The teams that we shall deal with, therefore, are teams built into the managerial hierarchy, and having to do with managers, supervisors, and project team chiefs getting their work done. Building and sustaining such teams requires that managers, supervisors, and project team chiefs create work environments which foster an easy flow of information and advice, bottom up, top down and across within the team (see figure 5.5).

This setting of shared information and advice generates true participation and is one way to meet subordinates' expectations regarding how they should be treated and valued as unique individuals. The usual format for sharing information and advice is to call a meeting of the team. There are two different kinds of team meetings and they produce very different results; namely, team business meetings and meetings in the team-working mode. The idea of the business meeting will be familiar. The team-working mode is that in which the manager and subordinates work together as equals, pro tem, using brainstorming and other idea generating techniques to try to tackle problems for which the manager has been

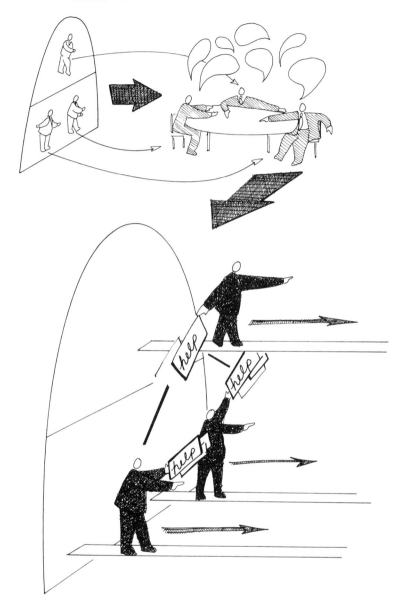

Figure 5.5 Immediate subordinate teambuilding

unable to find satisfactory solutions. The subordinates have been called together as a team of knowledgeable individuals who, by virtue of their work for the organization and their experience, may be able to shed light on a particularly difficult problem which the manager faces. How to use this mode of working with subordinates and its efficacious results are described later.

All managers and team leaders should know how to conduct each of these meetings and use them to their fullest. Both are required because both offer optimum conditions for subordinates to be kept informed about key issues and the big picture as well as to provide expert advice. The providing of such advice, to one's manager as well as to one's peers, in a setting of shared discussion, generates a feeling of true participation within a subordinate team.

Developing a true sense of participation, however, requires that the manager (or supervisor, or project team chief) does more than simply schedule sufficient team meetings. Every manager must ensure that in these meetings (as well as at the workplace in general) he or she is both receptive to feedback provided by subordinates and responsive to such feedback. In other words, team members have to feel that their manager is open to their input and advice, that the manager will give such input serious consideration, and that he or she will always provide subordinates with relevant responsive feedback to such advice or input.

If subordinates do not feel that they have some real upward influence with their manager, then over time they will simply stop providing such advice or feedback. Such a development can quickly result in subordinates feeling that the communication climate is one-way, top down. Subordinates in such a situation will feel no obligation to keep their managers out of trouble nor to help each other out, all of which can lead to a win–lose instead of a win–win situation.

Teamworking is not a substitute for individual accountability. It is only people who know what they are individually accountable for who can work together effectively. When individual accountability is not too clear, as, for example, in a crisis, individuals will often help each other at the expense of completing their own assigned tasks. While it is laudable that subordinates help each other out, particularly in difficult times, such help must not be provided at the expense of an individual's meeting his or her own assigned targets.

Team Business Meetings

Subordinates are frustrated if they do not have opportunities to get together at appropriate intervals to discuss issues. Thus, managers must schedule sufficient information-sharing meetings to ensure that subordinates are kept informed about critical business events. This gives them a chance to discuss the issues with their manager and with each other so that they develop a sense of teamwork. Every company's philosophy should favor such openness. But simply calling business meetings is not sufficient, by itself, to foster this sense of teamwork if the meetings themselves are not conducted properly. Most of us will recall experiences where we spent what seemed like an inordinate amount of time in meetings many of which were simply a waste of time and energy.

For meetings to be effective, they have to be carefully thought out and planned. They are costly in terms of the overall time they consume, and therefore need to be used effectively. Before a manager schedules a meeting, he or she must be clear about its purpose.

All information must be relevant to the subordinates' assigned tasks, or should at least be related to the overall context of those tasks, i.e. information describing the context of the work or how that context fits into the manager's larger context; or pertinent information relevant to the overall direction being pursued by the business unit or the corporation as a whole. Additionally, all information provided should be of an appropriate degree of complexity to be of use to team members, i.e. not too simple (too many details) nor too difficult (too many variables and/or too many interdependent relationships). It is equally important for the manager to ensure that problems are of an appropriate degree of complexity for team members to be able to grapple with all of the relevant variables.

When conducting team meetings it is important for managers to make their own points of view clear (see figure 5.6). All members should be encouraged to participate (see also section on team-working mode). The focus, however, on such participation should be on what each team member says and not on the individual. Managers must be open and approachable; they must accept bad news without prejudice and make it clear that messengers are not punished. By conducting team meetings effectively, a manager can build a high degree of team cohesiveness which further enhances a team's ability

Figure 5.6   Team business meetings

to overcome difficult problems and/or cope with high levels of stress and rapid change, characteristics which are necessary for succeeding in today's volatile business environment.

Team-Working Mode

One of the strengths of a good team is that subordinates collectively can often help to come up with more innovative solutions to difficult problems than can the manager working alone. This finding has been referred to in the management field as either "group problem solving" or "brainstorming." It has become the preferred mode of operating in so-called skunk works or off-site project teams. What is it that a manager must do to achieve the full benefits of good teamworking?

A manager must be able, when appropriate, to function in a team-working mode. This mode is one in which a manager gets together with one or more subordinates to find out how to tackle a problem which he or she is having trouble solving (see figure 5.7). The

Figure 5.7   Team-working mode

manager provides a setting – and all managers must learn how to do this – in which the manager and immediate subordinates can think and brainstorm together as pro tem equals, tossing ideas around in a free wheeling, no-holds-barred session. The manager then takes over to close the discussion and decide what to take out of it. Brainstorming teamwork is a powerful morale builder. It strengthens the constructive cohesion of the working group and it encourages independence of thought.

The team-working mode is to be encouraged in all TARR working relationships, and especially in project teams. Effective managers must seek to take advantage of this mode of interaction whenever the situation calls for it. Teamworking requires that the manager should value working with his or her team in this free wheeling, unstructured way. To be effective, this mode of working requires drill and practice.

In these sessions, authority barriers are down, thus permitting the manager to get the best possible information from his or her subordinates. When operating in this mode, the manager must be receptive to divergent views, be able to handle criticism, and recognize the usefulness of a speaker's ideas regardless of his or her status. The team-working mode implies that subordinates are actively encouraged to express dissent, to explore pros and cons, and to engage in vigorous debate, with each other and with the manager, regarding all issues. If there are decisions to be made, the manager must reassert his or her authority and make them. Functioning in a team-working mode does not imply that the team engage in a group decision-making process. In managerial hierarchical organizations, decisions are made by individuals; there can be no such thing as a group decision, and, as we have pointed out above, no such thing as self-managed teams.

Some Key Principles

Task-assigning role relationships (TARRs) are the primary way in which work gets done. They encompass the following features:

- They are the prime vehicle for implementing corporate and democratic values at the workplace.
- They are never one-way downward oriented, but are always two-way relationships and are always either improving or worsening.
- They are a set of organizational expectations regarding how people are to be treated and how work is to be done. These expectations are particularly relevant with respect to the issue of quality. They form the backdrop necessary for building and sustaining a new and refreshing focus on creating an environment that is properly oriented on quality issues.
- They are the primary mechanism for communicating.

Because TARRs represent the basic foundation of any organization's work system, there are some underlying principles that, if followed, will further enhance their overall utility.

- TARR leadership requires that only competent managers (those who have the necessary cognitive power, values, wisdom, knowledge, and skills, without disabling temperament factors [-T]) are retained

Figure 5.8 An effective manager accepts accountability for the work of subordinates

in managerial roles. Any tolerance of an incompetent manager shrieks the message that the company does not take seriously having decisive value-adding managerial leadership. For example, when ideas or innovations do not quite work out in a manager's team (or, for that matter, when anything goes wrong) and output suffers, is the manager willing to take the heat from his or her own manager for these problems and not to attribute them to his or her subordinates? This does not mean, however, that the manager does not take corrective action within the team. Alternatively, when things go well and ideas work out, does the manager give due credit to subordinates or does he or she take all the credit himself or herself? Is the manager personally seen as getting ahead in the organization by stepping on the backs of subordinates through callous misuse and/or continual overworking? Looking after one's subordinates is directly related to managerial competence; e.g. the more competent the manager the more likely it is that he or she will give credit to others or insulate them, if so required (see figure 5.8).

- TARR leadership means demonstrating concern about subordinates as valuable members of the company and of the manager's team. This means that managers must treat subordinates equitably and with respect and dignity. For example, such treatment means never publicly ridiculing them for shortcomings. TARR leaders must be willing to spend the time and energy to get to really know their subordinates.

- TARR leadership must be based upon the successful establishment of a trusting relationship between the manager and his or her subordinates. Trust is the necessary foundation for innovation and creativity because it forms the basis for delegating sign-off authority to the correct stratum in the organization. Managers can build trust by being reliable and consistent in their actions; by practicing candor and honesty in disclosing information; by responding to subordinate advice and input in a timely fashion.

- TARR leadership means setting a proper example for others. Such an example includes going about one's own work in a dynamic manner; building confidence and a winning attitude amongst subordinates; not settling for mediocrity in one's own work or in subordinate performance; setting challenging but realistic goals; striving for and building pride in good performance; and standing behind one's subordinates in good times as well as bad.

6

Managerial Leadership

Organizations exist to get work done. But getting work done effectively is often more difficult to do than most managers are willing to admit. To do so requires not only a requisite organizational structure but also competent individuals at each organizational stratum and a set of work procedures and practices which facilitate the work process. Such procedures consist of more than simply telling subordinates what their manager expects them to do. The work process requires more than good communication. For work to get done effectively, there is a whole sequence of steps that must be followed. The following outline briefly describes these essential steps.

Managers must:

- Be clear on their own work, since they cannot assign tasks to subordinates nor set context for the subordinates' work if they are not first clear about the context and scope of their own tasks and goals.
- Develop a plan to achieve their own tasks and goals and then use that plan:
  - to establish the limits within which subordinates' tasks must be accomplished;
  - to encourage subordinates to discuss the plan before it is finalized, thus allowing subordinates an opportunity to affect their own limits and context.
- Formulate tasks to be given to subordinates, ensuring that:
  - the tasks are created within an appropriate range of complexity;
  - limits and methods are discussed with subordinates.

- Assign tasks, which entails:
  - specifying the task parameters, i.e. quality, quantity, resources, and expected completion time (what-by-when);
  - setting context for subordinates' task assignments within the shared context of the managers' task assignments.
- Establish task reporting procedures.
- Provide performance accounting and feedback.
- Coach as required.
- Conduct personal effectiveness appraisals.
- Decide and act on merit recognition as required.
- Carry out supporting actions, such as:
  - selection and induction;
  - deselection, retrenchment, or dismissal, if required.

As is evident from the nature of the above sequence, these steps constitute the very heart of managerial leadership. The tie that binds them all together is that they are all linked to getting work done on time and to standard (see figure 6.1).

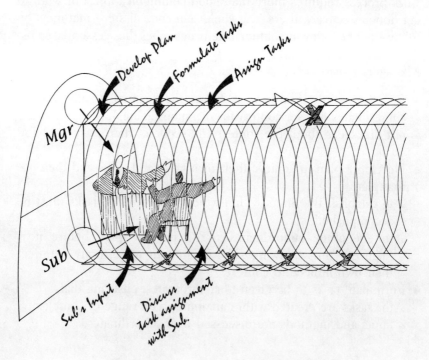

Figure 6.1   Managerial leadership

This sequence of steps represents an iterative process which should be followed each time a manager considers assigning a specific task to a subordinate. Often many of the steps can be quickly dealt with and for recurring tasks some steps can be skipped altogether.

The Planning Function

Managerial leaders must develop effective and innovative plans. If managers cannot develop plans (concepts of operation) which are sophisticated enough to encompass the full range of variables that operate at their organizational stratum, then it will be impossible for them to assign meaningful tasks to subordinates.

There is nothing mysterious about a plan; it represents a person's judgment regarding the best way to go about achieving an objective or desired goal. Plans reflect a desired pathway to the goal chosen within a set of limits which are established by one's manager. These pathways are constructed so as to anticipate obstacles and ways of overcoming them. Plans are important to the task assignment process, since the manager's plan establishes the context for his or her subordinates' work. Plans also provide the necessary linkage between the manager's work, the tasks assigned to his or her subordinates, and the work assigned to the subordinate's colleagues (this will be discussed in greater detail in the section on context setting).

Planning is a crucial part of the manager's own work. The formulation of plans cannot be delegated to subordinates because only the manager has the necessary cognitive capacity to handle the complexity of work at his or her organizational stratum. The manager's own creative imagination is nowhere more essential than in producing the ideas necessary for making a successful plan. If the manager cannot think up, and decide upon, better plans than any of his or her subordinates, it is a sorry state of affairs. Thus, for example, a stratum–V business unit president must have the competence to construct plans for critical tasks that will require 6, 7, or 8-year paths to completion. His or her subordinates, if they are at the right level for their own roles, will not be able to construct such pathways. They can work perhaps three or four years into the future, which can be useful in helping the manager to detail and develop his or her 7-year plan, but they simply cannot perceive the 7-year planning alternatives themselves.

It is too often thought that subordinates ought at least to be able to do the preliminary work of thinking up possible alternatives for the managers to pick over and choose from. Precisely wrong! How could a subordinate possibly find the imaginative, long-term outreach ideas that the manager is employed to have the competence to dream up? It is a manager's own creative competence in thinking up unusual ideas that creates competitive advantage. The key words are: "Managers must do their own work!" Nowhere is this slogan more true than in planning.

The planning process starts when an individual is assigned a task, either by himself or herself, or by his or her manager, or on request from some other authorized person. That individual must then construct and traverse a pathway which is sufficient to achieve the goal. The complexity of a given task/goal is determined by the problems (or obstacles) that have to be overcome in traversing the pathway. The questions are:

- How big are the problems?
- What needs to be done to overcome them?
- How complex are they?
- What resources will be necessary?

Managers must be able to encompass the full range of problems that they are likely to encounter on a given task. If the problems are less complex than the manager's own capability (type this letter, or answer this customer's request), the task might be delegated. There will be occasions, however, when a problem is too complex, and he or she should refer it upwards; for example,when a stratum-III unit manager encounters a task that will require the parallel processing of a number of interrelated serial projects to resolve it, that task should be handled instead at stratum–IV.

Let us assume, however, that our manager has chosen to work on a given problem himself or herself. The next step is to analyze the situation, envision a tentative concept of operation (method of attacking the problem), and generate alternative courses of action. Managers can of course enlist the help of their staff in generating additional alternatives. It is useful to do so, but only after they have personally determined the nature of the problem and have developed a preliminary concept of operation, utilizing their higher order of cognitive capability in doing so. The important point to remember is that every manager must develop his or her own plans, because only he or she is capable of dealing with the full range of variables (the complexity) that are operative at his or her organizational stratum.

The manager's plan is important also because it generates the context for the subordinates' tasks. By coming to grips with the full range of problems which the manager expects his or her subordinates to encounter, the manager is then in a good position to delegate sub-tasks to subordinates which are appropriate for their level of capability. This is one of the ways in which he or she sets the necessary conditions for getting everyone to move along with him or her in a common direction (see figure 6.2).

It is thus unfortunate that many executives tend to see their planning as something which can be handed over to their staff to do. While subordinates can assist in the development of plans, they cannot themselves develop the plan. They do not have the necessary cognitive capacity nor the wisdom to handle the full range of variables that their manager's plan must encompass. By the same token,

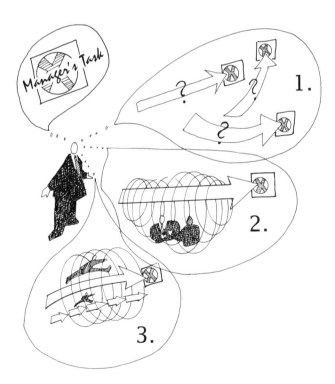

Figure 6.2 The planning function

subordinates' requisite time-horizons are likely to be too short for their manager's planning outlook. They are not likely to see the interdependencies and second order consequences of these variables (in other words, the pattern or weave of how the variables fit together into a comprehensive whole).

Subordinates can and should be expected to advise their manager on any planning issue that they know something about. This advice serves the dual purpose of helping subordinates to keep their managers out of trouble as well as giving them opportunities to participate in and influence the planning process.

Preparation of the plan is also an opportunity for managers to reach down into their organization and bring up specially qualified subordinates-once-removed (SoRs) to work with them in developing their plan. This type of direct interaction is a good way for managers-once-removed (MoRs) to get to know their SoRs better and at the same time it permits the MoR to make an assessment of the state of the immediate manager's working relationship with subordinates. But if an MoR is to give an SoR such an opportunity to help in detailing the MoR's plan, such work should not be delegated to SoRs through intermediate management levels. Such a procedure results in the SoR having to second guess or interpret what the MoR really wants. Second guessing an MoR wastes effort, stifles creativity, and wastes an important training opportunity in the direct working contact between an SoR and his or her MoR.

To the extent that a manager is capable of dealing with the complexity of problems at his or her level, in developing and articulating a coherent plan, he or she will be able to instill in subordinates a strong sense of confidence and trust. The ability to produce imaginative and workable plans is an important element in demonstrating managerial leadership competence.

Task Formulation and Assignment

The task assigning process lies at the heart of a manager's ability to get subordinates to respond in an effective and innovative manner. If it is carried out correctly, it will give appropriate freedom to subordinates and set the stage for an innovative and creative response; if it is done improperly, it will result in work not being done on time nor to standard. To understand how to make the task assigning process a particularly useful tool in the manager's tool box, one has first to come to grips with some basic concepts about tasks in general.

What is a task? A task is an assignment to produce a what-by-when; that is to say, a specified output (including quantity and quality) within a targeted completion time, with allocated resources and methods, and within prescribed limits (policies, rules, procedures, etc.). The output is thus the target or goal (see figure 6.3).

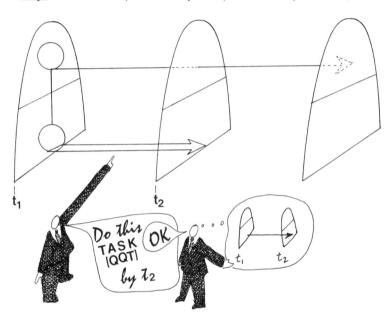

Key: **QQT** = a specific **Quality**; in a specific **Quantity**; within a specific **Time**

Figure 6.3   Task formulation and assignment

There exist two distinctly different types of task. The first type of task comprises those which are directly assigned by one's manager. The second type of task comprises those which are triggered as a result of a general responsibility that has been assigned by one's manager. A "general responsibility" is an instruction which applies indefinitely (unless amended) and specifies conditions which, whenever they arise, require a person to take appropriate action within prescribed limits, e.g. answer a request for data, or initiate a

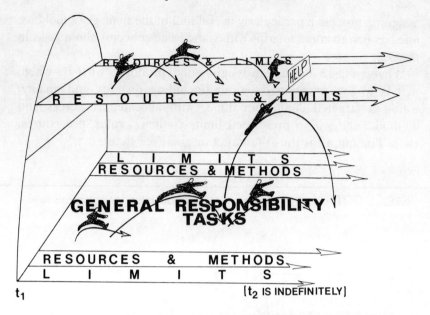

Figure 6.4   General responsibilities

particular task himself or herself, or respond to a customer request (see figure 6.4).

Distinguishing between the two different types of tasks is significant because the task assigning process is different for each. Although both require that the manager set context, the manager must set a specific context for each and every task that he or she directly assigns, but need not do so for each of the tasks stimulated by a general responsibility, only for the general responsibility itself. Clearly bounded general responsibilities paradoxically release initiative and creativity because the boundaries are clear. Unclear boundaries and lack of adequate limits always stifle initiative because people do not know how far they can push new ideas.

There is one absolute principle of delegation. It underlies the central managerial function of task assignment and is consistent with the central point in Edwards Deming's approach. It may be stated as follows:

The principle of delegation is that it is the manager who decides what he or she assigns to a subordinate, including quantity, quality, and targeted time of completion (QQT). The subordinate shall have no authority to vary assignments without discussion with the manager. Managerial leaders must be able to assume that the outputs associated with the tasks that they have assigned will be produced as specified unless the subordinates give advance notice to the contrary, and thus enable the manager to assess the situation and to decide what actions to take.

It is only under these conditions that a manager can be held accountable for the output of subordinates. Failure to inform one's manager that the assigned QQT might not be achieved is a matter of failure to adhere to a real rule and is not to be treated as a matter of inadequate judgment. It is a transgression and not to be judged in terms of a lapse in personal effectiveness.

The task formulation process provides managers with an important opportunity to establish solid, two-way, give-and-take discussions with subordinates prior to assigning them tasks. Such discussions are essential because they give subordinates a chance to participate in providing input to the manager regarding these anticipated tasks. This participation also allows subordinates to have an impact on the nature of the limits within which they are expected to carry out their assigned work. The opportunity to have this impact on work limits significantly contributes towards creating the conditions that allow subordinates to have some control over their environment and to keep themselves from being at the mercy of surrounding events (see figure 6.5).

The essence of good task formulation and assignment is to adhere to the following six steps.

- Be clear about what a subordinate is to do; i.e. the what-by-when.
- Allow for frank give-and-take discussions regarding task specifications and limits.
- Set a proper context for each assigned task.
- Ensure that assigned tasks enable subordinates to work at their full-scale capacity.
- Make sure that the task monitoring system operates effectively and provides responsive feedback as required.
- Ensure that the formulation and assignment process reinforces the building of an open and trusting climate (see figure 6.6).

It is essential to ensure that the level of complexity of a task fits the level of work in a subordinate role. There is a common tendency, which might be termed an inverted Peter principle, to delegate special projects to too low a level. Thus, for example, engineering improvement project work is delegated to stratum–II engineers or, if

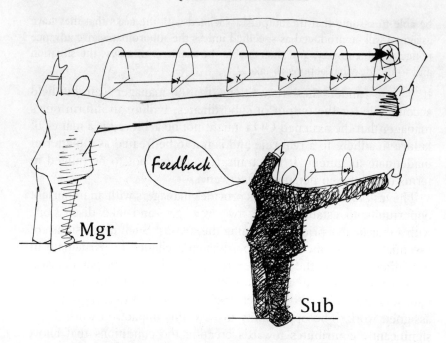

Figure 6.5 Feedback during task assignment

it is judged to be a difficult problem, to a stratum–III engineer. However, there are many times when engineering or other kinds of problems are complex enough to require that they be solved by using stratum–IV parallel processing of a number of stratum–III sub-projects. The problems may even be so complex as to require a conceptual attack upon them, say at stratum–V or even at stratum–VI for major corporation-wide problems.

If these more complex problems are assigned even one stratum too low, the consequences are highly predictable and all too familiar: budgets are over-spent, completion time targets need continually to be extended, and, should the project ever be completed, the quality of the result will be substandard.

Unfortunately, there is a widespread tendency not to set up above stratum–III the individual contributor roles that are required to deal with these more complex projects. Under these circumstances, the more complex problems, upon whose solution company survival often depends, are not handled satisfactorily. Effective task assignment is not possible, because the necessary level of human capability cannot be mustered by the individual assigned to tackle the problems.

It is essential to ensure that the complexity of tasks is appropriate for a subordinate's capability. All tasks should be appropriate in complexity to the level of capability of a subordinate. People want to be challenged to their full capacity but they can be turned off if they are stretched too far. For example, the notion of assigning complex and difficult tasks to subordinates to see how they cope can be an unfortunate practice, since tasks which are too difficult cause anxiety. And if a subordinate should be able to handle tasks at a category of complexity above that called for by the role, then that is a problem of career development. To continue to assign such tasks without advancement in status will create serious morale problems not only for the person but for colleagues as well.

It is essential to consider the task assignee's background. The task formulation process needs to be adjusted to take into account: the subordinates' time in role; their familiarity with the task; the foundation of knowledge and skill necessary to perform satisfactorily; the maturity of their relationship with their manager; and whether or

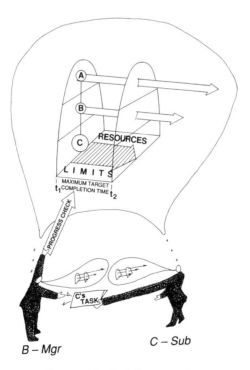

Figure 6.6 Building commitment

not they may value the assigned task. The task assignment process for mature subordinates, who have been around for some time, will be very different from that required for new personnel. For example, discussions between a manager and a seasoned veteran regarding limits and approved methods would vary considerably from those which would take place with a newcomer.

It is essential to build understanding and commitment. One of the most important steps in formulating and assigning tasks is that the manager and the subordinate must have a common language. It does no good for a manager to describe a task in terms which are meaningless to a subordinate. This is especially true for newly assigned individuals. It is up to the manager to ensure that the goal is clear and understood. Additionally, it is important that the manager sets methods and limits that capture the subordinate's enthusiastic and effective participation. The subordinate must have some say in the process.

It is essential to assign tasks properly. When assigning tasks to subordinates, managers must make the tasks clear in terms of what-by-when, i.e. quantity, quality, and time. In addition, they must also ensure that subordinates understand the resources and any approved methods or procedures which they are to employ while carrying out the task. While a manager must be able to assume that any assigned tasks will be completed on time and to standard unless he or she is notified by subordinates to the contrary, it is nevertheless up to the manager to ensure that his or her subordinates understand the task in the first place.

Context Setting

A central aspect of a managerial leader's adding value to a subordinate's work is setting an effective context for that work. This activity constitutes a sharing of the managerial leader's frame of reference with the subordinate. Understanding the manager's frame of reference allows subordinates not only to see how their work fits into the big picture but also to gain an appreciation of the types of variables and issues that the manager must grapple with in doing the manager's own work. Developing such an appreciation is an essential first step in helping subordinates to understand the fullness of their current role, as well as assisting them in exercising good judgment and discretion in being innovative and taking the initiative within the context of a larger perspective; that is to say, knowing where the managerial leader is going facilitates their going along in step.

Let us take an example (see figure 6.7). B sets context for C by outlining four things:

1 B's task (the what-by-when that A has assigned to B) and the limits within which B is to operate.
2 A's big picture (the context of B's task).
3 The nature of the pathway (the plan) that B has constructed to achieve his or her goal (accomplish his or her task).
4 The tasks that B has assigned to C's colleagues, and any interrelationship between C's tasks and C's colleagues' tasks.

The purpose of context setting is to ensure that C has a picture in his or her mind of what B intends for him or her to do and how that fits into B's overall plan. Knowing context, C is then in a position freely to exercise initiative and judgment because he or she is clear about the limits of freedom within which to act.

This kind of context setting gives genuine freedom, namely, freedom within appropriate limits. Requisite organizations are those whose managers maintain control over subordinates' actions by setting effective limits, that is to say, limits that are neither so wide as to leave too much uncertainty nor so tight as to constrict and choke off initiative and an individual's full competence and enthusiasm. Subordinates are in turn expected to exercise full competence and initiative within the overall confines of their manager's plan.

In setting context, managers should not complain publicly about the nature of the tasks or goals that they themselves have been assigned, e.g. "I don't know why we have to do this but . . ." or "this is stupid but do it anyway." Managers must take clear ownership of all assigned work. If they disagree with the nature of that work, they must take up any such disagreement with their own managers. However, once the manager's manager makes a decision regarding that work, the subordinate manager must be seen by his or her subordinates as being fully committed to such work. Adopting any position short of total commitment will seriously undermine morale and effectiveness.

Limits by themselves are neither good nor bad. Contrary to popular opinion, they do not inevitably constrain freedom. Effective managers are those who maintain control over subordinates' actions by setting appropriate limits. There is no such thing as total freedom.

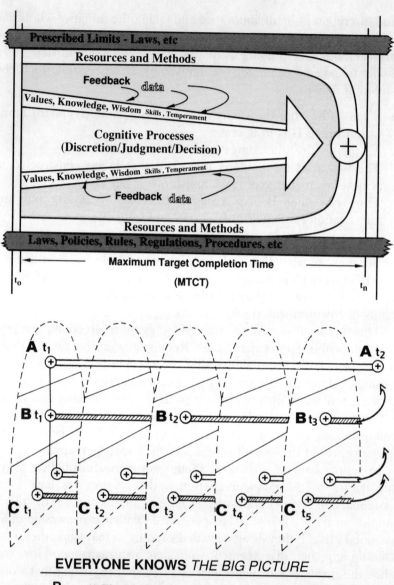

EVERYONE KNOWS *THE BIG PICTURE*

B	1) *The Big Picture* (**A**'s task and plan)
tells	2) **B**'s own task and plan
C	3) **C**'s task *and* **C**'s colleagues' tasks and plans

Figure 6.7   Context setting

Everybody has to learn to operate within certain specified constraints. That is what organizations and societies are all about. Freedom is affected only if the limits are too narrow or too broad. If too narrow, they stifle, i.e. constrain, the individual's level of work below his or her level of capability. If too broad, they are confusing and chaotic, i.e. the level of work is greater than the level of capability.

Thus, limits have an impact on the complexity of the task by increasing or decreasing the number of variables or by substituting certainty for choice. The methods and resources available to construct a pathway for completion of the task are limiting factors. Any limit must be congruent with the complexity of tasks at any given stratum. And limits can effectively be set for any one stratum only by someone capable of working at the next higher stratum.

Managers build trust by setting limits which establish task complexity at levels that are consistent with their subordinate's cognitive complexity. Trust and risk go hand-in-hand, just like accountability and authority, and one cannot build a feeling of trust without taking some calculated risks with a subordinate. This translates into actions such as assigning challenging tasks, setting appropriate limits, and checking progress and quality only as often as appropriate for the complexity of the work and the judged personal effectiveness of the subordinate.

The proper setting of limits constitutes the foundation of the organizational control system. Limits should release a subordinate's potential energy and not box it in. The purpose of setting limits is:

• To achieve integration (co-ordinated output).
• To avoid the unnecessary expenditure of energy by limiting the field (methods) for working on a task.
• To reflect the operating values and culture of the organization.

The difference between limits and context is that limits control the range of possible actions, whereas context provides understanding within those limits. Limits form the basis of control while context forms the basis of teamworking.

The following are types of limits: policies, rules, procedures, resources, methods and/or means of production, and level of work. Level of work is an especially important type of limit. If level of work is too low, the result will be wasted talent. Managers will find that discretion will be unduly constrained, with the effect of driving out their creative people. If level of work is too high, confusion is likely to occur because subordinates cannot handle the task complexity. If they are afforded the status and pay that goes with the work, they may try to hang on anyway. If such subordinates are also managers, no possibility of leadership exists because they cannot adequately set context, coach, assign tasks, or perform MoR duties.

Performance Accounting and Feedback

Effective managerial leadership in this area begins by managers making it clear that an assigned output (quantity, quality, and time) must always be achieved unless a subordinate notifies the manager differently. In the absence of such feedback, every managerial leader must be able to count on the output being achieved. If subordinates encounter problems, they must be expected to notify their manager accordingly so that he or she can do something about it, at the time it occurs, not later. At these junctions in the flow of the work, managers can assign more resources to the task, change the goal, or help subordinates to work more effectively.

Every managerial leader must also recognize the fundamental difference between performance accounting and personal effectiveness appraisals. An individual's performance is the relationship between targeted output and achieved output. Personal effectiveness appraisals are judgments made by an individual's manager about how well the subordinate has done in producing the outputs, taking into consideration all of the relevant circumstances. Thus, while accounting data and performance feedback are important, they do not, by themselves, tell how well or how poorly subordinates have worked at their assigned tasks. To tie individual personal effectiveness appraisals solely to quantitative information about performance imposes a serious injustice on subordinates.

Once this distinction between performance accounting and personal effectiveness appraisals is clear, it becomes equally clear that, while objective measures can be used for performance accounting, personal effectiveness appraisals call for managerial judgment (see figure 6.8).

Let us now consider performance feedback in its own right, separate from personal effectiveness appraisal. Any work system, in order to function effectively, requires a continual flow of reliable information. Such information is the lifeblood of the managerial control sub-system. It provides management at all levels with the

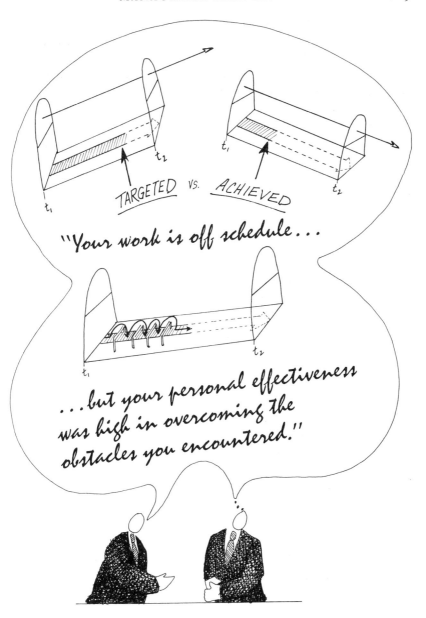

Figure 6.8 Performance accounting and feedback

necessary information for them to assess the progress of current work. This information, in turn, facilitates the exercise of judgment for making midstream corrections, if required.

Control systems are systems based upon the use of information for the purpose of controlling on-going operations; e.g. the just-in-time inventory system, the automatic re-supply system, sales levels, and project completions. Control systems require information which permits a person to compare his or her achieved outputs with targeted ones. If that person is a manager, he or she is in a better position to be able to decide what to do next, i.e. make adjustments in quality, quantity, or time; allocate more resources into the task; or assign additional tasks. Control systems provide subordinates with feedback about what is going on. But, to be effective, controls must be just right, not too narrow and not too broad, thus tapping a person's full potential.

One important feature of control procedures is that what is measured constitutes a *de facto* statement of what is important and thus should be carefully monitored because of its subsequent impact on individual behavior. For example, in a play-it-safe environment, there is a tendency to measure everything in order to be prepared for any eventuality, i.e. maintaining a just-in-case file. This file is kept to help managers to overcome possible questions about their judgment. The net effect of a play-it-safe environment is that it stifles subordinate creativity and initiative and subsequently makes it virtually impossible to develop trust. For example, in some organizations, managers not only have to get their budgets approved by their superiors but also have to get subsequent approval to spend the previously agreed upon budgeted amount. This latter approval wastes time and energy, further erodes the development of trust, and reduces effectiveness.

Feedback mechanisms are an important part of any organization's control system. Feedback, in order to be effective, must be more than a one-way downward oriented process. It must be responsive; that is, feedback must be provided to subordinate teams and individuals regarding the information that they have sent upward, in order to build and reinforce their participation. Such feedback should be timely and specific and is necessary to close the loop in the communication process.

It is equally important to note how receptive is the feedback process. Do managers crucify the bearers of bad news or are they open to suggestions and input from their subordinates, either individually or collectively? Subordinates must be able to perceive that it is possible to exert some upward influence on their managers in such areas as negotiating task limits, requesting additional resources, or changing task specifications.

Getting just the right degree of managerial control at each stratum has important consequences for everyone's sense of true participation, the openness or closedness of the organization's culture, and the development of trust.

Personal Effectiveness Appraisal

In the ordinary course of working, every manager should have sufficient contact with subordinates to be able to tell them when they are doing a good job or a bad one. This contact is the foundation of good everyday management: it must be an ordinary everyday management activity and managers must hold their managerial subordinates accountable for doing it. Such feedback must be provided in connection with a subordinate's efforts regarding on-going tasks. Failure to provide regular personal effectiveness feedback constitutes a major managerial shortcoming. It discourages subordinates and drains personally earned authority.

Judgments about a subordinate's personal effectiveness can generate intense feelings. Such judgments affect not only subordinates' pay and progress but also their sense of self-worth and self-esteem and their own judgment about how fair and just that they feel their manager (and the organization) has been. Hence, any judgment about a subordinate's having functioned below the manager's accepted standard must be carefully made. It is possible that what might appear to be personal effectiveness problems could have arisen more from inadequacies in the task formulation and assignment process than from the subordinate's personal effectiveness. Such judgments may sometimes be difficult for managers to make because of possible overestimation of their own competence in this area, with resulting blind spots.

Further, the feedback process between the manager and the subordinate may not be as good as the manager thinks. Research has found that most managers consistently overestimate the amount of feedback that they routinely provide to subordinates. Sometimes this overestimate is simply an oversight on the part of the manager. At other times, managers may be too wrapped up in their own work to find the time, or they may feel that their response is so obvious that it does not warrant feedback. Sometimes, the problem is merely that the subordinate interprets a given message not as feedback but as just another new message. Regardless of the cause, it is possible that in situations where a subordinate's effectiveness has been judged to be substandard, the subordinate may feel that he or she was not provided with adequate on-going feedback information, either about performance or about personal effectiveness, and that, as far as he or she was concerned, things were going satisfactorily.

Personal effectiveness feedback is vital to managerial leadership. It is the means by which companies convey work standards to their people. Good managerial leaders go the extra mile to ensure that they are feedback responsive: that their subordinates not only are provided with adequate feedback but also clearly understand that they have, in fact, received such feedback. Such communication does not just happen, it has to be actively worked at (see figure 6.9).

It is essential to determine the effectiveness with which subordinates carry out their work. Judgments regarding how well subordinates have carried out their work must be based on an assessment of the following factors.

- Were outputs produced consistently?
- Were the circumstances under which subordinates produced their results fairly ordinary, relatively free of unexpected difficulties, or were there messy surrounding problems with which subordinates coped or did not cope?
- Could a subordinate have been expected to have done better or worse under the circumstances?
- Did subordinates exercise discretion on assigned tasks within agreed upon limits?
- How well did subordinates work with their colleagues? Were they team players or did they prefer to go it alone? What was the nature of the subordinates' working relationships outside their team?
- What type of information and advice did subordinates provide to their manager? Was it relevant and useful? Did it show that the subordinates were able to grasp the important aspects of their manager's work?

- If the subordinates were in an advisory role, did they take the initiative in offering expert advice?
- Above all, was there any evidence that subordinates exercised initiative or creativity in achieving continuous improvement?

It is essential to conduct an on-going assessment of the personal effectiveness of subordinate managers. The personal effectiveness of subordinate managers can be judged by how effective they are in managing their own subordinates (see also the section on MoR

Figure 6.9 Personal effectiveness appraisal

oversight accountability). This judgment is heavily dependent on how managers have carried out the following four sets of tasks.

1   The capacity to develop adequate plans is a very important ability of any manager. Without it, managers will simply not be able to cope with the full-scale complexity of the work facing them.

   • How well have the subordinate managers carried out the planning process?
   • Have they been able to encompass the full range of variables confronting them?
   • Have they been able to develop successful plans for both their work and the work that they have given to their subordinates, taking into account all of these variables?

2   Managers must evaluate the overall quality of performance of immediate managers and their teams. Judgments must be reached about how well the managers have managed their subordinates. This judgment calls for an evaluation of the nature of the working relationship between managers and their subordinates. The manager can gain insight about this relationship by directly observing subordinate managers' behavior. Do the managers treat their subordinates with respect and dignity? By observing the behavior of subordinates two strata down (SoRs), managers of subordinate managers can determine the extent to which the SoRs work together effectively as a team. Do they behave in an open and trusting manner or do they apparently keep to themselves?

3   By observing the SoRs, the manager can evaluate the nature of the information regarding subordinates two strata removed which was provided upward by the subordinate manager. Was the information relevant and accurate? Did it coincide with the senior manager's own judgments regarding the subordinate manager's subordinates (the SoRs)?

4   Judgments of personal effectiveness of managers must take into account whether or not any continuous improvement projects have been initiated, progressed or successfully completed.

Managers must, from time to time, record significant examples of better or worse instances of personal effectiveness of subordinates. These brief records are essential to be able to refer back to when carrying out an annual personal effectiveness and merit award review.

Managers should always ensure that their subordinates are apprised of any recorded judgments. There should be no surprises.

Judgments about ineffectual personal effectiveness levels must trigger coaching and training.

Coaching

Coaching of subordinates must be an ordinary part of every manager's daily activities. It involves the routine sharing with subordinates of the manager's own knowledge, skills, and experience pertaining to the subordinate's work. The purposes of coaching are as follows:

- To help subordinates to understand the full opportunities in their roles, that is to say, the full range of task types available to incumbents in the role; and to get a picture of what they need to do to take advantage of these opportunities.
- To assist subordinates in learning new knowledge, i.e. methods, technology, and procedures.
- To bring subordinate values more in line with corporate values and the corporate philosophy.
- To assist subordinates in developing wisdom, i.e. building on the manager's experience to help subordinates to grow wise in the ways of the world.
- To help subordinates to smooth out any rough edges in their temperament (behavior that may have possibilities of becoming dysfunctional at work if it continues is -T). Coaching does not, however, involve trying to change a subordinate's personality; that is not a concern of the manager. If there are major temperament problems, then the manager must make it clear that continuation of the problem is unacceptable and the manager should make time available for a subordinate to seek full-scale, off-site professional counseling, if he or she should so desire.

Effective managerial leaders maintain a delicate balance between, on the one hand, situations where the managers permit subordinates sufficient leeway to use their own discretion in trying out new ideas which allow the subordinates to profit from their own direct, hands-on experience, and, on the other hand, situations where the managers assist subordinates to take full advantage of others' experiences with new ideas and innovations. The balancing act is to release sub-ordinates' full capabilities and energy by providing them with sufficient opportunities for creativity and innovation in achieving continuous improvement, guiding them in such a way as to avoid wasting resources or undue energy. Setting correct limits is all part of the manager's daily role in adding value.

Managers should be careful when coaching to avoid actually doing the subordinate's work. They may demonstrate techniques, perform one iteration of a procedure, but they must always ensure that subordinates have ample opportunity to perform similar tasks. It may often take more time to coach subordinates about a particular task than it would to do the tasks themselves. Coaching is another way in which managers add value to their subordinates' work and it can be a time consuming process. However, it is central to building subordinate confidence, loyalty, and sense of teamwork. As part of coaching, a manager should share with subordinates any unique knowledge and skills gained from his or her own work experiences. In addition, managers may choose to pass on any lessons learned from other personal experiences if they appear to be relevant to the subordinate's current situation.

Coaching begins with a manager's pointing out opportunities for subordinates to extend the range of work to which they are being assigned, if only they could overcome given weaknesses, or learn new knowledge, or gain greater skill in using what they know (see figure 6.10). Arising out of such a discussion, or as part of it, the manager might teach or train, or arrange for teaching or training. In order for this teaching and training, which goes beyond the basic tasks of the role, to be effective, it must be valued by the subordinate. If the subordinate expresses a lack of value for certain kinds of new knowledge and skills, this must be taken into account when assigning new tasks and special projects and when discussing the subordinate's possible progress in the current role. The outcome should be continual improvement in the capability of subordinates.

Coaching should also take place when subordinates are experiencing problems. It is appropriate for managers to ask subordinates to identify areas where they might be experiencing problems. Problems may be related to the manager's task formulation and assignment process, e.g. the tasks may be too complex or may not be divided up sufficiently for the level of the subordinate's capability, there may be difficulties regarding methods, or difficult limits. These are matters

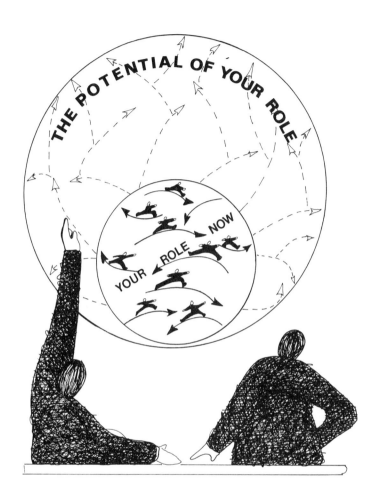

Figure 6.10 Coaching

to be sorted out by discussion between the manager and the subordinate.

Other problems may be associated with the nature of on-going working relationships. Often these types of problems stem from subordinates being unclear about their accountabilities and authorities in relation to others. In the absence of specification, people make their own rules about what they can and cannot do in relation to one another, causing interpersonal conflict and mistrust. Given such problems, coaching about the nature of role relationships is called for. Other working relationship problems may arise as a result of temperament (personality) problems in subordinates. Managers need to handle such situations judiciously. As we have already observed, it is no business of the manager to try to change the temperament of any subordinate *per se*, that is up to the subordinate himself or herself. It is appropriate, however, for the manager to point out the need for greater self control in areas where a subordinate's temperament is seen by the manager as interfering with his or her ability to get work done.

Managers will come across coaching opportunities as a normal by-product of the on-going personal effectiveness appraisal process. Whenever managers identify subordinates' performance deficiencies, they should set aside sufficient time to discuss such issues with the subordinates, as part of the ordinary coaching process.

The above processes cannot be left to managerial goodwill. Managers-once-removed (MoRs) must see to it that their managerial subordinates actually do it. To that end, MoRs must themselves act as appropriate role models with their own subordinates.

Training

Every manager is accountable for maintaining a proper balance between meeting current work demands and preparing for future requirements. Training can play a key role in achieving such a balance. Training programs reflect a corporate philosophy which stresses that individuals should be given all of the tools they need to do the work in their current role effectively, and that the company is willing to invest in its human capital in order to prepare for future requirements.

Training, as used throughout this book, is the process of helping individuals to develop or enhance their skilled use of knowledge, that is to say, to become so proficient in using their knowledge as to be able to apply it without having to think about it, thus freeing up their discretion and judgment capabilities. For example, the basic steps to go through in carrying out a personal effectiveness appraisal and merit review can be learned and ingrained by training practice, leaving a manager free to devote energies and judgment to the content of the discussion itself, and to the outcome decisions.

The manager's role in training is to ensure that it occurs routinely in conjunction with normal coaching activities. All training should be relevant to work success and should be conducted personally by the manager, as appropriate. Managers must provide subordinates with on-going feedback regarding their achieved proficiency. Subordinates should never be held back from training as a disciplinary measure.

One type of training need may arise when a manager notes that some tasks which are common to a number of subordinates (for example, the need to use a particular software program for project management or to develop a budget or to fill out expense forms properly) are not being executed effectively and that the execution of those tasks could be improved by a training session for the group rather than one-on-one sessions. Having identified such tasks, the manager must ensure that the steps, procedures, proper sequences, and background knowledge have been specified in sufficient detail to be used for training.

Managers may consider using their most experienced skilled subordinates to identify the most effective steps and procedures for executing particular tasks (see figure 6.11). If the more experienced subordinate is also skillful in verbalizing what the others need to know, and in demonstrating the steps and procedures necessary for successful completion of the tasks, the manager may want to ask this subordinate to train his or her colleagues. This new training task for the subordinate then becomes an opportunity for personal growth and training as the manager coaches the subordinate to deliver the training sessions.

A second source of training needs flows from analyzing current problem areas which are identified during the on-going personal effectiveness appraisal process. The manager must determine if such problems are related to skill deficiencies. The introduction of new equipment also creates another major source of training needs. New equipment often calls for new procedures and any personnel assigned to work with such equipment may need to be retrained accordingly.

A final source for the identification of training needs is directly related to impending personnel decisions regarding transfers, promotions or the induction of new individuals. MoRs need to play an active role in this process. When MoRs discuss the future of SoRs with them, it is important to include the training implications in the plans for the development of the SoRs.

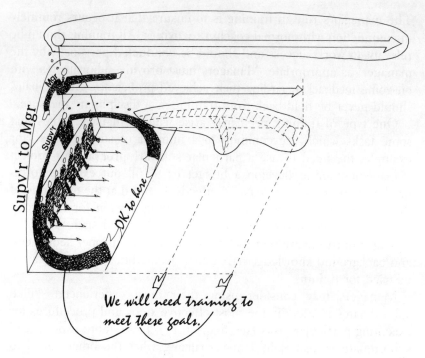

Figure 6.11   Training

Recognition of Personal Effectiveness

A manager's appraisal of the personal effectiveness of each subordinate naturally leads to some form of positive or negative recognition of the subordinate's work. These appraisals constitute a major influence on subordinates' behavior. Recognition cuts right to the core of an individual's identity and sense of self-worth. It represents more than merit awards or pats on the back. Both positive and negative recognition personify the corporation's philosophy and values, and demonstrate how the organization treats its employees in terms of fairness and justice.

We use the terms "positive" and "negative recognition" rather than "rewards" and "punishment," because we are dealing with adult subordinates and not children. There is no room in the workplace for paternal attitudes toward employees. Recognition, both positive and negative, has to do with judging the level at which subordinates are operating in their work, as part of the managerial process of personal effectiveness appraisal. Such appraisals are concerned with adult recognition of entitlement, and not with reward and punishment. These processes are very different from each other.

A sound company philosophy with respect to recognition includes the following practices:

- A basic employment contract (often verbal and supported by the employee handbook) which assumes energetic and effective collaboration.
- All managers recognizing that people want the opportunity to use their fullest capability in their work.
- The company's recognition that effective managerial leadership cannot motivate people but can release blocked energy, and create an environment in which subordinates' natural desire to work to their full capability is supported and channeled toward company goals.
- Recognition by pay increases is tied to taking on increasing levels of work.

The following practices are modes of recognition, sometimes verbal, sometimes written and recorded, which every manager must have available and use regularly as an integral part of his or her on-going management practices.

- Verbal recognition This comprises ordinary everyday indications of more or less satisfaction with work, expressed in words or non-verbal body language. No formal written record is kept. Verbal recognition may be noted informally for the manager's own use for personal effectiveness appraisal and then destroyed.
- Task recognition This entails reinforcing verbal recognition by assigning tasks with more or less growth opportunity. No formal record is kept. As with verbal recognition, the manager may keep notes to be used for personal effectiveness appraisal and then destroyed.
- Recorded verbal recognition This is given in an away-from-work situation, with an opportunity to discuss agreements or disagreements. It is recorded and held on record until taken into account in annual review.

- Broadened or narrowed task type Subordinate is given more complex or less complex task types. This is recorded as part of permanent employment record.
- Merit award Manager decides whether or not subordinate gets an annual merit increase in pay. This is recorded as part of permanent record.
- Recommended upgrading or promotion, or initiated transfer This is recorded as part of permanent record.

Managers should keep in mind that not all recognition needs to be financially expressed. People value being told when they have done a good job or a bad one. The military, for example, gets mileage out of recognizing individuals with decorations. Managers must ensure that individuals get the recognition they earn. They should make use of the full range of available methods of recognition techniques: pat on the back, verbal comment or recorded statement.

Penalties and Dismissal

Penalties have nothing to do with judgments of personal effectiveness, but rather they involve the use of sanctions when an individual has violated rules or limits. Transgression of prescribed limits for most people will be a rare event, so that penalties may never be meted out. We do not expect any special recognition for obeying rules but we certainly can expect to get penalized for violations. If a manager lets a subordinate get away with transgressions, it can demoralize the rest of the team; "If he or she can get away with doing wrong things or doing things wrongly, why should I try to do things correctly?"

Penalties result from misdemeanors where policies, rules or regulations have been broken; for example, persistent lateness, substance abuse, fighting, excessive rudeness (abusive language), acts of neglect, misappropriation of property, blatant use of office supplies for personal use. Managers must ensure that the choice of penalty fits the crime. For example, extreme lateness, when repeated, might deserve suspension without pay for the day. Serious misappropriation of property could warrant immediate dismissal, as could physical fighting on the premises. Persistent minor misdemeanors should lead to recorded warnings and, if there is no improvement in subordinate behavior, subsequent dismissal (see figure 6.12).

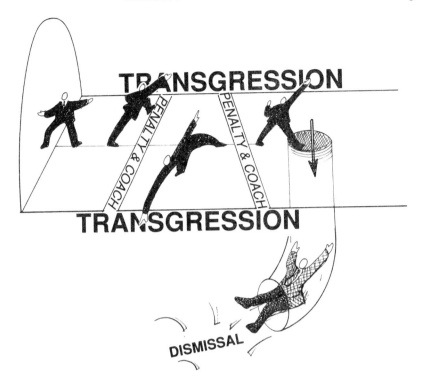

Figure 6.12 Penalties and dismissal

A subordinate who comes to work impaired by drugs or alcohol may be suspended for the day as an appropriate response for the first offense. However, if it happens on more than one occasion, the manager should invoke company policy regarding appropriate external resources for the employee's personal management of the problem.

The ultimate penalty (sanction) which is available to a company for use against individuals who violate rules or limits is dismissal. The employee loses all entitlements, such as outplacement service, notification period, or separation pay. Certain acts should be explicitly identified as the subject of instant dismissal, for example, stealing, fighting, or gross safety violations. In such situations managers should be given the authority to impose the dismissal; this should always, of course, be subject to appeal.

Penalties should be applied as quickly as possible after a transgression and, once a penalty has been handed out, the manager should move on and not dwell on it. All penalty actions, especially dismissal, should afford the affected party due process. Deselection and retrenchment must not be used as penalties. These two reasons for an employee leaving the company are discussed on pp. 215–20.

A dismissal action differs fundamentally from a deselection action. Dismissal is triggered by either serious breaches of regulations or a history of accumulated negligence whereas deselection is brought about by inadequate effectiveness in role.

There are thus two types of dismissal: instant dismissal for an extreme transgression, such as for conduct that is dangerous or illegal, and those situations where a manager recommends to the subordinate's MoR that the individual be dismissed because of accumulated problems. Policies pertaining to situations calling for instant dismissal should be clearly understood by all employees. All dismissal actions should be immediately reviewed if appealed.

Remuneration

Current methods for establishing corporate remuneration systems are among the worst practices in management. They are based upon a number of false assumptions about human nature. For example, they assume that we are all inevitably greedy and out to get all that we can for ourselves, regardless of the entitlements of others; or that we will all work more effectively if we are paid piece-rates or other kinds of bonus. These assumptions are patently false. People want to be paid at comparable levels for comparable work but, in the absence of any clear measurement of comparable work, all kinds of magic and tricks emerge with respect to pay, all of which arouse anxiety and mistrust.

It is instructive to look at some of the common misconceptions underlying the design of most pay systems. There is the tendency to count the number of subordinates whom a manager can garner as an important factor for determining his or her worth to the organization. This approach seriously under-recognizes the creative work of the independent contributor. A large number of organizations world-wide have been talked into using this dysfunctional view of work and remuneration. Relying on so-called market value is no better, since there is no way to compare one role in company ABC with a role in company XYZ other than through similar titles which may bear little relationship to the levels of work in either of the roles.

There is also the common failure to differentiate between achieved performance and personal effectiveness. These difficulties are dealt with on pp. 207–10.

Then there are the host of false principles dealing with output related pay. A prime example is group bonuses. This pay system is completely counter-productive. It is individuals who make decisions and take actions. Groups cannot be held accountable for results unless, of course, a company is willing to dismiss an entire group for lack of performance, ignoring individuals in the group whose personal effectiveness was satisfactory; or, in the case of excellent group results, which have been achieved primarily through the efforts of one or two individuals, a company is willing to pay bonuses to the other individuals who may not have been personally effective in the work they were given to do. Paradoxically, these so-called incentive schemes are in fact disincentives in the long run because they focus attention on the short term and cause people to push aside the difficult and longer term developmental work.

Output related performance pay systems (piece work, individual bonuses, group bonuses) are the arch enemy of effective managerial leadership for two reasons. First, they remove managerial judgment of an individual's personal effectiveness and hence undermine manager–subordinate relationships regarding effectiveness. The net effect is to turn managers into little more than paper pushers. Second, they undermine effective work organization, because they allow the subordinate to decide for himself or herself whether to produce below, at, or above the target assigned.

Instead, people desire pay systems which are built around the following principles.

- Pay brackets are tied to the level of work bracket in each role, i.e. roles with the same level of work carry the same pay bracket.
- Opportunities are provided for individuals to move within their pay bracket, in accord with recognized merit and based on their personal effectiveness appraisal.
- A fair and just pattern of pay differentials, related to differentials in level of work, is used to determine the range of pay.
- In the special case of personnel shortages in the market-place, scarcity premiums are paid separately from wage and salary and are noted as an anomaly which disappears when the scarcity disappears.

In a fair and equitable pay system, everyone must have the opportunity to progress in level of work and pay in accord with the growth of their working capacity. Recognition of individual effectiveness has already been discussed in the section on merit recognition. Cost of living increases are added across the board to the salary structure which is assigned to each respective stratum. Provisions must be made for *ex gratia* payments; for example, a one-off payment for outstanding work above and beyond the line of duty.

In order to reinforce decisive, value-adding managerial leadership, companies should establish pay brackets for each stratum, by setting pay levels for each stratum boundary. The pay bracket for each stratum should then be divided into three pay bands, to provide pay bands that are about 25–30 percent wide. This amount gives individuals a realistic immediate pay progression target to aim for (see figure 6.13). Next, roles should be classified within a pay band by time-span analysis or complexity analysis.[1] Managers should then assign individuals to roles within a given pay band. Subordinates must always be in one of the bands in the next lower stratum from their manager and never in a lower band within the same stratum. Personal

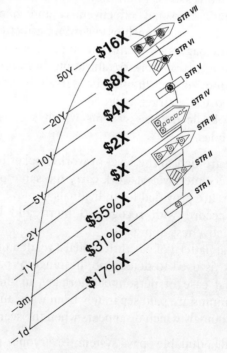

Figure 6.13 Remuneration

assistants (for example, secretaries) can be more than one stratum lower.

Annual Review of Personal Effectiveness

The annual review must be based on the fact that managers have conducted periodic personal effectiveness appraisals throughout the year. Indeed, managers who have not done so should not be allowed to conduct an annual merit review. The annual review is an opportunity to reflect on the past year's events, including the attempts at coaching and the assessment of how useful they have been. It is the time for the manager to tell the subordinate the type of merit award that he or she is proposing, remembering that any merit award must be supported and reinforced with data recorded throughout the year. How the manager handles this annual review is important. Handled well, the annual review gives managers another opportunity to continue to develop a relationship of trust and respect with their subordinates.

Without a doubt, conducting the annual review is a delicate process emotionally. When engaging in this on-going process, managers must not rely solely on their memory. There is a human tendency to recall more vividly instances of low or poor personal effectiveness as opposed to adequate or good instances. (For example, there is more than a shred of truth to the saying that it takes only one "that's no good" to offset ten "at-a-boys.") To overcome any such tendency, effective managers maintain a notebook where they record, on a regular basis, significant instances of a subordinate's personal effectiveness, both satisfactory and not.

If a manager does not have a notebook listing his or her judgments throughout the year, then he or she has a problem in doing the annual review. There must be no surprises at the end of the rating period. If a manager is going to tell a subordinate that he or she has not been achieving the manager's accepted standard of personal effectiveness, then the manager must be able to cite numerous examples where personal effectiveness was substandard and had been discussed with the subordinate at the time. An effective manager should also be able to refer to specific situations where he or she provided coaching and/ or training to assist the subordinate in achieving the standard. To rely on one's memory is not good enough!

In carrying out an annual merit review, managers must review the subordinate's role accountabilities, looking at basic assignments, special projects, interaction internally and externally, and overall team collaboration. Next, they must muster facts upon which to base the overall judgment of the subordinate's personal effectiveness during the year, going back over their periodic notes on the various instances of satisfactory and possibly unsatisfactory performance issues, coaching sessions, and the subordinate's responsiveness to corrective actions taken by the manager (see figure 6.14).

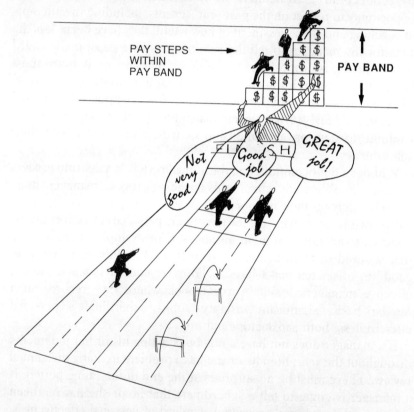

Figure 6.14 Annual review of personal effectiveness

Private, uninterrupted time for the review discussion must be arranged by the manager. Managers should review their findings with their subordinates and outline their judgment of the subordinates' personal effectiveness over that last twelve months. Subordinates should be given the opportunity to tell their manager their own assessment of their personal effectiveness, giving examples to support their assessment. The subordinate's judgment should then be compared with that of the manager. If the judgments do not agree, managers should allow sufficient opportunity to discuss differences and agreements. It is useful, in pulling together material for this annual review, for the manager to identify ways in which the subordinate can improve his or her effectiveness, and then to discuss these with the subordinate, working out a mutually agreed program for continued improvement by the end of the review process. Managers must schedule sufficient time to follow through on such a program.

Adjustments to employees' pay within pay bands are made in connection with the annual personal effectiveness review. Effective merit recognition practices require that a company has established a requisite differential pay structure with salary levels assigned to the boundaries of each stratum and to the appropriate pay bands within strata (see Jaques [1989]). The starting point for merit awards is a role in an allocated pay band. The immediate manager decides where he or she places an individual in the pay band in terms of his or her judgment of whether that individual is effectively working towards the bottom, the middle, or the top of the level of work range that is represented by the pay band.

In connection with merit pay awards, the size of increase, or decrease, is important. A 5 percent merit increase, for example, feels like a significant increase, whereas a 2 percent merit increase is a hardly noticeable difference, anything less than which seems like nothing at all. Managers can also decide upon no increase or, in negative circumstances, an actual decrease. Deciding upon a decrease is allowable only if the subordinate has been notified that his or her personal effectiveness has been lagging, and has been coached seriously throughout the year and given sufficient opportunity to improve.

Merit awards are to be clearly differentiated from performance related bonus systems which award increases for output performance regardless of the manager's judgments of personal effectiveness. Bonus systems are counter-productive. They run totally counter to effective task assignment because they give special recognition to people for outputs which they ought to be achieving anyhow rather than for personal effectiveness.

Once the annual review session is completed, managers should write up their evaluation. This evaluation is then made a part of the employee's permanent file and the manager's notes, which were used to prepare for the review session, are destroyed. Last, but certainly not least, the manager is now engaged in observing the subordinate's progress into the ensuing year, based on current assignments and the on-going improvement plans.

Selection

When positions become vacant in a company, individuals within the company who feel qualified are entitled to expect to have a fair chance at the vacant position. At lower organizational levels this means a chance to apply for a given position. At higher organizational levels (stratum–IV and above), managers generally accept the fact that vacancies are not always advertised. Nevertheless, people at these levels strongly value the opportunity to be at least considered for any vacancy. One way of ensuring that such consideration will be given is by means of the manager-once-removed (MoR) process (to be described in Chapter 9) in which every manager-once-removed nominates qualified subordinates for higher level roles. It is important for all subordinates to be able to feel that they have at least been considered for a short list of candidates, whether or not they are ultimately selected. It is equally important that qualified personnel should never be held back simply because they play a critical role in the current work system (see figure 6.15).

In preparation for the selection process, it is necessary for the manager and the MoR to review the role. As part of this review, the manager must examine the functions encompassed by the role so as to determine if these functions could be combined with those of another role or if they are sufficiently complex to warrant a stand alone role. Based on this review, the MoR must determine if the role is necessary and so either authorize the vacancy or delete the role and agree to how the tasks will be assigned to other roles. The manager and the MoR must also ensure that the level of complexity of the work of the role is right for the given stratum.

In order for any company adequately to address the selection issue, it must first have an adequate concept of individual development. Chapter 11 describes a prototype corporate development strategy. As illustrated in that chapter, an important part of any development

Figure 6.15 Vacancies

strategy is the underlying model describing the variables which determine an individual's capacity to work at a given organizational stratum.

The selection process, to be effective, must be built around these essential variables. When considering an individual for a given position, the following information must be obtained (see figure 6.16):

- What is the applicant's current potential (cognitive category)?
- Does he or she value this kind of work or other kinds of work? (This is a major issue in deciding between managerial and individual contributor roles.)
- Is the applicant's behavior congruent with corporate values? If there are any incongruencies, are these likely to be modifiable?
- Does the individual possess the necessary knowledge and the skilled use of that knowledge?
- Does the individual suffer from any pathology in temperament?

The immediate manager must ensure that he or she interviews fairly and does not manipulate the role specifications in such a way as to confine the selection process to one individual. The selection process must avoid the "old boy" network.

For entry level positions and for individuals who have not been in the company long enough to have become known, it may be necessary to employ specialist assistance in assessing an individual's current potential (cognitive category). There are recently developed procedures, however, which can be taught to company interviewers to enable them to carry out this assessment.

For those who have been with the company long enough, their current potential will have been evaluated by their MoR. MoRs will have forwarded all such evaluations to corporate human resources (HR) personnel who, in turn, maintain a master file of the overall health of the corporate talent pool (see also Chapter 11). Based upon the latest MoR input, corporate HR personnel are able to provide the immediate manager with a short list of all applicants who are judged to be ready for work at the next higher stratum.

The manager interviews the applicants and chooses one from the short list. If there is only one person shortlisted, the manager's right of veto on appointment makes it possible for the manager to reject an unsatisfactory candidate and start the selection process over again. The real force of veto derives from the fact that both the manager and his or her manager know that he or she can exercise it. This veto option is tangible evidence that the company is willing to trust the manager, and reinforces his or her personal sense of accountability.

Induction

The use of induction programs reflects a corporate philosophy that people should be helped to adjust to their new tasks, new locations, and new organizations and should be properly oriented in a timely manner.

Newcomers have questions regarding their new role and their new site. Inadequate orientation can lead to dismay, confusion, and unnecessary stress which in turn ends up wasting time and energy. Confidence springs from knowing what to do and how to do it. It is essential that the immediate manager take part in the orientation process, although parts can be conducted by one of the manager's

Selection

Formula	How you get these components
 **CP** Cognitive Power	MoR evaluation
V Values	Opinion of others & interview
 **K/S** Knowledge/ Skills	Matter of record & tests
Wi Wisdom	Interview & reports
 **(-T)**	Interview & reports
 **CAC**	

Of those whose CAC passes muster for the position, the Mgr decides, based on his/her own best judgment, whom to pick.

Figure 6.16 Selection

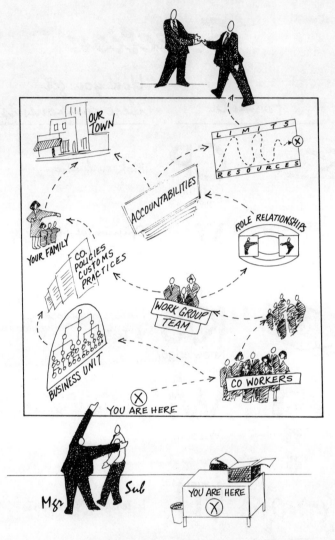

Figure 6.17 Induction

aides. The induction process, although short, has a long and lasting impact for better or worse.

Newcomers need two different types of help in adjusting. The first type can be provided by the manager's subordinates (the newcomer's colleagues), and includes: a picture of what it is like to work in this location; the overall conditions of employment; business unit and site policies, customs and practices.

The second type of help needs to be given directly by the manager and includes: various details of the specific role and how it fits into the overall work system, the context of work encompassed by the role, role accountabilities, limits, methods and resources pertaining to the role, relationships with other roles inside the team and outside the team, and standard reporting and other work procedures (see figure 6.17). This second type of induction is concerned with integrating subordinates into their new roles and their new management team. This integration process which is carried out personally by the manager represents the beginnings of the horizontal bonding process. Effective managers take this opportunity to provide all newcomers with an explanation of the accountabilities of the work group team members. The manager might want to consider assigning a team sponsor to a new subordinate, to help in the adjustment process.

Deselection

Deselection is the process whereby a manager initiates the removal of an immediate subordinate from being a member of his or her team, but without dismissal from the company. Deselection arises when a manager decides a sufficiently good match no longer exists between the role requirements and the role incumbent. There can be many reasons behind such a change; for example, the role has changed, the role incumbent has changed (-T), technology has changed. Whatever the reason, performance has not kept up, and the role incumbent is no longer the right person for the role.

To attempt to downplay or disregard a bad fit is to do everyone a disservice, no matter what the cause. For example, an incumbent has difficulty in adjusting to a change; subsequently, an initial small performance shortfall grows to become larger and larger as change continues. The individual no longer is able to cope satisfactorily. Should he or she be allowed to continue for humane reasons? Not at all. Such a situation is not in the best interests of the individual. It is cruel, and everyone else suffers as well. When a bad fit occurs, deselection with appropriate transfer, if possible, may be the only practical solution.

This issue is particularly serious when a subordinate is a manager, since the shortcomings put unacceptable stress upon that manager's subordinates. Sometimes managers are reluctant to use deselection because a subordinate has been a long standing good citizen of the company and it does not seem quite right to treat people this way. Managers in such situations will often respond that "we have to take care of our own." While treating people with compassion is indeed an appropriate corporate value, managers must balance this against the deleterious effect that inadequate performance has on other individuals within the organization.

Managers must always be on the lookout for early evidence of a subordinate's problems which, if left unchecked, could ultimately lead to a deselection action. The on-going personal effectiveness appraisal process should certainly identify someone who is showing signs of not doing well enough.

All subordinates are entitled to the following due process before a deselection action for unsatisfactory performance can be initiated. First, subordinates must be given an adequate opportunity to improve. This means that managers must inform them that their performance is substandard and then coach them and help them to improve. Next, managers must reappraise the subordinates' effectiveness, inform them accordingly, coach a second time, and reappraise once again. While going through this process for the second time, managers must warn subordinates that, barring adequate improvement, they could be deselected. This warning must be recorded and the MoR must be notified. This sequence must be carried out before managers are free to initiate the deselection process with the MoR, who must then carry it out within a reasonable time (see figure 6.18).

Having received a deselection decision from a subordinate manager, the MoR must take one of the following steps. He or she can explore opportunities for other positions for the individual; for example, a position at a lower level or at the same level but with a set of different functions. If the individual who is recommended for deselection is a manager, the MoR might consider moving him or her to a specialist role.

Regardless of the action an MoR ultimately takes, he or she must deal with the compensation issue. If the individual is moved to a lower level role, the MoR must decide if the pay is to be lowered commensurately or if it will be allowed to fall in line over time by not granting annual increases.

If the MoR finds that no alternative employment opportunities are available, then the employee will have to be laid off. Such a lay-off is not the same as dismissal for transgressions; it is the equivalent of

Figure 6.18 Deselection

retrenchment, and should carry the same entitlements, including outplacement services if such services are provided for retrenched employees. Retrenchment is described in the following section.

Retrenchment and Downsizing

Companies may encounter conditions which leave them with no choice but to retrench part of the work force; for example, the market has dropped, the company has lost a major contract, competition has captured increased market share, or technological improvements have significantly changed the production process. Such circumstances may strike at the heart of the business and may require drastic action on the part of management if the company is to survive. Retrenchment is one such action.

There are some actions, however, which every company should take long before they find themselves in a retrenchment situation, and which, if taken, can help to avoid the need for extreme downsizing cuts. First, companies should establish a requisite organization at the outset, since that avoids unnecessary roles and overstaffed functions. By having a requisite organization structure, with the requisite number of layers, a major problem which is associated with downsizing can be avoided; namely, combining downsizing with a "delayering" exercise, in which entire pay grades or so-called "layers" are simply chopped out, thus leaving unpredictable consequences to be faced.

Second, companies must not allow managers to abdicate their managerial accountabilities by failing to deal with subordinates who are substandard performers. This kind of inadequate managerial leadership readily leads to overstaffing and to eventual downsizing which is partly induced as a means of removing the very substandard performers whom the managers had not dealt with in a straightforward way. These organizations must learn to deal with substandard performers as they are encountered, by means of deselection. Managers who prove to be really incapable of handling this procedure, and who utter that lame complaint of "you cannot get rid of inadequate performers these days," ought themselves to be considered for deselection. Downsizing should not be the method used to deal with inadequate managerial personal effectiveness appraisals.

Third, before considering downsizing, corporations should take maximum advantage of normal attrition. A hiring freeze should be imposed and clamps should be put on normal replacement actions.

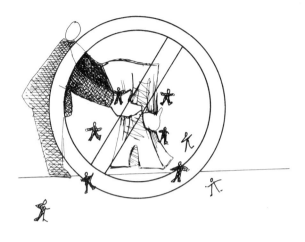

Figure 6.19 Corporate values in retrenchment and downsizing

Finally, overtime should be cut. Only if all of these actions are insufficient should companies turn to downsizing.

When downsizing is necessary, all managers should be required to decide which of the functions for which they are responsible could be cut, whether these be particular roles, or groups of roles, or whole departments or areas. If an insufficient number becomes available by this means, it may become necessary to impose cuts across the board. Managers must then examine the residual work that they have left after the retrenchment action and see if they can collapse it and/or reconstitute it with their remaining work force.

Having identified these roles, the next step is to identify the individuals who, under ordinary circumstances, might be assigned to these roles, and to deselect (see p. 215) those least entitled to stay, usually on the basis of length of service, other things being equal. Each manager must decide if there are individuals whom he or she needs to retain and so recommend them to the MoR, as appropriate.

How managers handle retrenchment actions (downsizing) can minimize or accentuate the problems associated with such decisions. Managerial leaders need to be candid and honest with the entire work force when considering retrenchment. To do otherwise can rapidly destroy whatever credibility a managerial leader may possess. Managers need to be aware that the actual treatment that is afforded to retrenched workers communicates an important message to the work force about how the corporation really values its human resources. Every manager must also clearly understand the rationale behind the retrenchment decision and be able to discuss it individually and collectively with subordinates.

Retrenched workers should be provided with career counseling and outplacement services as far as possible. They have not been dismissed for cause and are entitled to as much help as possible in locating new employment (see figure 6.19).

Note

1 This system of remuneration is set out here only in outline. It is presented in greater detail in Jaques (1989).

7

Supervisory Leadership

The title "supervisor" is currently used in many different ways. For example, it is sometimes regarded as being interchangeable with "manager," or it is used for someone who oversees work in a general way, or for a junior shop or office foreman. We shall use the title for only one specific role:

The role of supervisor is that shop or office role whose incumbent is held accountable for assisting a first line manager in developing and maintaining a team of subordinates who are capable of operating to their full capability; in directly overseeing their work, and in getting them to work in the direction set by the first line manager, so that each member exercises individual initiative and collaborates with the first line manager, supervisor, and colleagues to achieve shared goals.

Supervisors are required when a first line manager has operators who have difficulty working without direct supervision, particularly when technical problems or work assignment problems exist, and the manager's work is such that he or she cannot be on hand sufficiently to give the direction and help required. Such a situation would be a three-shift operation where there is an advantage in having one manager who is accountable for the entire three-shift operation for that section but who simply cannot be there all of the time (see figure 7.1).

Thus, supervisors assist first line managers; they do not replace them. As assistants, they do not possess the same set of accountabilities and authorities as the first line manager. Since supervisors are not full-scale managers, there exists a common assumption that they do not have any authority and therefore cannot be given leadership accountability. This assumption is not true. As we define the role, supervisors carry accountability for shift output, including significant

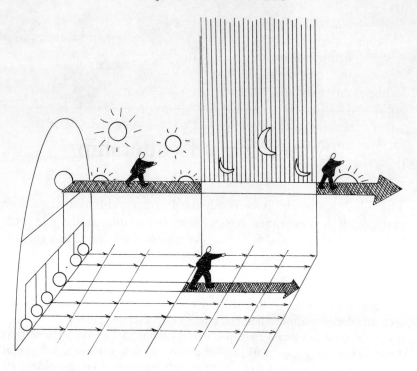

Figure 7.1 Supervisory work

recommending authority, and can be charged with leadership accountability on each shift. This leadership accountability is especially important under conditions where work planning and task setting are carried out on the assumption that employees will consistently achieve quality, quantity, and time targets (see figure 7.2).

It is important to note that, even though supervisors have less role vested authority than first line managers, they must nevertheless win personally earned authority (see Chapter 2) in order to discharge their leadership accountability. They are in a position to do so because they spend almost full time in face-to-face contact, helping, directing, and training operators. Because of the importance of winning personally earned authority, supervisors must be given adequate opportunities to learn and understand requisite practices which are central to the process.

There is a widespread tendency to establish too many supervisory roles. This tendency derives from a general assumption that operators and clerks will not work satisfactorily if there is not someone physically present to watch them. Such an assumption is the product of the failure to establish effective first line managers who can understand that most operators and clerks will work effectively without firsthand supervision, given half a chance to do so. The prime conditions for such independent work are that the manager will have to set clear context and directions and be focused upon effective training for all subordinates.

Before deciding, therefore, on the setting up of supervisory roles, it is wise to determine whether or not the operators or clerks are working at a level at which they are capable of self-supervision. Only if they are not should supervisory roles be established. It is inadvisable to go to the other extreme and set up so-called self-managing teams just because the operators or clerks are judged to be capable of self-supervision under good managerial leadership. Teamworking is fine in the managerial hierarchical organization but "self-managing" teams, without decisive accountable managers, will lead to a deterioration in work in the medium and long term.

Supervisory Task Formulation and Assignment

The task formulation and assignment process that is carried out by supervisors is very similar in practice to the process applying to managers, but with three notable exceptions. The three exceptions have to do with limits, context setting, and feedback.

Supervisors always assign tasks within the limits established by the manager. Managers must ensure that supervisors formulate tasks of an appropriate degree of complexity for their supervisees' capability. To formulate appropriate tasks, supervisors must first understand how such tasks fit into the manager's goal. The supervisor must then ensure that the tasks which are set are specific and reasonable and permit the supervisee to function at his or her full capacity, for the same reasons described under the manager's task assignment process.

It is the manager and not the supervisors who sets context for assigned tasks. Context setting contains the following elements: the immediate manager's task and context; his or her plan for accomplishing that task; any tasks that the manager has assigned to a given subordinate's colleagues, and their relationship with the subordinate's task. But even though it is the manager and not the supervisor who is accountable for providing context, supervisors must understand the context clearly enough to be able to explain it to their supervisees on the shift.

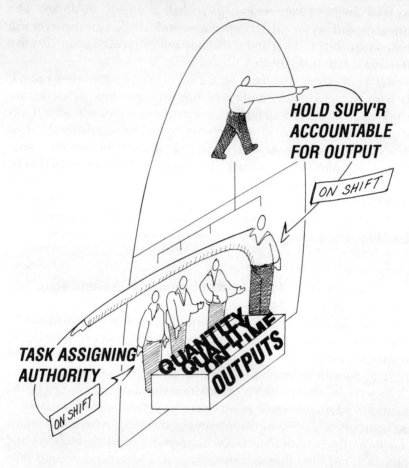

HOLD SUPV'R ACCOUNTABLE FOR OUTPUT

ON SHIFT

TASK ASSIGNING AUTHORITY

ON SHIFT

QUANTITY QUALITY ON TIME OUTPUTS

Figure 7.2 Supervisory leadership

Since everyone needs to know how he or she is doing, providing timely and accurate feedback is an essential managerial accountability. But supervisors, because they are face-to-face with operators/clerks, can and must play a key role in this activity. It is for them to keep an eye on the work being done during the shift, and to give on-going praise and encouragement or criticism and help. The feedback, however, is oral, because the supervisor is not authorized to record judgments on the supervisee's file. Recorded judgments must be made by means of recommendations to the manager.

The supervisor must be able to assume that the outputs which are associated with the tasks assigned will be produced unless the supervisee notifies him or her differently. Achievement of quality standards and continuous improvement must be built into the task assignment system. The system must assume accountable operators and clerks, and it is the task of the supervisor to reinforce such a system.

Personal Effectiveness Appraisal by Supervisors

Any manager must know when subordinates are doing well or badly and must tell them accordingly. In the ordinary course of working, however, first line managers with over thirty subordinates, or with subordinates on three shifts, may not always have sufficient contact to be able by themselves to make accurate judgments of each individual's personal effectiveness. In these types of situation, managers can be helped by the observations of their shift supervisors. Since supervisors are on shift with their supervisees, they must be expected to be making personal effectiveness judgments during each and every shift; they should be giving routine feedback on effectiveness through on-going comments about work observed at first hand, and should be providing information to the manager when something special comes up. Keeping a notebook with such observations is far better than relying upon memory alone.

Supervisors should keep supervisees routinely informed about how they are doing. They should encourage rather than pour cold water on attempts at innovation, as a support for continuous improvement. Because a supervisor's observations regarding a supervisee's personal effectiveness has a significant long-term potential impact on the nature of the relationship between the first line manager and the supervisee, supervisors must not be put in a position where they can be seen as spies and thus cause stress and tension. Such problems can be avoided so long as the recommending accountability and authority of the supervisor is clearly specified for all to understand, and the requisite practices are carried out (see figure 7.3).

Supervisors do not themselves prepare annual reviews. The first line managers must build up their own firsthand knowledge by

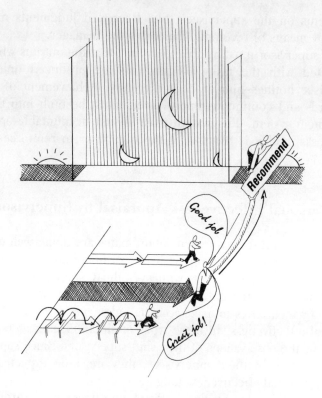

Figure 7.3   Personal effectiveness appraisal by supervisors

observing their people often enough. However, as mentioned above, supervisors take daily note of personal effectiveness and near the time of annual review can be asked for their recommendations on what the annual review appraisal should be for each supervisee.

Training

Training must be an ordinary part of every supervisor's daily activities. It involves helping supervisees to develop or enhance their skills through on-the-job practice. The supervisor's role in training is to assist the first line manager in ensuring that: (1) adequate training is provided prior to requiring supervisees to perform assigned tasks; (2) all training is relevant to job success; (3) adequate feedback regarding training proficiency is provided to each supervisee. In order to assist the manager, the supervisor must be proficient in the procedures for which on-the-job training is required.

The supervisor can also assist the first line manager in identifying future training requirements. For example, he or she can discuss with the first line manager current problem areas where training is a likely solution, such as deficiencies uncovered during ordinary personal effectiveness appraisals, or new work requirements based upon the introduction of new equipment or new procedures (see figure 7.4).

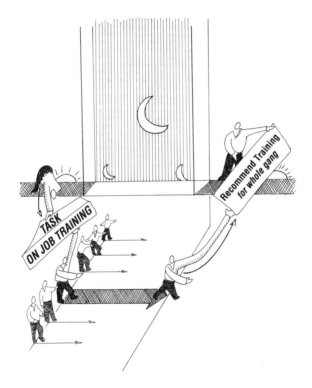

Figure 7.4   Training

Continuous Improvement Project Teams

Supervisors, because of their practical experience in handling day to day problems, can play an important role both as members of and as project chiefs for special project teams, in connection with continuous improvement projects at shop- and office-floor level.

Recognition and Merit Award

Supervisors must be taught to understand that people naturally like to work enthusiastically and to have the opportunity to go in a common direction, so long as they are able to do so, and are not discouraged by their organizations or their managers. The task of leadership is not to motivate but rather to operate in such a way as to sustain and allow for the expression of an individual's natural enthusiasm. A subordinate's effectiveness can be enhanced or diminished by how recognition is given or not given.

The supervisor gives positive and negative recognition directly to supervisees. He or she is immediately available to encourage and assist them when they are having trouble and to recognize them when they are doing well. Such recognition can range from something as simple as a pat on the back to a verbal or written acknowledgment given to the first line manager (see figure 7.5).

Supervisors must give recognition when supervisees have demonstrated personal effectiveness in overcoming unusual obstacles that have stood in the way of achieving or surpassing goals. Such recognition must be in a form that is of value to the recipient. Each company or unit will have several forms of positive recognition for high achievement. It may be the presentation of a special item that is used at work or worn to work; it may be adding the achiever's name to a list of others who have reached similar performance standards; or it may be as simple as announcing the accomplishment to everyone at the coffee break.

Supervisors must be very clear about the importance of recognition for unusual performance. If they promise recognition for a particular level of accomplishment, then they must ensure that they can deliver what they have promised and that all of the appropriate individuals receive it. The improper use of recognition can easily discourage supervisees.

Use of Penalties

Penalties involve the use of sanctions when an individual has failed to conform to rules or limits. The supervisor needs enough on-shift authority to sustain effective discipline. For example, a supervisor

Figure 7.5 Recognition and merit award

needs the authority to order a shift member off-site if that member is drunk or unruly.

The first line manager must also make it clear to all shift members that the supervisor has the authority to recommend supervisees for more serious penalties, such as unwanted transfer or dismissal.

Penalties should be used by supervisors only when someone has broken rules or acted outside the limits or guidelines specified by the first line manager. As in the case of managers, the guiding principles must be justice and fairness. Penalties should never be applied (or recommended) until the supervisor has convincing evidence that an individual has indeed violated limits and then the penalties should be applied as quickly as possible after the transgression. Supervisors should never threaten a penalty if they cannot deliver it or do not plan to use it as stated.

Selection

Supervisors assist the first line manager in assessing applicants for vacancies on the manager's team. Supervisors must be involved in any selection interview process. No first line manager should select anyone as a subordinate without the supervisor's input or recommendation. While the authority remains with the first line manager to make the final choice of new team members, because of the day-to-day contact between a supervisor and team members, the supervisor's recommendation must carry significant weight.

The supervisor must also be involved in recommending individuals from his or her sub-section or shift to the manager for promotion or selection consideration. Because supervisors are in daily contact with team members, they are in an excellent position to identify individuals who are ready to tackle more complex work. They must be careful not to overlook any qualified individuals, regardless of their importance to the team's overall effort.

Induction

Induction programs reflect a corporate philosophy stressing that: (1) people should be helped to adjust; and (2) all new employees should be properly oriented to their role, their site, and to their team. At shop- and office-floor level, supervisors have a key role in this induction process.

Effective managers can expect newcomers to have numerous questions regarding their new role and their new team. Inadequate orientation can lead to dismay, confusion, and unnecessary stress which, in turn, is likely to end up wasting time and energy. Confidence springs from knowing what to do and how to do it. While it is essential that the first line manager take part in the orientation

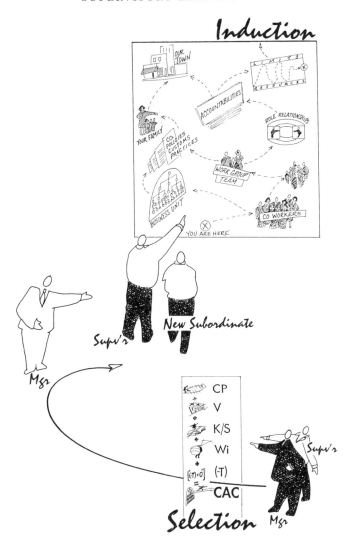

Figure 7.6 Selection and induction

process himself or herself, the supervisor must also be prepared to assist in orienting new employees (see figure 7.6).

For example, because the supervisor is immediately available, it is far more useful for him or her to explain customs and practices and required daily procedures than it is for the manager to attempt to do so. Second, it is a key part of the supervisory role to integrate new employees into the shift or sub-section. Supervisors can begin this process of horizontal bonding by introducing new members to colleagues and key people with whom they will be interacting and by informing them about their respective duties. Newcomers also need to be oriented on the nature of their expected working relationships with members of other sub-sections or shifts.

8

Project Teams and Expert Leadership

A project team is a group of people with a particular mix of expertise, who are brought together to carry out a designated project and who, when the project is completed or the project team is dissolved, return to their home bases. It may be noted again that we are not referring to the currently common notions of so-called semi-autonomous, self-managed teams and quality circles.

Companies form managerial hierarchies to get work done. These managerial hierarchies are made up of an established structure of individual roles, which are grouped in a particular functional alignment for the purpose of deploying people to carry out the work. But sometimes problems occur that cannot be handled by the established structure because they require a mix of expertise beyond that found in any of the existing work groups. Where a new circumstance is likely to continue, restructuring is called for. However, when the problem is unique, in that once solved there is no need for the group that solved it to continue in existence, then an *ad hoc* project team is necessary to tackle that specific problem. The challenge then is to assemble the required team for a discrete period of time to work on the problem in hand.

There are two main circumstances that give rise to the need to set up project teams. First, project teams are a way of life for companies that sell specialized services through tailor-made project teams comprising the necessary mixture of technical specialist staff; for example, construction contractors, who oversee the design and construction of buildings, roads, ports, power plants, electrical transmission systems, and so on, by providing specialized teams tailor made for each contract project, and who keep an organization of specialists available from which to build such teams. Second, project teams may be set up to deal with special projects within companies, such as special new product development and design projects; cost cutting exercises; overcoming a production technical problem; continuous improvement exercises.

Requisite and Anti-requisite Project Teams

A key characteristic of project teams is that they are not permanent. But they must have someone who is firmly accountable for the outputs of the team, whom we shall call the project team chief. The manager who initially creates the project team has to designate someone clearly accountable for driving the project through to completion. The project initiator must give the project chief the necessary financial and human resources required to accomplish the anticipated project work. It is the leadership accountability of the project chief which we shall address.

Project team members can be made up from one of three possible categories of people.

1 Attached subordinates: individuals working one or more strata below the project chief.
2 Attached colleagues of the project chief: individuals working at the same stratum in the organization as the project chief.
3 A mixture of attached subordinates and colleagues.

The three types of project team are called subordinate teams, colleague teams, and mixed teams.

The Project Team Chief

The leadership accountability of the project chief is discharged by carrying out some, but not all, of the requisite practices that are delineated in the manager–subordinate role relationship. There are differences in requisite practices between those that apply between the project chief and attached subordinate members of the team, on the one hand, and attached colleague members, on the other. We shall deal with each in turn (see figure 8.1)

Subordinate project teams (*attachment task forces*) In the case of attached subordinate members, the project chief must carry out all of

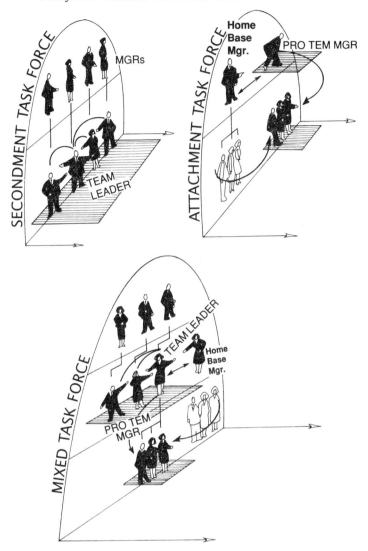

Figure 8.1 Project teams

the requisite immediate managerial leadership practices except one. The exception is that of annual personal effectiveness review and merit recognition. That is to say, the project chief must carry out the managerial practices of veto on appointment, induction, context setting and task assignment, communication about performance, on-going personal effectiveness appraisal and coaching, and deselection (back to home base), as necessary.

With respect to recorded personal effectiveness appraisal and merit recognition, however, the project chief makes a recommendation to the member's home base manager, who remains the one to make the decision about his or her subordinate's progress. The one exception to this procedure is the case of a special project that is planned to continue for more than one year. In this case, the project chief does decide the merit recognition, and the home base manager picks up the subordinate's progress on his or her eventual return to the home base unit.

These processes give the team chief the authority necessary to accept accountability for the progress of the project, and to exercise the leadership that can win the personally earned authority necessary for an effective and successful project outcome. The manager-once-removed relationship remains in the home base unit.

Colleague project teams (secondment task forces)   Here the project chief has colleague peers as members of his or her project team. These colleagues are on the team because they have expertise that the project chief does not possess. It would appear to be a difficult situation in which to exercise effective project leadership. That conclusion is not warranted.

Because the project chief is accountable for the progress and outcome of the project, he or she must have, as an absolute minimum, the authority to have colleagues with whom there is a reasonable chance of having an effective working relationship. That authority can be provided by allowing for veto on appointment, and by giving the authority of deselection, i.e. the authority to decide that a given colleague should no longer work as a member of the team. Given these authorities, and the obvious authority to decide task assignment, a workable situation exists.

Having structured a colleague project team as we have described, it will be apparent that the requisite practice that is most necessary for exercising leadership and winning personally earned authority is that of the team-working mode. The project team chief discusses major problems with colleague team members and gets their inputs and advice, particularly on how the colleagues' experience and expertise can be applied.

Indeed, the team-working mode should be used by the project

chief as a foundation for effective working relationships in the team. Everyone is an expert – that is why he or she is there – and the art is to bind this expertise into the unified effort necessary to get the work done.

However, it is important to note again that the project chief has been given the accountability for the end results and therefore must make the decisions regarding how the team will accomplish their individual and collective tasks.

Mixed project teams (mixed task forces)   The role relationships are as described for colleague and subordinate team members, the whole to be pulled together by regular team-working meetings.

Specialist Expert

Some project teams may require, as a member of the team, a specialist expert. This is an individual in the company who has developed a specialized expertise in a given area and whose expertise has been clearly recognized not only by personnel inside the company but also by an external sanctioning body or by established reputation.

Most specialist experts carry only advisory authority in relation to specified roles throughout the company. Because these are task-initiating role relationships (TIRRs), such specialist experts do not normally carry leadership accountability. There is one special case, however, where a company recognized expert may also carry leadership accountability and that is in a project team. This accountability must be decided and made explicit by the manager of the project team if he or she is going to hold an expert accountable for exercising leadership while serving on the project. Specialist expert leadership accountability is getting the project chief and other members of the team to go along willingly with the expert and to accept his or her technical recommendations; for example, a metallurgist in a team of production engineers, or an economist in a team of financial analysts. These highly technical experts win personally earned authority by virtue of having maintained sufficient contact with team members to understand the nature of the problems facing them, and the context of those problems, and by having demonstrated the ability to deliver competent help and advice for solving such problems. If an expert has been charged with leadership accountability, that expert has to go the extra mile to convince the project leader and team members to accept his or her expert advice (see figure 8.2).

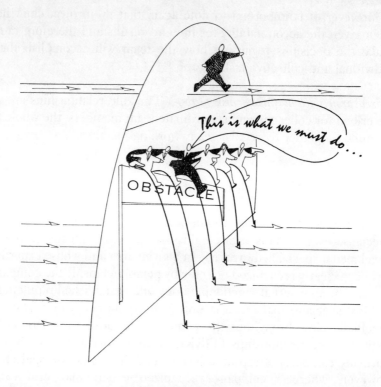

Figure 8.2   Specialist expert

A Note on "Matrix Organization"

This approach to project team leadership resolves the well-known problems that are attendant upon so-called matrix organization. "Matrix management" was developed in response to the need for tailor-made project teams, with their apparent "two boss" arrangement: the home base manager and the project team manager. But, instead of separating out the two different sets of accountabilities and authorities as we have done, a short-cut was taken by holding the two managers jointly accountable. And, to make matters worse, this organizational mix-up was generalized to a theory of all organizations and management and was applied everywhere, with continuing disruptive effects ever since.

Matrix organization will not work effectively any more than free-floating teams. They both undermine decisive managerial leadership and project chief leadership. Accountability for work progress and outcomes must always be clearly assigned and it must be assigned into the hands of one person only. Split accountability and "group accountability" cannot and do not work, and they most certainly are inconsistent with the requirements of competent managerial leadership. The project team processes that we have described provide for effective project team leadership without so-called joint management.

9

Manager-Once-Removed (MoR)
Leadership Accountability

The great importance of the requisite role of the manager-once-removed (MoR) has not been generally recognized. There are, by and large, no solid terms of reference for talking about the role. It is currently a rare situation in which MoRs are accountable for the career development of individuals; in most instances, they serve merely to rubber stamp the performance appraisal judgments of a subordinate manager. The manager-once-removed role is crucial in any managerial hierarchy.

The MoR role spans three separate organizational strata in the hierarchical structure: starting at the bottom of this three-stratum mutual recognition unit (described in depth in Chapter 10) with the subordinate at one stratum, his or her immediate manager at the next higher stratum, and finally the manager's manager (the manager-once-removed) at the second higher stratum from the subordinate. The subordinate-once-removed is referred to as the SoR. The MoR role thus involves on-going working relationships with both the intermediate level manager (his or her immediate subordinate) and the SoR.

The overall focus of MoR leadership is on carrying out the following main accountabilities:

- Ensuring that the quality of managerial leadership effectiveness of subordinate managers is satisfactory, including the quality of the task-initiating role relationships which have been set up by them.
- Being accountable for assessing the current potential of SoRs and matching their individual career aspirations with organizational requirements.

- Mentoring SoRs with respect to the use of their potential capability and career development and helping them to grow in wisdom.
- Building and sustaining three-stratum level teamworking, e.g. stratum–VII/VI/V; stratum–V/IV/III.
- Achieving equilibration across subordinate work units; that is to say, ensuring that opportunities and burdens, good and bad conditions, are applied equitably across all subordinate roles.

Failure to be clear about the requisite functions associated with the MoR role will undermine all other efforts at improving organizational effectiveness. Given a lack of clarity, many of the accountabilities which should be properly associated with the MoR role get piled on to the immediate manager's role. And because there should be a one category difference in capability between the manager and the MoR, tasks inadvertently assigned to the manager instead of the MoR will simply not get done effectively. Since the focus of the MoR role involves the future talent pool in the company as well as overseeing the quality of the organization's overall managerial leadership climate, any shortcomings in role specification will be serious. Organizations that want to get their people moving in a common direction with enthusiasm and initiative must pay adequate attention to this role, and establish its accountabilities and authorities.

The MoR has a special working relationship with his or her SoR. On the one hand, he or she is accountable for making decisions regarding key current issues such as assigning an SoR's role to a specific pay band or approving an SoR transfer, while, on the other hand, he or she is also heavily involved in the SoR's future through assessing potential, career counseling, and mentoring (see figure 9.1).

To carry out the full range of accountabilities, the MoR must have the following role vested authorities:

- Approving authority for all transfers and promotion actions which might be initiated by the SoR's manager.
- Final decision-making authority in the event of a dismissal action.
- Deciding within which pay band in a given organizational stratum an SoR role should be placed.
- Assessing the current potential of their SoRs.
- Deciding appeal actions pertaining to the SoR.

In many ways, for the SoR, the MoR represents the organization. The SoR's manager sets tasks and rewards personal effectiveness,

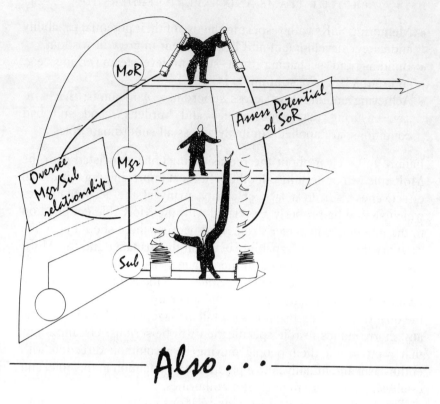

Also...

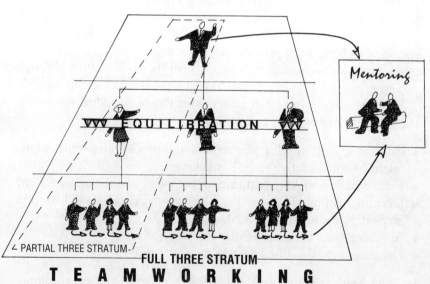

Figure 9.1 Manager-Once-Removed (MoR) leadership accountability

but it is the MoR who personifies the organization in providing longer term career opportunities for the SoR. It is the MoR who has the accountability to recognize potential and to ensure that the SoR has the opportunity to contribute to the organization's objectives to the full extent of that potential. And it is the MoR who is accountable for ensuring that the SoR is being fairly treated by his or her immediate manager. Finally it is the MoR who mentors the SoR about career aspirations and possible development action.

The relationship, therefore, while based on the role vested authority of the MoR, is a very personal one since it applies so strongly to the SoR as a person and to his or her future. The MoR is seeking to ensure the retention of SoRs, who are judged to be of value, as a part of the company's talent pool and to ensure their development to accept more senior responsibilities in the future. In order to assess the potential of SoRs and to be able effectively to counsel them on their future careers, MoRs must be proactive in getting to know their SoRs.

Such a relationship will not be effective if the SoR does not respect and trust the MoR. This leadership recognition must be personally earned by the way in which the MoR carries out the requisite practices; for example, MoRs must be proactive and consistent in their efforts in getting to know their SoRs. Not only must MoRs be competent in carrying out potential assessments but they must also ensure that they know their SoRs well enough to be able to make such judgments in the first place. MoRs must be open to discussion and to the initiatives of SoRs regarding their career development aspirations, and they must see to it that any mutually agreed development actions are carried out. MoRs must demonstrate fairness and openness in promotions, transfers, and dismissals.

It requires tact and skill on the part of MoRs to ensure that they do not weaken or interfere with the relationship between SoRs and their immediate managers. They can accomplish this aim by clearing all contacts with SoRs with the SoR's immediate manager and by never allowing any discussions with an SoR to focus on the immediate manager. It is important that the MoR does not solicit or accept any views that SoRs might offer up regarding their manager. In other words, there should be no surprises as far as the immediate manager is concerned as a result of MoR discussions with SoRs. MoRs are to remain focused on mentoring and career development by conducting potential assessments and discussions regarding the SoR's prospects in the company.

Finally, MoRs should not get involved in coaching, task assigning, or personal effectiveness appraisals, since these are critical leadership accountabilities of the immediate manager, and must not be interfered with.

Overseeing the Quality of Managerial Leadership

MoRs need periodically to evaluate the leadership effectiveness of their subordinate managers. The manager–subordinate relationship is a delicate one, in that it places a great deal of authority in the hands of the manager that could adversely affect the subordinate. When organizations are set up requisitely, managerial authority needs to be tempered by the presence of strong MoRs performing their oversight function. MoRs can perform the oversight function by observing the behavior of their SoRs either directly or as a normal result of carrying out their MoR accountabilities. Such observations can suggest to them whether their SoRs are focusing their energy on assigned tasks and working at the full capability required of the role. Further, MoRs can assess the quality of existing working relationships by observing the extent to which SoRs appear to collaborate and work effectively together and with outsiders.

MoRs can also directly observe the behavior of the subordinate manager. Does the manager treat subordinates with respect and dignity? Are tasks being carried out in an apparent climate of fear or one of trust? Do the managers look after their subordinates or appear to use them for their own benefit? Each of these respective indicators, while not necessarily constituting perfect predictors in and of themselves, can combine to form a generalized picture for MoRs of the leadership effectiveness of their subordinate managers.

MoRs need to be especially on the lookout for possible clashes between subordinate managers and SoRs. Sometimes such clashes are easily observed, whereas at other times they can only be discovered by carefully analyzing the quality of the manager–subordinate relationship, looking for the presence or absence of commitment, openness, trust, and collaboration in the behavior of the SoRs. By and large, SoRs will not readily confirm that they may be experiencing problems with their manager, unless their situation has deteriorated into something very negative. To complain about one's manager ordinarily runs counter to individual and corporate values of loyalty, or it may be that an SoR could simply be afraid of repercussions or be inhibited by guilt. Thus, many SoRs simply grin and bear it and go about their work in the best way that they can. Such situations are hardly conducive to reinforcing enthusiasm, initiative, and trust. It is incumbent upon the MoR to be watchful and wise in his or her observations (see figure 9.2).

Figure 9.2   Overseeing the quality of managerial leadership

MoRs must take advantage of opportunities to get to know their SoRs through periodic meetings and through work. In addition, they should create opportunities that require their subordinate managers and their subordinates-once-removed to work together as a team in meetings with the MoR present and they should evaluate the overall effectiveness of the manager–subordinate interaction.

The mentoring process required of the MoR, which is described in depth on pp. 253–5, offers another opportunity for data gathering, During this process, the MoR is expected to develop some sense of how SoRs feel about the opportunities in their work. Cumulatively, he or she will get an impression of SoRs who feel that they are being given challenging work and are respected by their managers, and those who do not have positive feelings about the work that they have been given to do and/or the way in which they are treated by their manager.

MoRs should look for signs of possible stress in the SoR. For example, has the SoR become very formal in his or her working relationships; do SoRs collaborate with others only as a result of outside pressures? MoRs should also be on the alert whenever one of their immediate managers complains about the quality of work being produced by an SoR. Such complaints could signal the beginning of possible long-term problems with an SoR which, if left unsettled, are eventually brought to the MoR's attention anyway in the form of an adverse pay decision, deselection, dismissal or other similar personnel action. When apprised of continued deficiencies in an SoR's personal effectiveness, the MoR is entitled to know what the immediate manager plans to do about the situation. The MoR must judge how effective the plan is and subsequently how effective the immediate manager's techniques were in attempting to correct the situation. It may be necessary to make a visit to the workplace of the SoR to assess the situation in its natural setting.

MoRs should also be on the lookout for mixed signals or inconsistencies when talking with SoRs about their career development aspirations, but should take care not to jump to premature conclusions from any one conversation or piece of information regarding a particular SoR. He or she must make judgments by interpreting a combination of all the data collected.

The judgments made by MoRs about the quality of the managerial leadership of their immediate subordinates, who are managers, must become an active element in personal effectiveness appraisal discussions. Such discussions, plus coaching related to quality of managerial leadership, are among the most powerful instruments available to any company that seeks to sustain high-quality, decisive managerial leadership.

Assessing SoR Potential

One of the major responsibilities of MoRs is to make judgments about subordinates' current potential capability, that is, the level at which an SoR would be capable of working if the SoR had had full opportunities to gain the necessary knowledge and skilled use of that knowledge and experience for the work. These assessments are always subject to change and must always be checked against the SoR's own assessment.

There are many faulty assumptions associated with the assessment of potential. First, there are unrealistic beliefs about what others are striving for, such as the incorrect belief that, career wise, everybody in the organization aspires to move upward and that people below us in the hierarchy want to be where we are, or even that everybody wants to be at the top. Second, we tend to underestimate how realistic individuals are when assessing their own potential. Individuals do not seek to break themselves by progressing above their felt capability. They do seek work which is consistent with their current potential and for progression to match their future potential. There can, however, be differences between the more inflated view that people might state publicly about their current potential, in order to bolster their self-esteem, and that which they state and know privately.

An important safeguard in achieving sound evaluations of an SoR's potential is to require the MoR to share and discuss all assessments of potential with the SoR before firmly committing himself or herself to a judgment. If the SoR is not happy with the assessment, then the MoR should have to leave the judgment open pro tem until he or she has had a chance to investigate it more thoroughly or, at the very least, formally note that the SoR does not agree with the assessment.

Many organizations teach interviewing skills and make reference to reading body language and other communication techniques, such as neurolinguistic programming, when carrying out the assessment process. Our experience, however, is that the teaching of knowledge about cognitive complexity together with holding substantial discussions with an SoR about opportunities within the company are much more powerful, accurate, and meaningful instruments.

MoRs may experience guilt and anxiety about making judgments concerning an SoR's current potential capability, since these judgments are of such importance to the SoR (and his or her family). It is of the greatest importance, therefore, to recognize that assessments of potential are not value judgments about the individual's character or personality, but rather an attempt to reach an accurate evaluation of potential in the best interest both of the individual and of the company.

A second safeguard with respect to the evaluation of SoR potential by an MoR is to implement firmly the requirement that no judgments of potential shall be made unless accompanied by mentoring. It is in the mentoring process (which is described more fully below) that the SoR can experience the full consequences of the MoR's judgment, and can have the full opportunity to put forward his or her side of the issues. Such mentoring is a process that ensures that every individual can be treated with due care and concern and can have the opportunity for continued justice.

The following are a series of on-going actions to be taken prior to the actual assessment. MoRs must engage in a number of serious talks with their SoRs. It is also useful if, with the agreement of the SoR's manager, opportunities can be made from time to time to bring the SoR up to work on projects with the MoR. This opportunity allows the SoR to become acquainted with some of the issues and problems at this higher level in the organization and allows the MoR opportunity to observe first hand the extent to which the SoR has matured in his or her cognitive processing. MoRs must also evaluate the quality of the SoR's approach to current work. For example, is there evidence of novel approaches? Is the SoR at ease with the difficult tasks in the current role? Are interactions with others appropriate and within limits? Does the SoR approach his or her work with enthusiasm?

By observing the SoR in his or her current role and in project work with higher level individuals, the MoR can evaluate whether the SoR is beginning to be able to do the level of work required of his or her manager. One of the most important techniques that MoRs can use is to see if they can picture the SoR working directly for them. If an MoR can picture a subordinate-once-removed as a direct subordinate and can envision that person handling work at the immediate subordinate level, the MoR must recognize the SoR's matured capability and put him or her forward for promotion to the next level within the immediate unit or elsewhere in the organization (see figure 9.3).

Finally, MoRs can assess the cognitive processing of SoRs by

Figure 9.3   Assessing SoR potential

means of recently developed methods for identifying the use of each of the cognitive processes. Such an approach is one of the practical applications of the description, presented in Chapter 2, of cognitive processes, orders of information complexity, and categories of cognitive complexity and how to recognize them.

Before conducting a mentoring interview, the MoR must set aside time to think about the career of the SoR. The MoR should check his or her sources and ensure that he or she has adequate first hand experience, as well as other reports concerning the SoR. The MoR must be confident that this evidence is sound. The SoR must also have been given adequate time to consider his or her own future and, prior to the interview, the MoR might want to prompt the SoR to think about significant events in his or her career to date.

Prior to the actual evaluation interview, the MoR should make a tentative judgment with regard to the SoR. The MoR is accountable for these judgments and must recognize that evidence may come forward in the interview to change the judgment. The critical questions to consider and answer are shown in figure 9.4.

In the light of these judgments, the MoR should sketch out a possible career development program for the SoR which will be the primary focus of the discussion in the interview. The MoR should initiate the discussion by obtaining the SoR's view of significant achievements in his or her career to date and career aspirations. The MoR should then relate these views to his or her judgment of the SoR's potential. There is little point in discussing any future development program until these judgments are clear. If there is disagreement and the SoR believes that his or her potential has been underestimated or overestimated, this disagreement must be resolved prior to the development program discussion.

Once an individual's potential assessment has been completed, the discussion should turn to career development needs. These needs should be discussed in terms of areas of development, the general objectives, specific means of achieving these objectives, by whom and by when. It may not be possible to specify all of the actions at the interview or to be sure of who will do what, since development may involve training by the manager, transfer, or other courses of action.

When the outline of the development program has been agreed upon, there may be the need to do further work to confirm the details (i.e. specific actions and accountability). Also the MoR must note the comments of the manager and the SoR once the program is confirmed and a review date set with the SoR. By closely following these necessary procedures for assessing potential, MoRs have set an example for all of their SoRs who may currently be accountable for groups of their own SoRs or who in the future may be assigned an MoR role.[1]

Gearing the MoR's Judgments of Current and Future Potential Capability of SoRs

There are two possible major distortions of the judgment by MoRs of the current and future potential capability of SoRs. The first distorts judgments of particular individuals. The second generally overestimates or underestimates the potential of all of their SoRs. The following procedures can prevent such distortion of judgment. Both procedures

1 Is the SoR's current potential capability sufficient for the level at which his or her current role is established, i.e., the level at which the role is being paid? (In other words, would the individual be just right if he or she valued the work, had the necessary knowledge and skilled use of that knowledge, and the experience in using it; or, perhaps, would he or she be just right for some other role in the same organizational stratum but in a different type of work?)

YES ☐ Sufficient for established level of current role
NO ☐ Insufficient for established level of current role

(a) If the answer is NO, at what level below the current role does the subordinate have the current potential to operate; and what do you propose to do to correct the situation?

(b) If the answer is YES:
    (i) Would the individual be placed in the bottom, middle, or top third within the stratum in terms of his or her current potential, i.e. is he or she only just in the stratum, solidly in it, or approaching the top?

    Bottom ☐ Middle ☐ Top ☐

    (ii) Does he or she have any problems with respect to:

    Values ☐ Skills/knowledge ☐
    Wisdom ☐ Temperament (-T) ☐

    (iii) What do you propose to do about any problems?

2 Do you think that the SoR has, or will have, the potential to work at the next higher stratum, for example, as one of your immediate subordinates?

Immediately: if so, is his or her current potential only just in the stratum, solidly in it, or approaching the top?

Bottom ☐ Middle ☐ Top ☐

In 1–3 years ☐
In 3–5 years ☐
Beyond 5 years ☐

If so, what is your development plan?

Figure 9.4 MoR's pre-interview evaluation of SoR

are based on the mapping of judgments of potential of SoRs on progression data sheets, as described in Chapter 11.

The first gearing procedure is for an MoR to plot his or her judgments of the current potential of all of his or her SoRs on a progression data sheet. Then the MoR should examine the mapping with two aims. First, he or she should compare the judgment of the current potential of each SoR with that of the others, adjusting these judgments until satisfied that the SoRs are placed at proper levels in relation to each other with respect to current potential.

Next, the MoR should examine the consequences for future potential of each individual by extrapolating along the progression bands into the future. It is useful to plot the current potential of two or more of the MoR's immediate subordinates (i.e. individuals currently in the next higher stratum to the SoRs whose current potential is well established and known to the MoR). Then the MoR should compare his or her judgment of each SoR's potential with that of the others, so as to gear them with respect to their relative position in following up the same or higher or lower progression bands (modes).

By this procedure, MoRs can examine the consistency of their judgments about their own SoRs.

The second gearing procedure is for the immediate manager of a group of MoRs to sit down with all of them together, and to compare the general pattern of each one's SoR judgments with that of the others. For example, a stratum–VII CEO sits down with his or her stratum–VI EVP subordinates. The MoR judgments of the stratum–IV SoRs of each of the EVPs are plotted on one progression data sheet with a different color for the population of SoRs of each EVP.

By this multi-colored mapping, the CEO and the EVPs can compare the general level of judgment of each EVP. Thus, for example, one EVP might have a population of SoRs most of whom are judged to be towards the top of stratum IV in current potential, while another EVP's SoRs have been judged to be largely towards the bottom of stratum IV. In such a case, the CEO and the EVP colleagues can consider whether this difference would seem to reflect an accurate picture of the situation, or whether they judge that one or other of the EVPs, or both, are generally biased upwards or downwards with respect to their judgments. This kind of gearing exercise has a salutory effect upon MoRs in tightening up their judgments.

Mentoring

All subordinates yearn for someone above them to sit down with them and discuss their careers and the future opportunities available within the company. This applies to not only those subordinates with continued growth potential ahead of them but also those who have matured to full potential but none the less still seek assurance of continued employment. The presence of such opportunities can make an extraordinary contribution to effectiveness supported by high morale and commitment. It is the MoR who must be held accountable for such mentoring discussions.

Mentoring is not a process that can be taken lightly as something that takes place only if and when an MoR finds time. SoR development is too important to both the SoR and the company to be left to chance. Every organization must devise a carefully thought out strategy, properly emphasizing and matching career development needs with future organizational requirements. Too often, however, the process boils down to a few lucky individuals being taken under the wings of a patron who takes it upon himself or herself to look after their careers. Such arrangements are all well and good for the lucky few, but what about the rest of the human resources of a corporation; are they left simply to fend for themselves? If so, corporations must be willing to accept the consequences on individual behavior and morale. Such consequences may be that many of these individuals look out for themselves and develop a sense of careerism or eventually leave. A process that values focusing unduly on one's own individual needs is likely to be at odds with and undermine the development of a more desirable set of corporate values.

Every corporation needs a planned strategy to ensure that all of its people are afforded an opportunity to meet with their managers-once-removed and discuss their careers, their continued growth in wisdom and experience, and their future in the enterprise. The organizational role best suited to take up this accountability is the MoR role, for two reasons: first, it is the MoR and not the immediate manager or human resource specialist who needs to be held accountable for succession; second, it is the MoR and not the immediate manager who is far enough removed from the SoR in terms of capability and experience to be able to discuss the SoR's current potential and likely future career opportunities. Every corporation's human resource development strategy must firmly root this accountability in the MoR role and not in the personnel or human resources department. Here is a definition of the process.

Mentoring is the process by which a manager-once-removed helps subordinates-once-removed:
- to understand their potential and how the full use of that potential might be developed to achieve as full a career growth in the organization as possible;
- to grow in wisdom and the exercise of judgment, and to achieve as full a use of their capabilities as they themselves seek and as opportunities in the company allow for.

People, with few exceptions, seek to work to their full capacity. This desire constitutes a prime individual value which everyone holds. Thus, companies must make provision, so far as work opportunities allow, for people to move up in level of work at a rate consistent with their maturation in potential capability. This kind of progress must be the cornerstone of any human resource development plan. The mentoring process is central to the building of such a plan (see also Chapter 11 on human resource development).

MoRs must sit down periodically with their SoRs and discuss their assessment of the SoR's current and future capability as well as the career needs of each SoR (see figure 9.5). This kind of discussion is necessary even for plateaued employees who need to be reassured that there is a continuing role for them in the company.

Next, MoRs must have in mind an individual career development program for every SoR. Such a development program for plateaued employees may include identifying future work experiences which would give the SoR an opportunity to expand his or her repertoire of skills in new areas, i.e. new technology or new production methods, within the same stratum of work. For the SoRs who are continuing to mature to the next stratum of work, this development program includes identifying future work experiences which would give the SoR an opportunity to grow, and helping the SoR to understand the frame of reference and full role requirements of work at the next higher stratum. These career development discussions and subsequent development programs constitute the link between the SoR's individual entitlement to have the opportunity to work at full potential and the working opportunities that are actually available.

MoRs are also accountable for maintaining their own SoR talent

Figure 9.5   Mentoring

pool. This means that MoRs must ensure that their high potential SoRs are given, as far as is practical, a challenging range of opportunities to work to their full potential. One method of doing this is by adding new functions, as far as the work allows, to an SoR role as these functions are needed or as they are available for reassignment from elsewhere. MoRs can also provide occasional opportunities for their SoRs to work for them as direct subordinates in a direct output support role (DOS). (This support role is fully described in Jaques [1989].)

Every MoR must also ensure that SoRs are never denied upward mobility because of current work demands. MoRs must be willing to approve positive transfers and/or promotions, as appropriate for the development of the individual and to meet the current and future needs of the organization for well trained, talented people.

Equilibration

MoRs need to ensure equity across their subordinate work units. An important safety valve is placed in the hands of the MoR in the form of appeals, but that is effective only after problems arise. There needs to be an additional constructive mechanism which goes beyond appeals and which satisfies an individual's need for a sense of fairness and justice.

Such a mechanism is the equilibration process. MoRs must maintain a fair balance by ensuring that all of their managerial subordinates operate in a consistent and fair manner. To ensure that equity is achieved, MoRs must make cross comparisons between the approaches to work and the practices employed by each of their subordinate managers. MoRs must provide SoRs with continuing evidence that someone is in charge of ensuring equitable treatment across the organization (see figure 9.6).

Figure 9.6 Equilibration

MoRs need to ensure that their managers, individually and collectively, are neither too easy nor too tough on their people. For example, some managers may tend to give higher merit awards, leading to subordinates being bunched at the top of a pay band when there is no evidence that their capability in fact falls at the top. The solution to this particular situation is for each MoR to be on the alert for such practices, and to correct them by coaching the particular manager involved. By contrast, it is counter-productive to try to correct or prevent such practices by requiring some artificial normal distribution. Such forced distribution systems serve as a crutch for poor managerial leadership and hurt an organization's good people.

MoRs also need to ensure that the task assignment process is seen as equitable in terms of opportunity, challenges, and interest. For example, in a stratum–IV operating unit, the stratum–III manager routinely volunteered (or at least tacitly approved of using) the people from one section for all of the so-called "trash" jobs, such as clean up detail, and for inconvenient overtime. Eventually, this practice frustrated the stratum–II first line manager of the constantly "volunteered" section, who was attempting to build a cohesive work team while simultaneously trying to rationalize the additional work load with his team members. This rationalization became an impossible task for the first line manager because he could not justify the work load with his people *vis-à-vis* other equivalent sections.

The stratum-III manager, throughout this period, was either oblivious to the unrest seething throughout the first line manager's team or he did not care. Meanwhile, the stratum–IV general manager (the MoR) was content because, as far as he was concerned, the work was getting done without any apparent difficulties. Unfortunately, the MoR was unaware of the depth of hostility that the problem was generating throughout the SoR's work group. It was only after the first line manager resigned that the MoR had any inkling of trouble.

This example of what happens when an MoR has failed to ensure work equity across his or her sub-units is not uncommon and can happen at all levels of the organization. It is specifically the MoR's task to ensure that inequities like this do not occur in his or her three-stratum work units.

Handling Tough Situations and Hearing Appeals

MoRs are accountable for ensuring that justice and fairness are operating values throughout their organizations. One of the ways in which they do so is in the handling of tough situations and appeals.

By tough situations we mean those where an MoR's immediate managerial subordinate wants to deselect, demote, or dismiss an SoR; or where there are real and serious personality differences between the manager and one of his or her subordinates. Such situations should not come as a surprise to an MoR. MoRs should be monitoring the gradual development of serious problems with SoRs as a routine part of carrying out their everyday managerial account-abilities. Appropriate monitoring allows MoRs to ensure that all possible preventive actions have been taken such as sufficient warnings, adequate coaching, and additional training. There should be no real surprises for an MoR, if the managerial system is working properly.

MoRs must be on the lookout for SoRs who may be heading for trouble. They may discover such individuals while assessing the quality of their immediate manager's leadership effectiveness or as a normal part of their mentoring and potential assessment process; or the individuals may be brought to their attention by subordinate managers as they are carrying out their normal managerial accounta-bilities. Regardless of how MoRs discover that someone is in trouble, they must ensure that prompt effective action is taken. For example, so-called clashes of personality are most often evidence of an anti-requisite organizational situation. MoRs would be wise to assume that such is the case until it can be proven otherwise. MoRs must identify what is wrong in such situations and take appropriate corrective action (see figure 9.7).

When a manager-once-removed first discovers possible problems with an individual SoR, the MoR must dig into the situation to ensure against any victimization. The MoR must keep a close watch on any such situation to ensure that the SoR is receiving adequate coaching. When a subordinate manager has made up his or her mind to recommend a specific action, the MoR needs to explore possible alternatives; if there are none, then he or she must be prepared to take such actions as to retrench, demote or downgrade an SoR to a lower pay band.

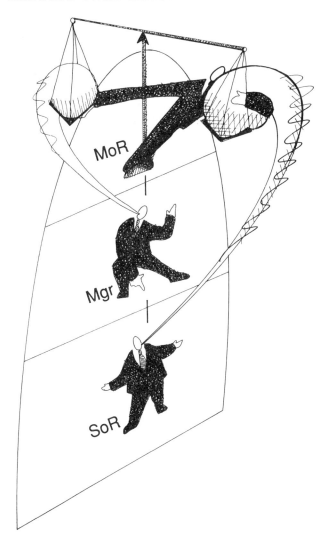

Figure 9.7 Handling tough situations and hearing appeals

In the final analysis, of course, the troubled SoR should be able to have recourse of appeal to the MoR. But if MoRs do their work properly, very few such appeals should occur, because the MoR should have seen and sorted out the problem beforehand. Effective MoR work of this kind not only supports the managers but also reinforces the trust of SoRs in the system.

However, when an appeal does occur, the MoR must attempt to handle it as judiciously as possible. He or she should sit down together with the SoR and the intermediate manager, and review all the facts as seen by both. This gives the opportunity to get a systematic picture of what has been going on. One matter that must first be considered is whether or not the SoR's appeal is really a dissatisfaction about some matter of policy which the manager had no choice but to carry out; in such a case, the manager must be exonerated, and the policy issue itself becomes the object of debate.

If the appeal is a true appeal (i.e. not an issue about policy), the MoR is faced with deciding whether the manager has in fact been behaving unjustly towards the SoR. Has the manager been too tough, or been handing out unfair assignments, or been giving inadequate opportunities, or been taking any of a hundred other actions that might give the SoR the feeling that he or she is being shabbily treated or victimized?

Such appeals are delicate situations. The MoR is faced with deciding whether or not a managerial subordinate is exercising fair and just managerial leadership, and whether the SoR is or is not justifiably aggrieved. One way or another, the MoR will have to decide, and the decision can be difficult.

The decision itself must be stated openly to both parties. But the matter does not end there. If the decision is for the SoR, then an immediate personal effectiveness appraisal and coaching discussion is called for with the intermediate manager. If the decision is for the manager, then an immediate mentoring discussion is called for with the SoR. Either way, a difficult situation has arisen and needs to be cleared away as constructively as possible by follow-up discussion.

On the negative side, every appeal is evidence of at least some degree of failure on the part of the MoR effectively to anticipate trouble and to take action to sort it out. On the positive side, however, the successful working through by an MoR of any appeal that does occur is a major contribution to the reinforcement of trust throughout the organization.

Three-Stratum Teamworking

In any large-scale organization, anonymity is a problem. There are two ways of reducing this problem. The first is to establish an organizational structure which is appropriate for the bottom three strata. The second is to establish and operate a three-stratum team at each level of the organization. Each of these will be discussed in greater detail below.

Anonymity sets in when a group exceeds 300 people in size, even if all of the individuals are working in the same room. To avoid anonymity, organizations need to create work units where all of the work members are able to at least recognize the MoR, the intermediate managers, and each other. Such a unit is called a Mutual Recognition Unit (MRU).

The ability to at least recognize each other is fundamental to the building of cohesion. Cohesion fosters a sense of identification and belonging and generates a feeling of participation. A cohesive unit is more flexible during stressful times. Cohesion is instrumental in building good morale, a necessary (but not sufficient) condition for the release of every individual's full potential and initiative.

The stratum–III MRU is the highest organizational level where all of the variables influencing the work situation are directly observable and the manager is still able to see his or her whole operation. By the same token, MRU managers must physically go to the work site of all of their output teams, since MRU managers cannot successfully lead their MRUs if the unit work force does not at least recognize them when they see them.

The three-stratum team is the foundation for building vertical cohesion in the corporation and for ensuring the development of leadership effectiveness. It is interpersonal in the sense that it is not anonymous. Because all of the players are able to recognize each other, the three-stratum team-working mode can be a powerful addition to a company's set of critical working relationships (see figure 9.8).

The focus of the MRU is to build unit cohesion by setting work practices which are consistent with the site and business unit philosophy and culture. MRU managers must ensure that they run mutual recognition units that consistently meet assigned targets and that they always act as credible role models in the process. MRU managers must be seen by their work force as having upward influence on their site managers. They can do this by exercising their advisory accountability and authority directly with the site manager, and not be seen as abdicating this responsibility to the site manager's staff specialists.

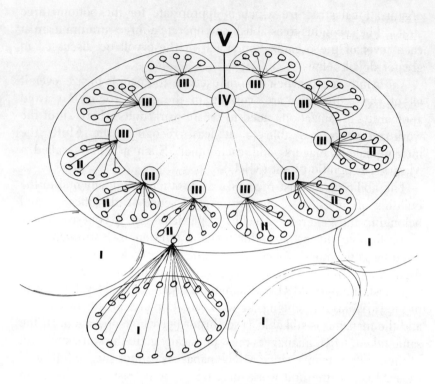

Figure 9.8   Three-stratum teamworking

MRU managers need to build cohesive mutual recognition units by ensuring that they set effective work practices. These practices must be consistent with the site and business unit culture and should never be seen as wasting subordinates' time, e.g. in ineffective and unnecessary practices. The MRU manager must also establish an effective MRU communication program. This can be done by ensuring that much of his or her time is spent physically at the site and by conducting periodic meetings of the entire unit. While on site, the MRU managers will want to focus on relevant effectiveness indicators (see Chapter 10, corporate culture) and to take any corrective actions necessary.

MoRs need to bring their three-stratum team together often enough to mold them into an effective working group. One useful means of doing so is to meet periodically with each of their immediate managers and that manager's immediate team of subordinates. Such meetings can be held, as appropriate for the occasion, either in the business meeting mode, to review performance results and plans and priorities, or in the team-working mode, to provide for free up and down exchange of views and ideas (see section on teamworking). MoRs must keep their three-stratum teams informed about each other's tasks and must provide for equilibration across the whole team, i.e. interchange personnel, if required, and assign tasks of comparable difficulty. Equilibration is described more fully on pp. 256–7.

While the above description is about the stratum–III to stratum–I mutual recognition unit (MRU), it applies equally to three-stratum teamworking at all levels: the corporate chief executive officer, executive vice-presidents, and business unit presidents (stratum–VII to stratum–V); the executive vice-presidents, business unit presidents, and general managers (stratum–VI to stratum–IV); the business unit presidents, general managers, and unit managers (stratum–V to stratum–III); and the general managers, unit managers, and first line managers (stratum–IV to stratum–II). When such teamworking cascades effectively down the organization, it can be a very powerful force for vertical bonding from top to bottom and can have a markedly enhancing impact upon working effectiveness (see figure 4.14 *The Cascading MRUs*).

Note

1 Development work is currently underway to validate training material and criteria to assist MoRs in making judgments about an individual's potential, as described in Chapter 2.

10

Organizational Leadership

A critical challenge facing all senior executives is how to exercise effective managerial leadership over their whole organization. In organizations with four or more strata, it is not physically possible for the CEO to build and sustain an effective interpersonal relationship with all employees. While all senior executives must continue to exercise good managerial leadership practices with their immediate staffs, they cannot rely on such practices when dealing with the entire corporation. Is there not something extra which must be done by CEOs in order to influence everybody or must they simply sit back and rely solely on the actions of subordinate managers operating two, three, four or more strata below them?

The answer to this question is that there is a set of specific practices that must be carried out if the senior executives in any organization hope to lay a strong foundation for everybody's moving in the same direction in an enthusiastic and innovative manner. These actions are not a matter of choice for a senior executive to carry out or not to carry out. They are executive imperatives. Together they constitute what may be referred to as organizational leadership.

In organizations with four or more strata, anonymity sets in. It is no longer possible for a manager to recognize each employee individually, as is possible within the three-stratum mutual recognition unit. This circumstance does not mean, however, that managers in these larger organizations can no longer influence their whole organization. But to do so demands that they adopt special means which we shall group under the heading of organizational leadership.

Thus, organizational leadership accountability is the exercise of leadership accountability from one to many. It includes accountability for setting direction and winning the collaborative support of all employees collectively, at all levels in the organization, to work effectively and to move in the direction set. In order to describe this process, we shall need definitions of two basic concepts: corporate vision and corporate culture (see figure 10.1).

Corporate vision is the longest forward direction for the corporation's business growth and development, which is set by a CEO in consultation with the board. It is the vision and direction that establishes the time-span

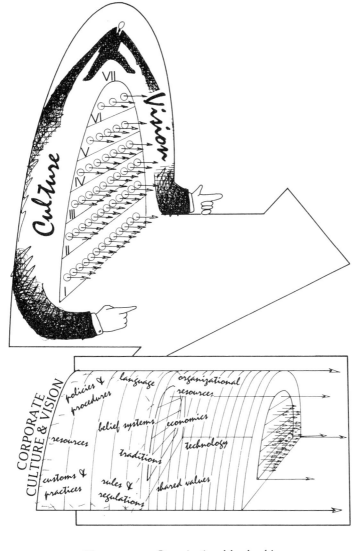

Figure 10.1 Organizational leadership

and priorities of the CEO role. Indeed, it is the ability to set a practical operational vision and to work towards it that expresses the time-horizon and therefore the level of capability of the CEO.

Corporate culture comprises the established ways of thinking and doing things in the institution and includes the company's policies, rules, and procedures; its customs and practices; its shared values and belief systems; its traditions and assumptions; and the nature of the language used to communicate throughout the company.

The essence of organizational leadership is that the managerial leader is in a working relationship with all subordinates at all successive strata at one and the same time, even though he or she does not know them all or communicate face-to-face with them all. The manager delivers the same message to everyone at the same time, using various company-wide communication processes, and establishes a common context with everyone in the same way, not relying on interpretation by intermediate managerial levels. This process is essential for achieving a shared outlook across the whole organization and for establishing a unified company culture.

Organizational leadership accountabilities vary by strata, each stratum being in a nested relationship with all lower strata. That is to say, each manager, when attempting to apply policies, clarify procedures, and establish traditions, values, and beliefs about the nature of the organization's goals and how they are to be achieved by employees, must take into account both the vision and the culture set by the most senior manager (and, where it applies, the interpretation of his or her own manager).

In particular, stratum–VII CEO organizational leadership is concerned with setting and sustaining an effective corporate vision and culture which exemplifies the vision and culture of the board for which the CEO works. Stratum–VI is concerned with the interlocking/gearing of the corporate culture and vision with and between the stratum–V business unit cultures. Stratum–V business unit presidents give organizational leadership to their whole unit by maintaining a sound business unit culture which is consistent with the corporate culture, and so also do stratum–IV general managers on separate sites. The output of effective organizational leadership is to forge a sound corporate context within which people can work together effectively and creatively towards achieving the overall direction set.

Corporate Culture

CEOs can win the hearts and minds of their people by creating a corporate setting that provides the necessary conditions for encouraging all employees to move in a common direction, to operate at their full individual capacity, and to do so willingly and enthusiastically. CEOs can achieve such a setting by building and sustaining a corporate culture that establishes appropriate constraints for subordinates within which to carry out their work.

By modifying the various elements of culture, the CEO has a direct impact on behavior because culture sets limits for each individual's behavior. A prime act of CEO organizational leadership is to create and sustain a corporate culture that provides a strong setting for an effectively working company (see figure 10.2).

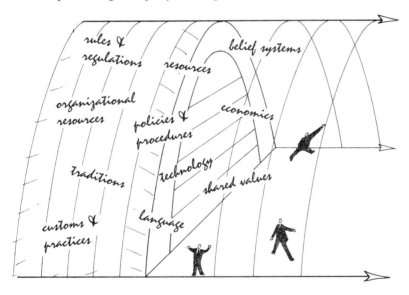

Figure 10.2 Corporate culture

In addition to its culture, every institution is made up of the following major interdependent components, each of which has a pronounced impact on individual and unit performance.

• Technical resources   The underlying nature of a corporation's basic technical orientation; the technology of the production process; the focus of the research and development efforts.

- Economic resources   The institution's capital assets; the sales and marketing process; stocks; inventories; and other financial resources.
- Organizational resources   The size of the establishment of work roles for the whole company, and the numbers and types of roles available at each stratum.
- People   The capability and outlook of the actual people employed.
- Corporate direction   The vision and goals for the institution which describe both the type of organization that it is intended to be in the future and the overall position that is sought for it in the world economy.

Recognizing the interdependent nature of these components, the CEO can integrate them so as to achieve a multiplier effect on individual and unit performance. Effective integration requires that the CEO set clear direction for the corporation and communicate that direction effectively to all employees. The CEO must then allocate the resources necessary to accomplish assigned tasks and missions. He or she can check on what subordinates are doing by reviewing resourcing issues and synchronizing the allocation of resources with the corporate planning process. Failing to resource subordinate efforts adequately undermines the building of an optimum corporate culture. Underpinning effective organizational leadership is the continuous achievement of long-term economic success of the enterprise, such that individual employees are able to develop a feeling of stability and job security.

CEOs win personally earned authority from their whole company by carrying out the above tasks effectively and by demonstrating a firm grip on their work. In addition, they must demonstrate the ability to sustain a sound corporate culture, modifying existing culture as necessary to achieve their on-going corporate vision. In order to carry out these critical CEO tasks, they must conduct periodic culture reviews by determining the internal congruence and soundness of existing policies, rules, practices, traditions, values, and beliefs; by reviewing and evaluating the corporate climate, and by assessing morale.

As we have noted earlier, culture is made up of a number of interrelated parts. Because it is generally described as one comprehensive whole, it has been difficult to examine the parts in relation to the whole. It is possible to feel overwhelmed when addressing culture issues and thus to ignore or overlook the effects of any change of individual parts on the whole. And, even if we address specific aspects of culture individually, it is often difficult to assess the resultant effect on an institution's culture as a whole. These difficulties can lead to unwanted or unplanned inconsistencies or negative effects.

Overseeing and adapting culture is a major part of CEO organizational leadership. As CEOs drive their corporations towards the desired future objective, they need to ensure that the corporate culture is consistent with getting there and that the parts are internally consistent with each other. Therefore, top level corporate executives must periodically review the various parts of the culture to discover any possible inconsistencies and must consider such questions as:

- Do compensation policies actually pay more salary to employees who perform more complex tasks?
- Do the vagaries of managerial language stand in the way of training for decisive value-adding managerial leadership?
- Do restrictive financial control procedures conflict with the company's valuing of individual initiative?
- Have customs and practices that inhibit continuous improvement grown up?

A company's culture either facilitates the accomplishment of the organization's goals and objectives or it interferes with the process; it is never neutral.

Changing an organization's culture is not a separate goal in itself. Culture changes are designed to achieve future corporate objectives. In contemplating changes which are necessary to pursue the company goals, CEOs should make good use of their senior corporate staff by seeking their advice and counsel regarding the likely impact of any culture changes. Prior to implementing any actual change, for example in corporate policies or procedures, CEOs should allow time for their executive vice-presidents to discuss the anticipated changes with their own subordinates. This process allows the stratum–V subordinates to anticipate the likely effects of any proposed changes on their unit's effectiveness and to discuss the impact of such effects with their stratum–VI executive vice-presidents. In taking part in such interplay, the stratum–V executives are actively participating in the culture development process. This outcome is essential for guarding against the negative effects of unplanned or unwanted change and for gaining commitment regarding the planned change. It is important to note that there are pieces of the corporate culture which are driven right down to the shop- and office-floor level (such as corporate compensation policies) and other aspects of the culture which stop at various organizational strata (such as foreign exchange policies, which apply primarily at stratum–VII to stratum–V). Taking these differences into account is necessary in order to determine how far down in the organization that discussions should take place as part of the process for achieving culture change.

Once a change has been adopted, but prior to full implementation, CEOs should make use of the three-stratum team-working process (described on pp. 260–3). Using this three-way interplay allows executive vice-presidents to discuss any impending change with their stratum–V executives and to help them to understand what is likely to happen. Knowing what is likely to happen allows the executive vice-presidents and stratum–V executives to figure out how best to absorb the change into the stratum–V organizations. Sharing experiences and wisdom, in adapting to change, with stratum–V executives is one of the ways in which the stratum–VI executive vice-presidents add value in an organization.

At least once a year, the stratum–VII CEOs should bring together all of their stratum–VI and stratum–V executives in a working meeting to review the corporate culture by discussing overarching issues affecting the corporation. It is at such meetings that some of the more seemingly abstract aspects of culture can be reviewed; for example, the creeping growth of counter-productive customs and practices, or subtle shifts in values or beliefs or assumptions which might be deleterious. Having such changes identified, formulated, and then widely understood is the necessary foundation for modifying them.

Corporate Values

If CEOs want to win personally earned authority and use it to get everyone in the organization to move in the direction set, then they must find ways of achieving corporate values which not only are consistent with the business aims but also enable employees to feel that their own personal values and the company's values are in line with each other. Aligning corporate and personal values is no small trick, since values are elusive and often difficult to articulate. Yet, the resultant impact of values on behavior is pronounced.

Values are the prime drivers of behavior. They determine what we choose to do and how much energy we put into each effort. It is critical for CEOs to be sure that the values existing within the corporation are supportive in getting all of their people to move effectively, enthusiastically, and with their full capability in a common direction.

Values can serve as a great unifying force, provided that both organizational values and individual values are reasonably congruent, because they bind people together as they move toward the achievement of the objectives of the organization (see figure 10.3).

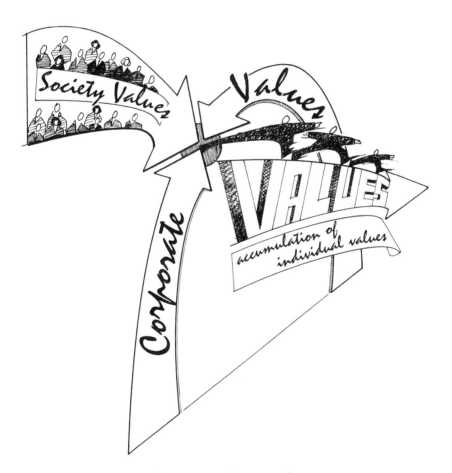

Figure 10.3 Corporate values

Alternatively, dissonant and conflicting values are great generators of friction and stress, which undermine managerial leadership and stand in the way of movement in a common direction.

Every organization's culture is shot through with a web of interdependent values. Some of these are the values that individuals hold, some are clearly articulated organizational values, and some reflect the operating values of the CEO and his or her corporate managers acting as significant role models.

Sometimes there is conflict between various sets of values; for example, the valuing of a flat versus a high differential pay structure, or the placing of different values on managerial versus individual contributor roles. Or, there may be inconsistencies between stated values and actual behavior. For example, a CEO publicly stated that he encouraged candor throughout the organization but, whenever confronted with bad news, he punished the messengers. The CEO's staff, having witnessed their manager being continually stressed by the presence of a seemingly endless parade of problems, put out the word to everyone to couch all CEO briefings in an optimistic vein. While the CEO felt better, none of the hard issues was being properly addressed. His subordinates were frustrated: one resigned, and two others sought transfer. The organization suffered as a result.

To the extent that the web of values is internally consistent, work performance can be enhanced. To the extent that there is inconsistency, performance will be diminished. It is a prime act of CEO organizational leadership to ensure not only that these value sets are consistent with each other but also that each and every manager throughout the company comports himself or herself in a manner consistent with the values.

Every institution must embrace a set of general core values which are fundamental to developing effective working relationships within the organization. We would suggest that the organizational philosophy must, as a minimum, place strong value upon the following.

- Mutual trust, confidence and reliability   Working relationships are specified in such a way as to build a solid foundation of mutual trust between people; everyone is confident that the organization has sought and retained sufficient human assets who possess the necessary capability to perform assigned tasks; people can be counted on to carry their weight.
- Fairness and justice   People are treated equitably, recognition is

related to personal effectiveness; there are opportunities for individuals to appeal against felt injustice or unfair treatment.

- Openness, with freedom from fear and central decree Everyone is free to express their true opinions within working relationships; opportunities for participation in context setting and policy making are available.
- Recognition of the value of the individual Everyone working at every level in the company is entitled to be treated with respect and dignity as a valued employee of the institution.

The corporate organizational structure, systems, principles, and policies must be consistent with the organizational philosophy (embracing the values described above) and must be seen obviously to be so.

In addition, there is a set of values which is stated by the company as the kind of behavior that it expects from its employees:

- Integrity: to behave honestly.
- Commitment: to express one's full potential capability and energy in work.
- Reliability: to be counted upon consistently to do what is expected or required.
- Initiative: to originate new ideas or methods without being asked.
- Co-operativeness: to work together with others for the common purpose.

Finally, there is a category of values which encompasses what individuals are entitled to expect as employees of the corporation:

- Clear accountability and authority specifications for all roles.
- Competent managers.
- Opportunities to participate in task assignment and policy development.
- Challenging work: opportunities to use individual working capacity to the fullest.
- Timely managerial feedback regarding personal effectiveness.
- Fair differential remuneration based on level of work.
- Assurance of continued employment so long as there is no redundancy and the individual continues to be capable of doing the work.
- Entitlement to be adequately advised of vacancies and to be provided with an equal opportunity to apply and be considered.

These value sets are interdependent in the sense that each affects the other in an exchange process. Individuals are likely to become committed, trustworthy, innovative employees provided that the organization offers a setting in which the values are genuinely shared and genuinely expressed in both planning and the implementation of plans, and in actual behavior. The onus is on the company to take the first step in this exchange process because it is the employing organization. If the company's managers treat people in accord with the company's core values, it has the right to expect everyone to respond accordingly with commitment and effective work.

CEOs need to ensure that the organization's policies, procedures, and practices reflect both the general core values and those values stated as important to the individual employees. Because of the significance of role modeling on subordinate value development, the CEO's personal conduct assumes particular importance. CEOs must function as appropriate role models for the whole organization. Their personal behavior must reinforce corporate values. If they cannot operate within the corporate philosophy which embodies the various value sets, they cannot expect their subordinates to do so. The consistent carrying out of the requisite practices that we are describing is one of the most important role modeling actions that any CEO can take.

Corporate Vision

It is impossible for CEOs to get all of their people moving along in a common direction if they do not have a clearly articulated conception of where they are trying to take the company. A vision of where the organization is going and what it might look like in the next 10 to 20 years sets the long-term direction. CEOs must personally take the lead in setting the corporate vision. This task cannot be delegated to subordinate strategic planners. It is the CEO who must be clear in the first place because the issue has been worked over in his or her mind. The confidence of all employees is heightened from knowing that their CEO has a clear idea of where he or she is going, is setting the pace to get there, and understands the necessary processes.

This vision statement is essential for inculcating throughout the organization the secure feeling that the CEO is on top of things and knows where he or she wants to take the company. Specific corporate objectives to be pursued in the future flow from this vision statement. The articulation of a corporate vision statement allows subordinate organizational elements to align their own sense of purpose and direction and is essential for building group-wide consensus (see figure 10.4).

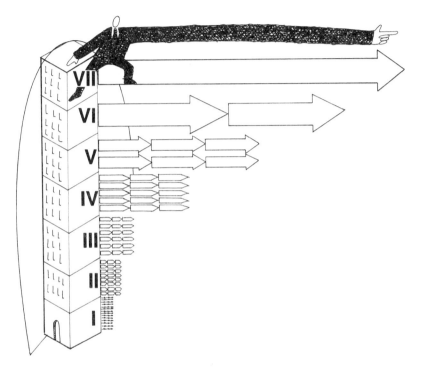

Figure 10.4 Corporate vision

The CEO, having identified where he or she wants to go, must devise the means for getting there. Corporate strategy states the pathway that the CEO wants to follow in striving to achieve his or her vision. Corporate strategy flows from the company's mission statement and consists of the major thrusts that the CEO sees the company embarking upon in order to achieve the objectives flowing from his or her vision of the corporation's future. The CEO must make clear to his or her people how corporate strategy is developing, so that they may be able to know where they are going and what will be expected of them to get there. Strategic thrusts, in turn, have to be broken down into critical tasks by each stratum–V business unit as part of the corporate planning process. It is this process that conveys to employees the realities of the CEO's vision and of the corporate strategies (see figure 10.5).

Figure 10.5 Impact of corporate culture

The Gearing Function at Stratum–VI

The prime act of organizational leadership at stratum–VI is helping to interlock or gear corporate culture and the CEO's actions with the culture and work of each business unit. The CEO's vision, strategy, and major strategic thrusts constitute the context for the goals and objectives at lower strata. The linkages between corporate strategy and business unit plans need to be clear and well geared to each other. It is up to the stratum–VI managerial leader to ensure that a good fit is achieved (see figure 10.6).

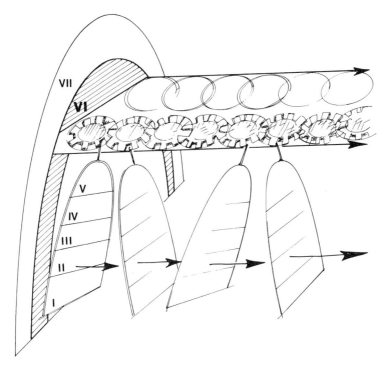

Figure 10.6 The gearing function at stratum–VI

Stratum–VI organizational leadership includes the following sequence of seven critical tasks:

1 EVPs should provide business unit presidents with a clear picture of corporate culture and an overall understanding of the larger context of the corporation's business.

2   EVPs should secure necessary resources for the optimum utilization of individual business unit assets by negotiating within the corporate collegial group for the resources needed by each business unit president.

3   EVPs should strive to create as friendly a business environment as possible for each business unit by working to change and adapt the political, economic, social, technical, and intellectual (PESTI) (see Jaques [1989]) environment to the advantage of each business unit; for example, by seeking changes in government policies, or in the priorities of research institutions, or in the outlook of financial institutions toward the company.

4   EVPs should continually work to secure a good fit between business unit requirements and corporate strategy and planning.

5   EVPs should assist business unit presidents in translating the CEO's directional statements and the corporate philosophy into appropriate policies for each respective business unit.

6   In collegium (as a group of equally empowered members), EVPs should help to develop corporate-wide systems for implementing corporate policies and principles; for example, the remuneration system.

7   EVPs should evaluate business unit experience in order to determine instances where the corporate culture may need modification and should take appropriate recommendations back to the CEO for consideration.

In discussing proposed culture changes, the stratum–VI executive vice-presidents must work closely with the stratum–V business unit presidents and in such a way that there is real input from the latter in policy development. The stratum–VI executive vice-president performs an important gearing function in the stratum–VII to stratum–V mutual recognition team (see Chapter 9 for expanded discussion of this concept) with regard to resource allocation changes, vision or strategy changes, and culture changes. After the stratum–VI executive vice-presidents and the CEO have agreed to a culture change, the stratum–VI executive must help the business unit presidents to figure out how best to absorb the change into their business units.

   Stratum–VI executive vice-presidents must be sensitive to the impact and consequences of changing culture upon the working effectiveness of the organization. They can use their three-stratum

(VI–V–IV) mutual recognition teams as a sensing device for discerning where business unit presidents and general managers stand on given culture issues. The three-level mutual recognition team should also be the forum for bringing issues into the open where corporate change is required.

Stratum–V Business Unit Leadership

It is the organizational leadership accountability of business unit presidents to set effective business unit culture. Each business unit has its own unique culture within corporate culture and, as with corporate culture, the effects of business unit culture are never neutral; they either facilitate getting work done or detract from the process.

The corporate culture at stratum–VII/stratum–VI sets the limits within which business unit presidents must run their organizations. Every business unit has its unique set of policies, rules, and procedures which is specific to that entity (see figure 10.7). For example, policies regarding working relationships with unions can vary widely across business units, as can safety regulations. Whenever business unit policies, rules, and procedures become inconsistent with their corporate counterparts, problems emerge.

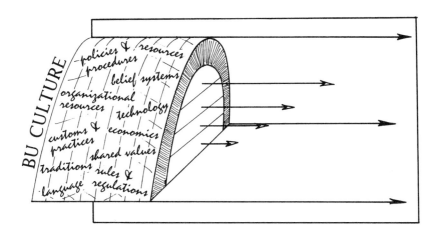

Figure 10.7 Business unit culture

Similarly, every business unit will have its unique values. Stratum–V leadership must be oriented towards the creation of values within the business unit which are a consistent expression of the broader context and objectives. These values include the sense that people have about how they should or should not behave, about the kinds of behavior that are favored or frowned upon, and thus affect their personal status, chances for meaningful work, and opportunities for the future. These business unit values are very much in the foreground, silhouetted against the corporate culture in the background. When the business unit values are inconsistent with the corporate values, confusion exists. Such confusion reduces everyone's working effectiveness. Some individuals will take advantage of competing values and adhere to those which best meet their needs. Inconsistencies between the business unit values and corporate values will undermine the efforts of the business unit president to get everyone to move along in a common direction effectively and creatively.

Just as leadership at stratum–VII must be oriented towards setting values and culture for the total organization, so leadership at stratum–V must be oriented towards the creation of a culture within the business unit that is a consistent expression of the broader corporate context and its objectives.

Stratum–V leadership, expressed via business unit culture, is thus the organizational means of linking corporate values to the actual working behavior of each individual. Without such a link, corporate values remain static and irrelevant, and so a matter of indifference to people. If, however, policies can connect the valued commitment that is sought from everyone with the valued entitlements that individuals seek from the company, then the whole place can come alive, and everyone is freed to express their initiative, enthusiasm, and imagination in their exercise of discretion and judgment and in their decision-making. A useful example would be not only the placing of strong value upon continuous improvement but also the demonstrated expression of this value in such practices as the establishment of *ad hoc* project teams to deal with stubborn problems, and in the responsive recognition by managers of improvements achieved by subordinates in the ordinary course of their work. Given such active expression of stated values, the sustainment of effective continuous improvement is no longer a problem: It simply occurs.

The business unit president exercises organizational leadership by attending to the business unit policies, rules and regulations, customs and practices, and values of the business unit culture (see figure 10.8). It is these control mechanisms that convey the most powerful messages about what is acceptable, even more so than any stated values could do. Thus, if it is desired to establish a culture and climate of mutual trust and creative initiative, there must be control mechanisms that allow for these things, rather than rules and regulations that mitigate against the use of imagination, and scream out that no one can really be trusted. Just as personal freedom requires structure and is impossible in anarchy, creativity and innovation also flourish best in a nurturing structure.

Social structure and organizational values must be consistent, or else people become confused and develop cynical attitudes towards the organization. Sustaining a sound organizational structure is the necessary foundation for business unit organizational leadership. There must be an optimum alignment of functions to satisfy the

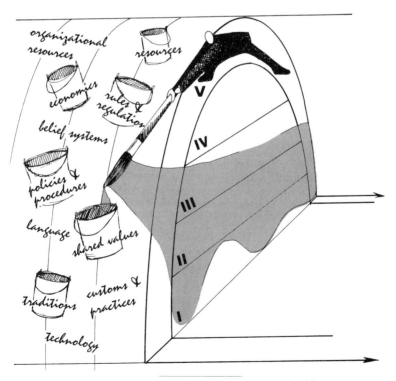

Figure 10.8   Stratum–V business unit leadership

needs of customers. The president must identify all essential functions and ensure that each is clearly assigned to a general manager role. The president must periodically review all of the functions to ensure that conditions have not become so altered that it is necessary to differentiate out a given function into a separate stand-alone role. This means that the president must review the work assigned (or associated in any other way) to each stratum–IV role to ensure that there is adequate time for the role incumbent to accomplish all tasks associated with each critical function. Presidents must not hesitate to realign functions to roles, as required.

Effective communication with the entire business unit must be maintained, including making good use of the three-stratum team-working mode, involving meetings of the president with general managers and unit managers. Such meetings can be an excellent means of getting feedback from the entire business unit organization.

Presidents should regularly visit major business unit sub-units and talk with subordinate managers and their teams. They should use these opportunities to keep the work force apprised of the current business unit status. Presidents should be careful, however, to avoid dealing directly with individuals at lower strata on specific issues. Any details pertaining to such issues must go through the regular managerial line. The president can, however, accumulate information regarding specific issues to get a generalized feel of the effectiveness of the unit and its culture.

On appropriate occasions, the president should consider communicating directly with the whole business unit about events of major importance to the entire work force, such as the approved business unit annual plan.

Presidents should seek means of giving personal recognition to individuals who are identified by their managers as having manifested superior effectiveness. Such recognition reinforces standards of excellent work throughout the unit.

Finally, business unit presidents can have a most substantial impact on the deep-seated establishment of continuous improvement within a company. They can do so, for example, by means of policies and procedures that require the regular and sustained use of special project teams at all levels in the unit, who are engaged in overcoming the unanticipated problems that will always be encountered and that do not fall neatly within the on-going established accountabilities in any specific role.

Stratum–IV Site Leadership

It is the site general managers who play a critical role in the communication of the organizational philosophy so that it really has an impact upon those at stratum–III to stratum–I, the people who carry the heavy load of the large-scale, cost-generating production work. And where there are free-standing sites, located away from headquarters, the site general manager has duties similar to the business unit president in maintaining a healthy site culture, as described in the previous section.

Whether on a separate site or not, however, it is the stratum–IV general managers who are at the highest level where it is still possible to have a direct sense of the social climate and working effectiveness of the shop and office floor. General managers are at the level where the culture, including the values flowing down from above, meets the operating values and experience flowing up from below. The general manager has to manage discrepancies as they arise, modify what he or she can, and interact with the business unit president where he or she considers that business unit culture needs to be changed.

In order effectively to perform this critical organizational leadership role, stratum–IV general managers are required to establish a two-way mutual communication interaction with the three layers of organization below them; with stratum–III managers as immediate subordinates, stratum–II managers as subordinates-once-removed, and stratum–I employees who are key opinion formers (see figure 10.9).

This last point must be duly noted. The interaction with key opinion formers (stratum–I individuals who occupy influential positions with their peers), either on an *ad hoc* or an institutionalized basis, can be extremely valuable for seeking consensus on shared values and commitment when there are wide spans of control. Whenever the stratum–IV general manager is able to interact with key individuals working at stratum–I, this allows for true two-way leadership interaction in the formulation of local values and of agreed ways of doing things.

The general manager should make regular use of the three-stratum team-working mode, i.e. general manager–unit manager–first line manager. General managers should meet face-to-face with each of their unit manager-led teams at least quarterly to keep them

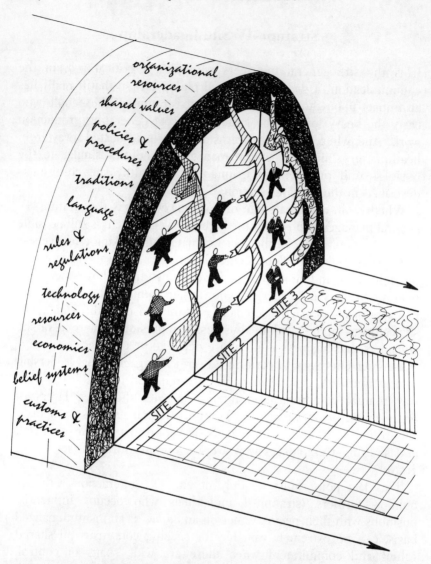

Figure 10.9 Stratum–IV site leadership

informed about how the site is doing. In addition, site general managers should talk to their entire work force from time to time to inform them of the overall site picture. General managers can and should talk to the whole work force more often when the situation demands, such as when there are major technological changes and problems, or a major change in strategy.

Organizational Communication

Organizational communication is necessary when organizational leaders wish to convey the same information to all of their subordinates at the same time and in the same way (or as near simultaneously as circumstances will allow). These organization-wide communication events are necessary in order to describe directly, to everyone at the same time, changes in vision or strategy, the introduction of new policies, and/or major business developments. Managers should use organizational communication whenever there is a situation which affects all members of their organization equally, regardless of role (see figure 10.10).

When a manager wishes the same information to reach everyone, he or she should convey that information to everyone by the most appropriate media and not leave it to managers to pass the

Figure 10.10   Organizational communication

information down through the managerial hierarchy, i.e. he or she should not use subordinate managers as telephone switchboards.

Managers should, under ordinary circumstances, call a meeting with their immediate subordinates before making an organization-wide communication. This type of team meeting could include using the three-stratum team-working mode.

In the case of stratum–VII/VI communications, which impact on the whole company, it is more effective to communicate via the stratum–V business unit president and to leave it to the stratum–V executive to decide how best to handle the communication within the business unit. Various communications can stop at different strata in accord with the judgment of the business unit president. Thus, the business unit president acts as an important gate-keeper in the organizational communication process.

11

Managerial Leadership Development Program

What we mean by a managerial leadership development program is a program for ensuring that a company has the necessary supply of managerial leadership talent of the right kinds and also the numbers flowing up the hierarchy at a rate necessary to fill the oncoming company requirements for managers with strong competence in all respects including the discharge of leadership accountability.

A managerial leadership program is not a crown prince program. It does not tap individuals on the shoulder and designate them as the future CEO of this, or the future president of that, or the next EVP of the other. Those decisions can be made only at the time a vacancy occurs or is planned for. No company can give advance guarantee of any specific role for anyone, unless and until someone's impending retirement or transfer has been announced and someone else is appointed as a designated successor, to take up the role immediately and to be assisted in induction by the existing incumbent.

Nor is the managerial leadership development program, which we believe to be requisite, a program for modifying people in this or that psychological trait or temperamental characteristic. Teaching an understanding of the underlying nature of human behavior is useful, but for an employer to try to modify and manipulate the personalities of employees focuses attention away from the hard down-to-earth work that needs to be done, and is likely to prove ethically questionable into the bargain.

Nor should it be a program for somehow matching the personality make-up of members of teams so that the sum total of the personal qualities of the members is conceived to meet the personality requirements of the "group." Nor should it be a program in which managers and subordinates share personality analyses of each other so that they can handle each other better. We have tried to emphasize that effective managerial leadership development lies elsewhere. It lies in the hard realities of sound organization with competent managers (with the necessary cognitive capability, values, knowledge, and wisdom) using requisite managerial practices, and in everyone's behaving in their own natural manner while exercising self-control over possibly disruptive personality characteristics.

The managerial leadership development program that we shall propose has two essential components. The first component comprises methods for translating the changing company plans into numbers and types of role which will probably need to be filled, and for reviewing and evaluating the existing personnel in terms of the match between a future requirement, say in 1 year, 3 years, and 5 years, and the appearance of the available company population at those times. The second component is a program for the evaluation and career development of individuals, to fit in with the over-arching company plan.

We shall deal with these issues in this chapter. First of all, we shall present means of looking at categories of current employees at all levels, and ascertaining the relationship between what a company may have in various categories at various levels and what it may need now and in the planning future.

Second, we shall look at the conditions for individual career development within the requirements of the company, focusing upon the provision of experience and education that will extend knowledge and its skilled application and enhance wisdom by teaching and by use.

Underlying this program is the assumption that a managerial talent pool control room will be set aside. This is a room in which a stratum–VII CEO and his or her stratum–VI EVP subordinates can survey all of their stratum–V and stratum–IV subordinates, whose photographs, ages, and qualifications are displayed on small magnetic plaques which are set out on magnetic panels, organization by organization and in categories of future potential.[1] The room should be available for use also by stratum–V business unit presidents and their stratum–IV subordinate general managers.

At least once a quarter, and as frequently as once a month during periods of rapid organizational change, the corporation CEO and his or her corporate team of EVPs (or the stratum–V president and

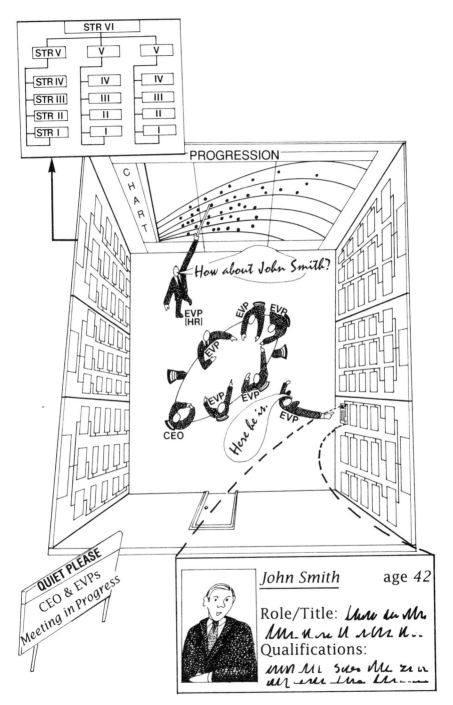

Figure 11.1 CEO's managerial leadership talent pool control room

stratum–IV GMs) should meet in the control room to consider their up-and-coming talent for filling their likely vacancies for the succeeding one to three years, taking into account retirements, new ventures and developments, and possible circumstances such as unexpected leaving, or illness, or sudden market shifts, or other business crises or opportunities (see figure 11.1).

The problem, of course, is how to represent the talent pool in a way that gives a meaningful picture of its development, of what it will be like in one, two, three, or five years. Just such a method of representation becomes possible by the use of the cognitive progression data sheets that we discussed in Chapter 2. We shall now illustrate their use in "K Corporation."

Mapping the Corporate Talent Pool

We have described a number of practices that, once used, facilitate the construction of a comprehensive picture of the available talent in the company. These practices include:

- MoR appraisal of potential of SoRs.
- MoR mentoring and career development of SoRs.
- Application of the concept of the maturation of potential capability in terms of mode, as set out on the potential capability progression data sheets.

Given the data from these practices, a picture of the talent pool can be created as shown in figure 11.2. This chart is displayed on a board in the talent pool control room and, once one has learned how to read it, it makes it possible to see all at once the total movement of the potential corporate talent pool that is subordinate to one of the operational EVPs. The particular chart illustrated shows the judged current potential of all of the immediate subordinates (5) and all of the subordinates-once-removed (38) of "John Appleby," who is the Stratum–VI operating EVP of K Corporation.

K Corporation is an integrated corporation, organized in 7 levels – or strata – and employing 17,000 people. It trades through 8 separate strategic business units, organized into two groups each of which is subordinate to an operational EVP. It has two large corporate research laboratories led by an EVP, a range of corporate finance, legal, taxation, and related services, and a small international shipping fleet. Its corporate human resources (HR) work is carried out by an EVP–HR who is assisted by a small high-level staff at stratum–V.

Appleby (JA) himself is 54 years of age, is judged (by the board) to have the current potential to work at mid-stratum–VI, and is being employed and paid at that level. He is judged as mid-mode–VII in

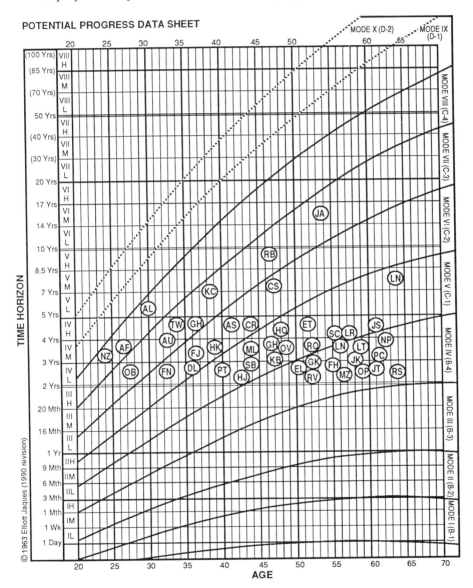

Figure 11.2   Mapping the talent pool

future potential but has been told (and he himself realizes) that, by the time he matures in potential to low-stratum–VII, he will be just too old (60 years or more) to be in the running for the corporate CEO position that will become vacant when the CEO retires, as he has stated that he plans to do, in three to four years' time.

Appleby has a good and effective group of immediate subordinates. The judgment of potential of those subordinates has been made by Appleby's manager, the corporate CEO, who is their MoR. AL, KC, and CS have settled in well to stratum–V work; AL in particular, who is 30 years of age, shows great promise for corporate-level work in a stratum–VI EVP role by his late 30s.

RB, however, is an active problem: he is clearly ready now for stratum–VI work but no opportunity is immediately available in the corporation. The CEO has mentored him, however, on a number of occasions over the past few years, and he has agreed to stay on for the time being, because at least two stratum–VI EVP positions (one by retirement, a second by new growth) will become available in the next few years and he is to be considered for both of them (i.e. considered along with others, not promised the vacancy). LN will be retiring, and possible replacements are available at stratum–IV (see figure 11.2). At stratum–IV, Appleby has 38 SoRs, every one of whom he has mentored on several occasions during the past three years, in addition to having seen each of them at work and socially on many other occasions, in site meetings, on special projects, and in other circumstances. He has a number of excellent and stable situations and also a number of problems.

First, there is a strong and stable group in mode–V, all but one of whom (ET) are at least six to seven years away from the stratum–V boundary. This group currently expresses its future potential in greater imaginativeness at the stratum–IV stage of their maturation. They will be strongly bolstered by the high-flyer (fast track) group of 12 mode–VI, mode–VII, and mode–VIII individuals, all but four of whom (GH, AS, CR, and TW) have four or more years before they will be ready for stratum–V work. These last four, plus ET, constitute something of a problem group, since all of them are now ready for promotion to stratum–V and will become restive if they do not have the opportunity to progress.

In fact, Appleby began discussions with each of them two years ago, against a background of discussions in the CEO's HR co-ordination meetings, at a time when there were reasonable possibilities of opportunities opening up for all of them in the divisions of his colleague-EVPs. But conditions have tightened since that time, and he is in the process of arranging for planned leaving for two of them. The other three have decided, pro tem, to hang on for one or two years to see what opportunities at stratum–V, for which they might apply, will actually occur. The CEO supports this move, since it retains three of his highest future potential people ready for work at stratum–V, where they will strengthen the talent pool of potential stratum–VI EVP replacements in 10 to 15 years' time.

The Corporate Talent Pool

The overall pay-off, however, from this method of charting the talent pool comes from consolidating the EVP chart shown in figure 11.2 and similar charts for each of the other EVPs into one chart showing all of the stratum–VI to stratum–IV personnel. Such a chart is presented in figure 11.3. Although it may appear crowded at first sight, the eye can quickly enough learn to pick out a range of features (and it is, of course, much easier when it is possible to use multiple colors).

First, direct comparisons can be made of the state of human resources in various EVP divisions. One of the operating divisions is jammed into mode–IV and mode–V, and is making no contribution whatever to the corporate talent pool. Its performance has been solid but lackluster for some time. In sharp contrast is the treasurer's division ((●) see figure 11.3): nearly every one of its members is a fast tracker, and it is likely to continue making a substantial talent contribution at corporate levels. This prediction is strengthened by the fact that, although not shown here, this division also has a rich supply of young mode–VI to mode–VIII individuals currently at stratum–III.

It is this composite chart that is the centerpiece at the CEO's meetings for co-ordinating human resources. The CEO and the EVPs have in front of them the following information.

● Who is retiring when.
● Who is ready for promotion to the next higher stratum:
  ● now;
  ● in a year or two;

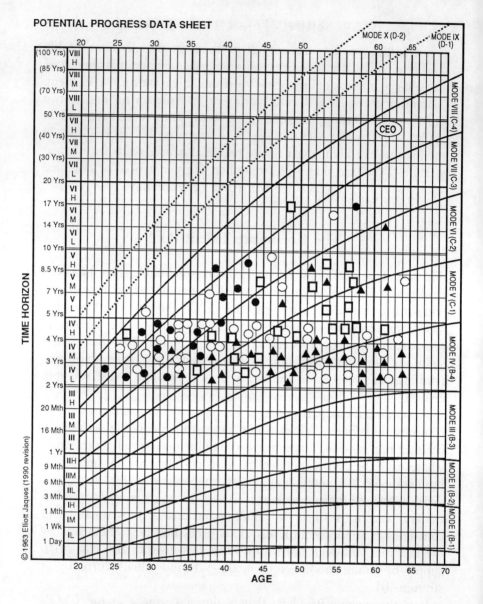

Key

▲ = Operating Division
● = Treasurer's Division
○ = Manufacturing
□ = Engineering

Figure 11.3 The corporate talent pool

- in three to five years;
- in five to ten years.
- Where the talent pool riches are.
- Where there are too many pressing into the next stratum.

The issues can then be elaborated and detailed by reference to each of the division charts which are also hung on the boards, thus facilitating consideration of the possible domino effects of changes, or the need and opportunities for lateral transfer to foster the development of particular individuals.

CEO Succession and Other Mappings

As an aside, it will be apparent that the corporation also has a potential problem at the very top. The stratum–VI group has reasonable potential, but not strikingly so. The only likely internal successor, within the next four years, for the current CEO is the corporate treasurer. As it happens, he is considered by the board to have the necessary knowledge, skill, and values for the position. But, even so, it is likely to be eight to ten years before he has matured far enough into the mid-stratum–VII level of capability needed to sustain the corporation's competitive position. It is unfortunately only in the last year that the board has come to face the fact (aided by its first use of this talent pool mapping process) that it might want to search outside for a successor to the CEO, who ideally would be in mid- to high-mode–VIII and would already have the potential to work at least at low- to mid-stratum–VII.

This datum, the current (and future) potential of the CEO or, indeed, of a manager at any level, in relation to that of his or her immediate subordinates, is probably the most important single piece of information that a board (or a manager-once-removed) can have. Figures 11.4a and 11.4b illustrate two more such situations. Figure 11.4a is relatively balanced, in that the CEO is ready to move across a boundary and, if all goes well, will take the organization into the next higher stratum, with a group of five immediate subordinates all ready to move up to a next higher stratum. Figure 11.4b, by contrast, manifests a problem: a CEO towards the bottom of the stratum, with at least two younger thrusting subordinates beating against the boundary of promotion but with no obvious place to go. The possible patterns are obviously infinite.

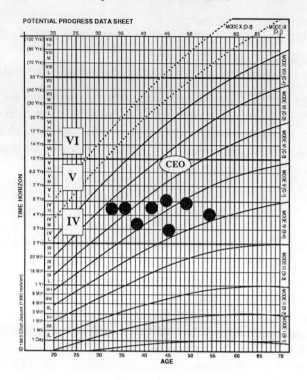

Figure 11.4a   CEO Succession

In addition, many other analyses and models can be set out. These models are not illustrated here, but their description should be self-explanatory, as should the value of their application. Here are just two such examples:

- Plotting of all of the members of particular professions or those with special qualifications, e.g. all accountants; all engineers; all computer specialists; all marketing and sales executives.
- Plotting everyone who is known to be either under- or overpaid for the level of work that they are carrying, and/or employed at a level of work either above or below that consistent with their judged current level of potential. All that is necessary is to place a colored dot on the marker of all individuals whose judged current potential is significantly out of line with their current level of work or their pay. Such a chart allows a review of all personnel anomalies and can show up starkly those areas of the organization that have more than their share of anomalies.

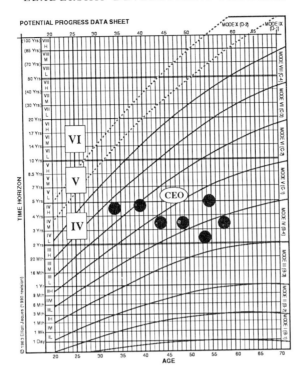

Figure 11.4b CEO Succession

The foregoing describes a comprehensive method for mapping the talent pool of a corporation in dynamic terms; it is not only a mapping of the present situation but also a mapping of the present in such a way as to show the potential of the current pool unfolding into the near-term, mid-term, and long-term future. As we said at the beginning, however, there are substantial assumptions built into this method that must be clearly recognized: namely, a basic standardized system for the structuring of organizational layers, i.e. the strata from I to VIII; a means whereby systematic manager-once-removed judgments can be made of the current potential capability of subordinates-once-removed; and the progression data sheet whose curving bands, we suggest, represent the natural maturation of potential capability throughout the full period of early, middle, and late adulthood. These assumptions are far-reaching and need to be argued. Before doing so, let us draw attention to two principles that we have been using; we shall explain their rationale in the course of our argument below.

The first principle is that we have taken mode–V to mode–VIII to contain the so-called high-flyer or fast track group of individuals. We have done so for two reasons. The first reason is that the individuals in these modes are the ones with the potential eventually to reach the true corporate strata, which, as we have shown, occur at stratum–V and above. The second reason is that practical experience has shown that senior corporate executives understand that these individuals hold the corporate future in their hands, and it is precisely this group that is consistently and intuitively picked as the "high-flyers."

The second point is that we have limited our mapping of the corporate talent pool to those currently in stratum–IV and above. This stratum is the one that can be encompassed by the corporate CEO (at stratum–VII or even at stratum–VIII in the super-corporation), with the help of the stratum–VI EVPs. And, having moved into stratum–IV, this group contains those who are moving to within shooting distance of the corporate levels at stratum–VI.

Stratum–V BU Talent Pools and Graduate Interns

A complete mapping of the total membership of a corporation's talent pool requires the establishment of a second set of talent pools; namely, a talent pool for each stratum–V business unit and containing everyone at stratum–III to stratum–I. The procedure operates in the same way, except that it is now the president of each strategic business unit who carries the accountability for reviewing his or her talent pool up to stratum–III, aided by the team of stratum–IV subordinates. By examining these mappings, the corporate CEO, the corporate HR EVPs, and other corporate executives can obtain a picture of their corporate talent pool in great depth; i.e. the population of mode–VI to mode–VIII people who are currently at stratum–II and stratum–III and who will become the corporate executive candidates in ten and twenty years' time. In short, the assessment of potential and career development of individuals should occur in the business units when they are still at stratum–I, II, or III. When, however, they are promoted to stratum–IV, their career development and future opportunities should move up to become a corporate matter.

In the same vein, graduate interns (or associates or management trainees, as they are sometimes called) need to be evaluated within the business units at general manager and president level. General managers should act as MoR to the interns who are judged capable of working with category B–3 complexity projects, and the president should act as MoR to those judged capable of category B–4 work.

The president together with the general managers should review the intern population at least half-yearly. The purpose of the review would be to pool knowledge so as to increase the accuracy of evaluation of the potential capability of each intern, and to ensure that the interns were being effectively employed and progressed (see figure 11.5).

One of the outcomes of such a review would be to identify those interns who have already matured to category B–4 cognitive capability. Those individuals would be brought to the attention of corporate HR, so that they could be taken into account by the company CEO and EVPs when they review the corporate talent pool.

The current category B–3/4 interns should also be displayed on the company talent pool development charts, since that gives a more complete picture of the corporate talent pool, in terms of the richness of the pool in relation to the ten-year-plus corporate outreach.

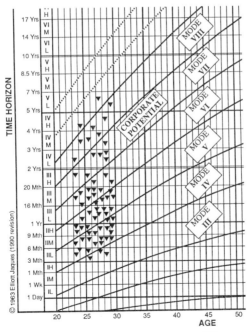

Figure 11.5 Graduate interns (▼)

Development of Individual Talent:
Coaching and Mentoring

It is a basic principle, to be made clear to everyone, that individuals are accountable for their own personal and career development, for setting their own goals, and for seeking opportunities to fulfil them. No company can guarantee a career or any individual position for anyone. But a company can ensure that it has procedures which enable individuals to know what opportunities might be available, which help individuals to clarify their goals in relation to opportunities, which provide fair and reasonable educational opportunities, and which sustain fair and effective procedures for judging potential capability.

We have so far described procedures for evaluating the total talent pool situation and keeping it under review:

- The stratum–V presidents watch the business unit pool at stratum–III to stratum–I.
- MoRs watch their own SoR pool.
- The board watches for potential CEOs.
- The stratum–VII CEO watches the corporate pool at stratum–V and stratum–IV.

But what about the development of each individual? We have already dealt with that subject as well, in the requisite practices that we have described. Here is an integrated summary.

Immediate managers should deal with in-role issues. They must coach regularly with a view to helping subordinates to realize their full capabilities for the full opportunities which are available in the role. Coaching is mainly teaching (training in the skilled use of knowledge may be provided where relevant) and covers extension of knowledge, skilled application of knowledge, focused articulation of values, and reinforcement of wisdom. Any problems of (-T) should be pointed out to subordinates and discussed, so that they may have a better opportunity to get them under self-control, or to get personal professional help.

Managers-once-removed deal with individual career development issues. They should evaluate current and future potential and periodically review those evaluations. They provide information about career opportunities in the company, and help SoRs to settle on personally desirable goals to be pursued if and when opportunities become available. They should ensure that their own MoR subordinates are aware of the potentialities for the company of SoRs, and of desirable transfer opportunities for their optimum development.

Moreover, an MoR should foresee the point where an SoR is likely to be shifting into the next higher stratum in cognitive capability and should discuss specific opportunities, if any. Although no commitments for promotion can be made in advance, the SoR can be encouraged to pursue relevant opportunities and the MoR can put the SoR forward for such opportunities.

If a particular SoR is not regarded as having a sound future in the company, the MoR must be frank about the situation, and should encourage and help the SoR to seek and find employment elsewhere. Planned leaving of this kind is both helpful to the individual and reassuring to everyone else, since everyone can realize that there are no nasty secrets in the closet.

Career Ladders and Qualifications

The practice has grown in recent years of having double career ladders, one managerial, the other technical. This practice is mechanistic and unsound. Individuals should be encouraged by their MoRs to make their next move to where they can get the experience best suited for their personal development within the needs of the company. It is important, however, for the company to make clear the kinds of qualifications or experience that are deemed useful, or perhaps essential, for given types of senior roles to which individuals might aspire.

This simple procedure makes it possible to consider for any given vacancy not only those with formal qualifications for the positions but also any others who might be suited by experience and values for the work but who are not necessarily formally qualified. The consolidated progression data sheets thus make it possible to identify both the best of those on the functional slate of possible candidates for a vacancy and also the "best of the rest."

✴ Managerial Leadership Teaching and Practice

Hierarchical systems *par excellence* demand unified action that moves up and down the organization, and from side to side as well, to concentrate the efforts of the hundreds, or thousands, or tens of thousands of people performing equally as many different functions, all of them essential for secure survival and success against the competition.

We have described the role of effective managerial leadership in this process of getting everyone, from top to bottom, working and collaborating willingly and enthusiastically as they move together towards a variegated array of goals, all focused on one common encompassing direction. This leadership activity is exercised in every immediate managerial mutual knowledge unit (MKU), in supervisory and project teams, in MoR three-level mutual recognition units (MRUs), and in the harmonizing of the whole through interleaving organizational leadership work from stratum–IV to stratum–VII.

Unified effort in a common direction, however, cannot by itself achieve success. Success first demands that the direction be fit and wise, and that it be altered sharply and efficiently to meet changing circumstances.

Figure 11.6 Managerial leadership teaching and practice

Choice of best direction is a simple function of the competence of each and every managerial leader from top to bottom. Managers at lower levels must alter the directions that they set so as to steer along in concert with the directions coming from above.

Thus, we have put our emphasis upon what we consider to be the hard core of managerial leadership (rather than what we have come to regard as the fuzziness of charisma, special personality traits and qualities, and emotional make-up and relationships).

These hard-core requirements need to be re-emphasized:

- A structure of managerial roles that provides for effective managerial leadership work and working relationships.
- Every manager competent in role.
- A comprehensive system of requisite managerial practices which facilitates managerial work and which, carried out effectively, ensures that every manager will win the full complement of personally earned authority that is necessary to bring his or her subordinates willingly and effectively on line.

We have reviewed in this section the main features of this hard-core approach to hierarchical leadership development. There is one more piece, however, which we have not mentioned and with which we shall bring this book to completion. This piece comprises leadership teaching and training. We are not, however, referring to the idea of training in esoteric leadership "skills" such as communication or listening skills. We have argued that, in addition to the necessary cognitive complexity, values, wisdom, and freedom from (-T), every manager needs to have crisp and clear knowledge not only of all of the requisite practices that we have described but also of the principles and concepts that underlie these practices.

We thus come to a practical process of managerial leadership teaching and training which is made up of two main elements (see figure 11.6). First, there is the straight educational teaching process, the presentation of lecture–discussions in all of the material set out in this book. Second, there must be the opportunity to rehearse the use of the requisite practices via discussion of case studies and actual role practice.[2]

In short, effective managerial leadership can be unequivocally and efficiently taught, but there must be in place a requisite organizational structure plus principles and practices which can be imparted and by means of which managerial leaders can thrive and flourish once they have learned them.

Notes

1 These panels, based upon the potential capability charts developed by Jaques, are available in a range of sizes and materials from the publishers, Cason Hall.
2 Our publishers, Cason Hall, are preparing relevant practical text and video teaching packages.

Outline and Summary

Basic Propositions about Leadership

1   This book has been written with a very practical and specific purpose. We are concerned with the problem of how to release the full commitment of the millions of people who are employed in the managerial hierarchies that now provide the wealth of our industrial societies, and with the achievement of two great and proper social aims: to maximize the effectiveness of these organizations in line with the democratic values of our society; and to do so in such a way as to give everyone who works in them the opportunity to satisfy that deep-seated human need to be able to gain creative fulfillment as well as economic security from work.

2   The achievement of such desirable outcomes is commonly associated with what is called leadership. We must, therefore, start with a clear and unequivocal definition of leadership, as follows.

3   Leadership is defined as that process in which one person sets the purpose or direction for one or more other persons, and gets them to move along together with him or her and with each other in that direction competently and with full commitment.

4   This book is limited to leadership accountability in managerial hierarchies, that is to say, in organizations made up of layers or strata, with manager–subordinate relationships between roles in one layer and roles in the next lower layer.

5   Not all roles carry leadership accountability. Examples of some that do so are:

- Managerial roles.
- Military commander roles.
- Political representative roles.

- Parental roles.
- Elementary and secondary school teacher roles.

For the purposes of this book we have examined leadership accountability in managerial roles.

Examples of some roles that do not carry leadership accountability are:

- Salesperson roles (a salesperson tries to persuade a client to do a particular thing but does not try to get the client to move along willingly and enthusiastically in collaborating to help the salesperson to move in a particular direction).
- Friendship roles.
- Acquaintance roles.
- Service-providing roles.
- Auditing roles.

Even though these role relationships do not carry leadership accountability, they do carry varying kinds of accountability and authority.

6   By this definition there is no such thing as a free-standing leadership role. By the same token there is no such thing as a leader *per se*. There is managerial leadership, military leadership, but not detached "leadership" or "leaders" all by themselves.

7   This definition also implies that there cannot be some people who are "managers," some people who are "leaders," and some who are both managers and leaders, as though they were separate and additive. That makes no more sense than to say that some objects are fruits, some are oranges, and some are both oranges and fruit. They hang together.

8   This point of view (that there can be managerial leadership but not managers and leaders separately) gets rid, once and for all, of those misleading questions of whether a good manager needs to be a good leader, or whether someone can be a good leader but rather weak on the managerial side, or whether higher-level managers need to be good leaders but lower-level managers do not, or whether management, leadership, and administration are the same or different.

Managerial accountability includes leadership accountability as an integral part of the role. One cannot be an effective manager without getting one's subordinates to go along in willing and enthusiastic collaboration with one, any more than one can be an effective manager without being good at deciding what tasks one wants to assign to one's people.

9   The emphasis in leadership competence is thus thrown upon competence in role rather than upon some generic leader competencies, for example, upon competency in managerial roles rather than upon leadership competency which is separate from managerial competency or an add-on to it.

10   Our research over many years reveals that there are no special traits or personality qualities which are associated specifically with something called leadership. Charisma is the negation of effective role leadership, since it leads to blind followership and diminishes competent working together. And qualities such as courage, initiative, proactivity, energy, flexibility, open-mindedness, imaginativeness, and all the other factors that appear on lists of "leadership qualities" are nothing more than the everyday qualities that are needed for ordinary working in a wide range of roles.

11   The qualities that make for effective managerial leadership are precisely the qualities for effective managerial work. These are:

- The necessary level of cognitive complexity to carry the level of task complexity of the specific managerial role.
- A strong enough sense of value for the managerial work and for the leadership of others.
- The appropriate knowledge plus experienced practice and skilled use of that knowledge.
- The necessary wisdom about people and things.
- The absence of abnormal temperamental or emotional characteristics that disrupt the ability to work with others.

12   Along with these psychological conditions, which are required for effective managerial leadership, there are two essential organizational conditions: an organizational structure that places managers one category of task/cognitive complexity above their immediate subordinates, and a full range of requisite managerial practices as summarized in this book.

13   Effective managerial leaders are neither made nor born: given the necessary psychological and organizational conditions, anyone who values managerial leadership work can exercise effective in-role leadership. All of the conditions except one are open to some degree of human influence and modification. The non-modifiable condition is that of level of cognitive complexity; but even that can be adjusted

by ensuring that everyone is appointed only to roles with levels of work for which he or she has the necessary cognitive capability, and that the level of work is increased as his or her cognitive capability matures.

14   In short, everyone who genuinely wishes to do so is "born to lead," given the necessary conditions. There are, of course, people who are forced to take managerial positions because they so frequently pay better than individual contributor technical work, but who would not want to do so if they did not need the money. Such people are unlikely to become effective managerial leaders, not because they are not "born leaders" but because they do not value doing so.

15   In order to be able to discharge the leadership accountability in a managerial role, it is necessary (as with any accountability) to have the requisite managerial authority. This authority is described in the foregoing material. But role vested managerial authority can achieve only the minimum contractually required collaboration. The achievement of willing and effective collaboration requires that a manager should be able to win personally earned authority over and above the authority that is possessed by virtue of the role. This result is accomplished by having the necessary capability for the managerial role and by effectively carrying out the requisite practices which make up the bulk of this book.

16   An effective managerial leader inevitably adds value to the work of subordinates.

The Managerial Hierarchy

17   The managerial hierarchy is the type of organization by means of which most of the work gets done in industrial societies. Such hierarchies comprise the employment systems in industry, commerce, and in civil service, social service, health and educational organizations.

18   These managerial hierarchies are necessarily made up of successive layers of organization which are created by the cascade of manager–subordinate role relationships, roles in any layer being at the necessary level to carry managerial accountability for roles in the next lower layer.

19   A managerial role is one whose incumbent – a managerial leader – is held accountable for the work of subordinates, for maintaining a team of immediate subordinates who are capable of

doing the required work, and for the exercise of leadership in relation to those subordinates. It is this accountability for the work of others that is much too often overlooked or even denied by those organization experts who seek the demise of the managerial hierarchy.

20 True managerial leaders require as an absolute minimum the authority, in relation to immediate subordinates, to veto an unacceptable candidate for a vacant role, to decide the types of task to be assigned to subordinates, to decide how effectively they judge their subordinates to be working and to award merit recognition, and to decide to remove from their immediate team a subordinate who is judged to be unable to do the work required.

21 In addition, managers are accountable for winning from subordinates the personally earned authority that will enable them to gain the subordinates' willing and effective collaboration. We describe in detail in Chapters 5–11 just how managers can do so.

22 For a manager effectively to exercise leadership and add value to the work of subordinates, that manager must be in a category of cognitive complexity which is one quantum step higher than that of any immediate subordinates, and engaged in tasks that are one quantum of task complexity greater than the complexity of the tasks assigned to the subordinates.

23 Complexity is a function of the number of variables operating in a situation, the ambiguity of those variables, the rate at which they are changing, and the extent to which they are interwoven so that they have to be unraveled in order to be seen.

24 Cognitive complexity and task complexity come in a hierarchy of recursive packets, or categories; that is to say, each higher category nests each of the lower categories within it.

25 The big finding about organizational layering is that there is an optimum pattern of organizational layering in which there is one organizational layer for each quantum step in cognitive and task complexity. This layering makes it possible to have an organizational structure in which each layer contains roles within the same category of task complexity. These roles can then be filled by people of the same category of cognitive complexity. A beautifully effective organization can thus be realized, whose structure provides the constraining mold into which roles and people can be poured with the assurance that they will conform to the conditions that are absolutely fundamental for effective managerial leadership. The highest levels

of task complexity in each role will be within the cognitive capacity of the individual who is given the work in the role. The use of this mold ensures that there will always be the correct number of layers and is the essential foundation for the suffusion of democratic values at the workplace.

26   The actual number of layers required in any given hierarchy is a product of its mission. Mission sets long-term vision, and that in turn creates the overarching time outreach of the organization. This time outreach sets the time-span requirements of the top executive role, and that time-span gives the stratum or layer at which that role must be placed, thus determining the number of strata/layers from the top to the shop and office floor.

27   Once the basic structural conditions have been established for any given managerial hierarchy, it becomes possible to fill the roles and to put requisite managerial practices into place. Descriptions of these practices make up the bulk of this book, in Chapters 5–11. They are the literal expression of democratic values at the workplace, and include:

- Task assignment and control, i.e. planning and context setting, task assigning, information and control, personal effectiveness appraisal, coaching, training, recognition and penalties.
- Support practices, i.e. selection, induction, and annual review.
- Three-layer interpersonal managerial work by managers-once-removed, i.e. oversight and review of quality of managerial leadership, assessment of potential of subordinates-once-removed, mentoring, and career development.
- Organizational leadership, i.e. culture, values, and vision set at stratum–VII to stratum–IV, and modified by means of policies, procedures, and regulations, so as to produce an effective trust-inducing basis for effective and energetic work.

28   Close adherence to requisite structure and practices is the core of managerial leadership based upon democratic free-enterprise values.

Hierarchy and Leadership

29   Hierarchical systems that employ people to get work done demand unified action that cascades up and down the organization, and travels from side to side as well, to concentrate the efforts of the

hundreds, or thousands, or tens of thousands of people performing as many different functions, all of them essential for secure survival and success against the competition.

30   The role of effective managerial leadership is this process of getting everyone from top to bottom working and collaborating willingly and enthusiastically as they move together in one common encompassing direction.

31   This leadership activity must be exercised in every immediate managerial unit, in supervisory and project teams, in three-level mutual recognition units. It must create the overarching harmonizing of the whole system through interweaving organizational leadership work from the levels of general management up to the top of the organization, i.e. stratum–IV to stratum–VII.

32   Unified effort in a common direction, however, cannot by itself achieve success. Success first demands that the direction be fit and wise, and that it be altered sharply and efficiently as necessary to meet changing circumstances.

33   The choice of best direction is a function of the competence of every managerial leader from top to bottom. Managers at lower levels must alter the directions that they set so as to step along in concert with the directions coming from above.

34   Thus, we have put our emphasis in this book upon what we consider to be the hard core of managerial leadership rather than what we have come to regard as the fuzziness of charisma, personality traits and qualities, and emotional make-up and relationships. What is required to ensure effective managerial leadership is:

- A structure of managerial roles that provides the necessary conditions for effective managerial leadership work and for working relationships that generate trust.
- Competent managers in every role.
- A comprehensive system of requisite managerial practices which facilitates managerial work and which, when carried out effectively, ensures that every manager will win the full complement of personally earned authority that is necessary to bring subordinates willingly and enthusiastically on line in the set direction.

Bibliography

Clement, Stephen D. (1985) "Systems leadership: a focus on the gestalt", in J. G. Hunt and J. Blair (eds) *Leadership on the Future Battlefield*, Pergamon Press, New York.

Clement, Stephen D. and Ayers, Donna (1976) "A matrix of organizational leadership dimensions", US Army Leadership Monograph Series, No. 8, Fort Benjamin Harrison, IN.

Deming, W. Edwards (1986) *Out of the Crisis*, MIT, Center for Advanced Engineering Study, Cambridge, MA.

DePuy, William E., Gen. US Army ret. (1988) *Army*, August 1988.

Jacobs, T. Owen (1979) *Leadership and Exchange in Formal Organizations*, US Army, OE School, Fort Ord, CA.

Jacobs, T. Owen and Jaques, Elliott (1987) "Leadership in complex systems", in Joseph Zeidiner (ed.) *Human Productivity Enhancement*, Praeger, New York.

Jacobs, T. Owen and Jaques, Elliott (1990) "Military executive leadership", in Kenneth Clark (ed.) *Measures of Leadership*, Center for Creative Leadership, Greensboro, NC.

Jaques, Elliott (1964) *Time-Span Handbook*, Cason Hall, Arlington, VA.

Jaques, Elliott (1989) *Requisite Organization: The CEO's Guide to Creative Structure and Leadership*, Cason Hall, Arlington, VA and Gower, Aldershot, Hants.

Jaques, Elliott (1990) *Creativity and Work*, International Universities Press, Madison, CT.

Stamp, Gillian (1988) "Longitudinal research into methods of assessing managerial potential", *Technical Report 819*, US Army Research Institute for the Behavioral and Social Sciences, Alexandria, VA.

Index

Note: Page numbers in *italics* indicate figures

Abedi, Agha Hasan xviii
abstraction concepts: third order complexity
  55
abstraction universals: fourth order
  complexity 55
accountability/ies 8, 17, 19, 112, 127;
  individual 166; made explicit 23;
  managerial 306–7; role-vested 106–7;
  various 305–6
accumulation: diagnostic 92, 94, 96
action: direct 91, 93–4
ADO *see* aided direct output
aided direct output (ADO) 159–61
Alexander the Great 5
annual review 225; as delicate process 207;
  how conducted 207–10
anonymity 260–1
argument: academic and real 66
assessment: faulty assumptions 247; of
  personal effectiveness 191–5; pre-
  judgements 249–50; safeguards 248
attitudes: negative 70–1
authority/ies 8; correct sense of 21;
  personally earned 10–11, 26;
  requirements of 111–12; role-vested 10,
  106, 123

behavior: employees 273; goal-directed 39;
  of SoRs 81, 83, 244–6
business unit leadership: and stratum-V
  279–82

capability/ies: current actual 45–6; current
  potential 46; future potential 46;
  maturation of potential xviii–xix, 83–8;
  potential 57–65
career development 183, 243, 253–5, 288,
  300
career ladders 301

case studies: level of capability/level of
  work 137–45
CEOs 35–6, 55, 69, 288, 293, 300;
  capabilities required 110; competence
  35–6; corporate 137, 147; and corporate
  culture 267–70; and corporate values 72,
  270–4; and corporate vision 102, 265–6,
  274–6; entrepreneurial 37; five steps to
  follow 152–3; and leadership 264;
  succession 295; as workaholics
  69
charisma 26, 30, 110, 147, 303, 307, 311
China 109
Churchill, Sir Winston xiv, 5, 6–7
coaching xix, 31, 89, 44, 46, 257, 300, 302;
  aspects of 195–7; opportunities 198;
  purposes 195
cognitive complexity 48–58, 83–6, 109–10,
  309
cognitive power: defined 49–50
cognitive processes 47–8; defined 48–9;
  four types 51–3, 58
communication xix–xx, 161–3, 282, 283,
  303; organizational 285–6
compensation policies 269, 270
complexity: defined 48; four orders xvii–
  xviii, 53–7, 91–3; handling of 51; and
  size 119–20
concrete things: first order complexity 54
context setting: importance 184–5; and
  limits 187–8; purpose 185–7
control systems 190
corporate culture 279; additions to 267–8;
  defined 266; overseeing and adapting
  269–70
corporate values 270, 274; behavior of
  employees 273; conflict in 272; core
  272–3; defined 271; individual entitlement 273

corporate vision 274–6; defined 265–6
counseling xix, 89, 90

data: making sense of 53–4
DDO *see* delegated direct outputs
de Gaulle, Charles 37
delegated direct outputs (DDO) 158–9
delegation 180–1
Deming, Edwards 157; on delegation 180–1
democracy 153
DePuy, William E. 37–8; quoted xxii
deselection: process of 215–17
direct output support (DOS) 159, 255
dismissal: two types of 204; as ultimate
    sanction 203
DOS *see* direct output support
downsizing *see* retrenchment/downsizing

education 75–6
EEI *see* essential elements of information
effectiveness: personal appraisal 191–5,
    225–6; personal recognition 200–2
equilibration 256–7; duty of 130
essential elements of information (EEI) 162
euthanasia: example of information
    organization 58–65
EVPs 35, 55, 288, 291–2, 293; seven critical
    tasks 277–8

Ford, Henry xviii

gearing: function at stratum-VI 277–9;
    procedures 252
Geldof, Bob xiv
goals 176; common 106
graduate interns 298–300, *299*
Graicunas 117

Hampden-Turner, Charles xiii
hierarchical systems 109–14, 124;
    responsive xiii; summarized 310–11
Ho Chi Minh 37
HR *see* human resources
human nature 15, 17
human resources (HR) 212

individuals: development of 88–90, 210–11,
    300–1
induction 212–15; programs 230–2
information 194; complexity 93; four orders
    of complexity 53–8; organization example
    58–65
integration: effective 268
interviews: skill of 247, 249

Japan: approach to quality 158; management
    approach xiii–xiv

Jaques, Elliott xiii–xxi, 112, 154
judgements: consistency 252; mapping 252;
    on personal effectiveness 191–5; pre-
    249–50
just-in-time inventory controls 158

K Corporation: as example of talent pool
    290–3
knowledge 48, 49, 83; defined 74; as
    necessary 75; shortage of 129–30

language: solid and hollow 66–8; use of 54
layering xvi, xx, 74; hierarchical 109–14,
    124; organizational 116, 309–10
LBOs *see* leveraged buy-outs
leader/s: effectiveness of 42; free-
    standing 44; good 15; notion of 6, 37–9;
    slack usage of term 7
leaders-followers 5, 6, 11–14, 17; Anglo-
    Saxon terms 13
leadership: accountability and authority
    8–10, 17, 19, 32–3, 107, 237;
    charismatic xiii; competence 35–6, 44–8;
    defined 2–3; different roles xxiii, 39;
    effective 15; failure 36; free-standing 44;
    good 1; maximum unit sizes 120–3; need
    for skill and knowledge 74–6; non-
    accountability 305–6; psychological
    conditions 25–7; requisite xiv–xv;
    responsibility 32–4; situational theory 7;
    and stratum-IV 283–4; summarized
    305–8; supervisory 126–8; task of 228; to
    win 145–7; true meaning 11; *see also*
    organizational leadership
level of competence (LoC) 36
level of work (LoW) 36
leveraged buy-outs (LBOs) 36
Lievegoed, Bernard xviii, xxi
limits, purpose 187
LoC *see* level of competence
LoW *see* level of work

MacArthur, Douglas 37, 38, 39
management: different approaches to xiii–xiv
manager-once-removed (MoR) 77, 81, 121,
    178, 199, 210, 300–1; accountabilities
    240–1, 253–5; assessing SoRs 247–50;
    authorities of 241; as crucial 240; hearing
    appeals 259–60; mentoring process 245,
    249; need to ensure equity 256–7; observe
    behavior of SoRs 244–6; relationship with
    SoRs 243–4; and tough situations 258
manager-subordinate: group 124;
    relationship 111, 154–5, 234; team 125
managerial hierarchy/ies 14–15, 17, 42, 82,
    97; flexibility in 108; fundamental
    proposition 114–16; summarized

308–10; why formed 233
managerial leadership: hard-core
  requirements 303–4; overseeing quality
  of 244–6; qualities necessary 307–8
managerial leadership development program:
  two components 288; underlying
  assumption 288–9; what it is not 287–8
managerial role: basic nature 112;
  competence in 145–7; three factors
  111
managers: and annual review 207–10; "big
  enough" 42–4; capabilities of 42, 43; and
  communication 161–3; debasement of
  role 19, 21; defined 22–3; effective
  151–3; essence of leadership 173–5; first
  line 229, 230; four authorities 24–5; as
  individual contributors 158–61; as leaders
  17–19; need for assurance 34; and
  planning function 175–8; and selection
  210–12; and subordinate appraisal 191–5;
  and teams 123–6
Masuda, Yoneji xiii
matrix organization 107–8, 238–9
mentoring process: defined xix, 89, 245, 249,
  253, 254
merit awards see remuneration
military organizations 28, 30–1, 118, 119,
  127–8; and information 162
mission 102–3, 108
MKU see mutual knowledge unit
MoR see manager-once-removed
motivation 69
MRU see mutual recognition unit
mutual knowledge unit (MKU) 121, 302;
  leadership in 123–6
mutual recognition unit (MRU) 121, 261–3,
  302; leadership in 128–31

Napoleon Bonaparte 5, 37
natural initiative theory 71
newcomers: and induction process 210–15

objectives 102
old boy network 212
organization/s: managerial slogan 19;
  maximum size 118–20; non-hierarchical
  xxiv; problems and shortcomings 43;
  requisite xv–xvi
organizational leadership: and
  accountabilities 264–6; conditions
  28–30; defined 131; and structure 131–4;
  see also leadership

parents: accountability, authority and
  responsibility 8–10, 82, 308
pay: felt-fair 112
payment-by-results 157

penalties: fitness and application 202–4; use
  of 228–30
performance: quality of 194
perfomance accounting: defined 188–9
performance feedback: defined 188–91
personality: concerns of xxv–xxvii;
  defined 79; factors 43, 46–8; variables
  80–1
Peter principle 181
pigeon-theory conditioning approaches xx
plans 31; alternative serial 92–3, 94, 96–7;
  development of 173, 175–8, 198
potential: evaluation of 129
potential progress data sheet 86–7
presidents: what they should do 282, 288–90
processing: assertive 52, 57, 58, 59–60;
  cumulative 52, 57, 58, 60; parallel 53, 57,
  58, 61–2; serial 52–3, 57, 58, 60–1, 64,
  162
programs: mutually interactive 93, 94–5
project chief 234–7
project teams (task force) 155–6; (anti-)
  requisite 234; colleague 236–7;
  continuous improvement 227;
  defined 233; mixed 237; and specialist
  expert 237–8; subordinate 234–6; why
  needed 233–4
promotion: in case studies 138–45

QQT see quality, quantity and targeted time
qualifications 301
quality, assumptions concerning 157–8
quality, quantity and targeted time (QQT)
  180–1
quintaves 57

Reagan, Ronald xiv
"real boss" 111–13, *114*, 124
recognition: positive/negative 200–1; types
  of 201
relationships: pattern of 106
remuneration: and merit awards 228;
  misconceptions 204–5; paybands and
  merit awards 209; principles 205; types of
  205–7
Requisite Organization (Jaques) 135
response: immediate situational 91, 95–6
retrenchment/downsizing 218–20
Revans, Reg xx
role competence 35–6; defined 44–8
role complexity 97
role relationships 3, 5, 6, 17
roles: classified 206; specialist 134–6;
  various 154–6, 307–8
rule of six 117

salesperson–purchaser relationship 82
selection process 230; preparation and concept 210–11; procedures 212
self-control 82–3
shift work 126
skill/s 48, 49, 83; defined 74
skunk works 73
SoR see subordinate-once-removed
span of control 116–18
specialist experts 237–8
Steiner, Rudolf xx, xxi
strata 116, 121, 123; in case studies 137–45; organizational xvi–xvii; various 131–3, 181–2, 252, 257, 263, 266, 269, 275, 286, 300; various, and talent pool 288–99
strategy: planned 253
stratum-IV: leadership 283–4
stratum-V: and business unit leadership 279–82
stratum-VI: and gearing 277–9
stress 246
structure: basic concepts 102–4; basic conditions 310; designated and perceived 112–13; family 108; heart of 109–11; organizational 104–6
subordinate-once-removed (SoR) 129–31, 178, 198, 199–200, 283, 301; assessed 247–50; behavior observed 244–6; development 253–5; future potential capability 250–2; relationship with MoRs 241, 243–4
subordinates 41, 309; accountabilities of 197–8; annual review 207–10; appraisal of 191–5; behavior 81, 83; and communication 161–3; and deselection 215–17; and influence 191; need for restraint 79; optimum numbers 120–1; and planning function 177–8; psychology of 83; and teams 123–6
supervisor–supervisee role 155
supervisors: and induction programs 230–2; and penalties 228–30; and personal effectiveness appraisal 225–6; and project teams 227; and recognition 228; role of 221–3; and selection 230; and task assignment 223–5; and training 226–7

T and minus T (−T) 79–82, 83, 86, 89, 170, 215, 300, 303; in case study 141
talent pool: corporate 293–5

talent pool control room 288, 289, 290; evaluation 300; mapping of 290–3, 295–9
TARRs see task-assigning role relationships
task complexity: categories 93, 97; second order 93–5; third order 95–9
task force see project teams
task-assigning role relationships (TARRs): defined 154; effectiveness 156–8; key principles 170–2; leadership 172; and teambuilding 163–70
task-initiating role relationships (TIRRs) 134–5, 237
tasks 115, 173–5, 176; assignment by supervisors 223–5; context setting 223–4; defined 39–40, 179; formulation and assignment 181–4, 257; problems 49; types of 179–80
teaching 89
teams: brainstorming 168–9; building 164–6; business meetings 164, 167–8; defined 163; mutual recognition 278–9; "self-managing" 223; three stratum 260–3, 270; two types 125, 164–6; working-mode meetings 168–70
Thatcher, Margaret xiv
time-horizon 86; defined 50–1
time-span 109, 111, 112, 115; analysis 206; cut-off points 113; defined 98–9; of discretion 97; measurement of 100–1
TIRRs see task-initiating role relationships
training 31, 86, 89; defined 198–9; and supervisors 226–7; three sources of need 199–200

values 69, 303; democratic xxiv–xxv; importance of 31, 72–3
verbal variables: second order complexity 54–5
vision 102–3

Washington, George 37
Watson, John 5
Weber, Max xv
what-if analysis 95–6
wisdom 31, 48, 49, 83, 86, 303; importance of 76–7, 79
work: changing variables 41–2; defined 39–40; level of 97–8

Index compiled by Geraldine Beare

Developmental Management

The following titles have now been published in this exciting and innovative series:

Ronnie Lessem: *Developmental Management* 0 631 16844 3

Charles Hampden-Turner: *Charting the Corporate Mind** 0 631 17735 3

Yoneji Masuda: *Managing in the Information Society* 0 631 17575 X

Ivan Alexander: *Foundations of Business** 0 631 17718 3

Henry Ford: *Ford on Management** 0 631 17061 8

Bernard Lievegoed: *Managing the Developing Organization* 0 631 17025 1

Jerry Rhodes: *Conceptual Toolmaking* 0 631 17489 3

Jagdish Parikh: *Managing Your Self* 0 631 17764 7

John Davis: *Greening Business* 0 631 17202 5

Ronnie Lessem: *Total Quality Learning* 0 631 16828 1

Pauline Graham: *Integrative Management* 0 631 17391 9

Alain Minc: *The Great European Illusion* 0 631 17695 0

Albert Koopman: *Transcultural Management* 0 631 17804 X

Elliott Jaques: *Executive Leadership* 1 55786 257 5

Koji Kobayashi: *The Rise of NEC* 1 55786 277 X

* Not available in the USA   All titles are £18.95 each

You can order through your local bookseller or, in case of difficulty, direct from the publisher using this order form. Please indicate the quantity of books you require in the boxes above and complete the details form below. NB. The publisher would be willing to negotiate a discount for orders of more than 20 copies of one title.

Payment

Please add £2.50 to payment to cover p&p.

☐ Please charge my Mastercard/Visa/American Express account
card number ☐☐☐☐☐☐☐☐☐☐☐☐☐☐☐

Expiry date _____

Signature _____
(credit card orders must be signed to be valid)

☐ I enclose a cheque for £_____ made payable to **Marston Book Services Ltd**
(PLEASE PRINT)

Name _____

Address _____

_____ Postcode _____

Tel No _____

Signature _____ Date _____

Please return the completed form with remittance to:
Department DM, Basil Blackwell Ltd
108 Cowley Road, Oxford OX4 1JF, UK
or telephone your credit card order on 0865 791155.

Goods will be despatched within 14 days of receipt of order. Data supplied may be used to inform you about other Basil Blackwell publications in relevant fields.
Registered in England No. 180277 Basil Blackwell Ltd.